Frederic Huidekoper

Indirect Testimony of History to the Genuineness of the Gospels

Frederic Huidekoper

Indirect Testimony of History to the Genuineness of the Gospels

ISBN/EAN: 9783337284572

Printed in Europe, USA, Canada, Australia, Japan

Cover: Foto ©Lupo / pixelio.de

More available books at www.hansebooks.com

INDIRECT

TESTIMONY OF HISTORY

TO THE

GENUINENESS OF THE GOSPELS.

BY

FREDERIC HUIDEKOPER.

NEW YORK:
JAMES MILLER.
1879.

PREFACE.

THE history of mankind evinces that civilization has been highest in communities where conscience and hopefulness have been most developed.[1] It further shows that these have been most developed in communities having most faith in a Moral Ruler of the universe, to whom mankind are responsible, and in whom they can trust.[2] Yet further: no community without belief in revelation has ever believed in such a Ruler.

If we now turn to the question of revelation we find at least two communications, one through Moses and a later one through Jesus, which claim to be from God, and the evidence for which, internal or external, claims respectful attention. The one through Moses is so buried in a remote antiquity as to furnish us with little or no external evidence save what we find in the Old Testament and in the influence which Judaism exercised on Greek civilization. The other, through Jesus, is at a date when

---

[1] See *Judaism at Rome*, pp. 364, 367 - 371, 382 - 386.
[2] See *Judaism*, pp. 367, 370, 386.

external evidence, direct or indirect, is more abundant and permits more thorough scrutiny.

Our knowledge of Jesus and his teaching rests chiefly on the genuineness and trustworthiness of four records termed Gospels. The direct evidence for their genuineness has been repeatedly given. The following work is an effort to present some of the indirect evidence.

There are individuals who in a question of this kind reject any evidence for what is supernatural. Some do this heedlessly because indifferent to the subject; some do it impatiently from antagonism to what they deem human credulity; others who appreciate the subject find themselves unable to credit an interruption to the laws of nature. For these last mentioned a suggestion is placed in the note.[3]

In the Appendix various fraudulent works by Christians are given in Notes A to K inclusive. In these no

---

[3] No fact can be better established than that the earth at no comparatively remote period was uninhabited by mankind. They now live upon it, and it is obvious from geology that they originally were, as now, distinct from, and independent of, any known animal. When the first human pair, or pairs, came into existence, it could not have been as helpless infants. They must have had capacity to care for themselves. This formation of two or more mature human beings, destitute of parents, must unquestionably have taken place. No recorded human experience has witnessed such an event, nor is there any natural law to which it can be referred. Yet this fact, though obviously a miracle, is one which it seems impossible to reject. Does not a consideration of it render easy the supposition that the Being who formed man would interpose for his education?

miracles are attributed to Jesus except those found in our Gospels. This claims especial attention in the earliest of them, the Acts of Pilate, wherein §§ 8, 9, should be studied. The inference is fair that in the first half, or perhaps in the first quarter, of the second century, the history of Jesus was so well established that even the author of a fraud, anxious to magnify the Master, did not venture in this respect to vary from it.

Of these fraudulent works some were translated by the author and some are given in extant translations. He had intended revising both, except in the Ascension of Isaiah, that being from the Æthiopic, of which he is ignorant. The condition of his sight has precluded such revision. Its absence will not affect the argument, but may the interpretation of particular passages. He could have wished also further time for research on more than one point. Other and more imperative duties, however, claim what remains to him of vision. In bringing his work to a close he must acknowledge deep indebtedness to Professor E. Abbot, of Cambridge, for valuable aid.

MEADVILLE, PA., July 28, 1879.

TABLE OF CONTENTS.

CHAPTER I.

CONTROVERSIAL WANTS OF THE EARLY CHRISTIANS.

Section	Page
I. These called for Jewish or Heathen Records of Jesus	1
II. They occasion Pseudo-Heathen and Jewish Documents	3
Class 1. Pseudo-Records concerning Jesus	4
" 2. Pseudo-Records concerning Christians	7
" 3. Pseudo-Predictions	7
" 4. Pseudo-Teaching	7
III. Alleged Uncanonical Gospels	7

CHAPTER II.

CONTROVERSIES.

I. Between Jewish and Gentile Christians	8
II. Between Jews and Christians	11
1. The Ceremonial Law	11
2. The Messiahship of Jesus	13
III. Between Heathens and Christians	14
1. Concerning God. Whether but One? Did He create the Universe? Was He Corporeal? Did He take Interest in Human Morality?	15
2. Concerning Jesus. His Divine Mission proved by (1) Old Testament Predictions, (2) Pseudo-Heathen Records, and (3) Character of his Teachings	16
3. Concerning Heathen Deities	17
4. " Idolatry	18
5. " Antiquity of Christianity and Heathenism	18
6. " Public Calamities	19
7. " Creation of Man	20
IV. Controversy between Catholics and Gnostics	20

CHAPTER III.

OPINIONS OF CHRISTIANS.

Section			Page
I.	Concerning	Heathen Deities	21
II.	"	Idolatry	27
III.	"	Christ's Mission to the Underworld	29
IV.	"	Resurrection of the Flesh	30
V.	"	the Millennium	31
VI.	"	Restoration of Jerusalem	32
VII.	"	Rome's Destruction	33
VIII.	"	Beliar, or Antichrist	34
IX.	"	Nero's Return	35
X.	"	Conflagration of the World	36
XI.	"	God devoid of Name	36
XII.	"	Old Testament Predictions	37
XIII.	"	Jesus as Deity of the Old Testament	38
XIV.	"	the Personal Appearance of Jesus	39

CHAPTER IV.

CHRISTIAN CUSTOMS.

I. The Sabbath 42
II. Sunday as a Day of Religious Gatherings 44
III. Eating of Blood 46
IV. Baptism 48
V. The Lord's Supper 50

CHAPTER V.

DESIGNATIONS FOR GOD 51

CHAPTER VI.

TERMS APPLIED TO CHRISTIANS.

I. Ἀσεβεῖς, Unbelievers 54
II. Atheists 55
III. Christians 55
IV. Third Race 56

CHAPTER VII.

TERMS USED BY CHRISTIANS.

Section		Page
I.	Ἀσεβής, ἀσέβεια, ἄνομος, ἀνομία	56
II.	Σεβόμενος, φοβούμενος	57
III.	Εὐσέβεια, εὐσεβής	57
IV.	Θεοσέβεια, θεοσεβής	58
V.	Ἀδελφοί, ξένοι, πάντες	58
VI.	Δίκαιοι, Just Men	59
VII.	Jesus Christ	60

CHAPTER VIII.

MISCELLANEOUS QUESTIONS.

I.	Public Games	61
II.	Slavery	64
III.	Two Wars	65
IV.	Philosophy	66
V.	Dress	69
VI.	Origin of Evil	70
VII.	Sibylla, Bacis, Hystaspes	71
VIII.	Prediction and Inspiration	72
IX.	Spurious Converts	73
X.	Chronology and Divisions of Time	74
XI.	Temporary Disuse of the Words Jesus and Christ	75
XII.	Natural Science	76
XIII.	Literary Heathens	78
XIV.	Persecutions	78

CHAPTER IX.

ROMAN POLITICS.

I.	Emperors	79
II.	Political Personages	81
III.	Contest with Greek Culture	81

CHAPTER X.

SUMMARY OF ARGUMENT. 83

CHAPTER XI.

DID PSEUDO-RECORDS REACT ON THE GOSPELS? . 86

No. 1. Dream of Pilate's Wife, Matt. xxvii. 19 87
" 2. Pilate washes his Hands, Matt. xxvii. 24, 25 88
" 3. The Dead of former Times arise, Matt. xxvii. 52, 53 . . . 88
" 4. The Tomb Sealed and Guarded, Matt. xxvii. 62–66 . . . 88
" 5. The Soldiers Bribed, Matt. xxviii. 11–15 89
" 6. Account of Judas, Matt. xxvii. 3–10 89

CHAPTER XII.

TWO FURTHER QUESTIONS.

I. Correspondences of Matthew, Mark, and Luke . . . 92
II. Style of John, the Evangelist 92

APPENDIX.

NOTE A.

Acts of Pilate 105
Prefatory Statement 107
§ 1. Character of Charges against Jesus 108
2. Respect of Pilate and his Attendant for Jesus 109
3. Regard of the Common People for Jesus 110
4. Homage of the Standards to Jesus 113
5. Message from Pilate's Wife 114
6. Answer to Imputation on the Mother of Jesus 115
7. Pilate's Conviction touching Jesus 118
8. Nicodemus testifies to the Miracles of Jesus 121
9. Those cured testify to the Miracles of Jesus 123
10. Effort of Pilate to save Jesus 125
11. Crucifixion of Jesus 128
12. Accompaniments of the Crucifixion 132
13. Joseph esteems and buries Jesus 134
14. Heathens testify to the Resurrection 138
15. Jews testify to the Resurrection 140

NOTE B.

	Page
Pilate's Report	142
§ 1. Longer Latin Form	143
2. Shorter Latin Form	145
3. Greek Form	146

NOTE C.

Correspondence of Abgarus with Jesus 149

NOTE D.

Letter of Lentulus 151

NOTE E.

Interpolations of Josephus	153
§ 1. Concerning Christ	153
2. Concerning John the Baptist	154
3. Concerning James	156

NOTE F.

Edessene Archives, or Pseudo-Thaddeus 158

NOTE G.

Correspondence opened by Seneca with Paul 161

NOTE H.

Letter of Marcus Antoninus 167

NOTE I.

Ascension of Isaiah 169

NOTE J.

Sibylline Oracles 172

NOTE K.

Hermes Trismegistus, Mercury Thrice Greatest 179

NOTE L.

Alleged Uncanonical Gospels 182

NOTE M.

Date when Jesus was Deified 190

NOTE N.

First Two Chapters of Matthew 201

NOTE O.

Publication of Mark's Gospel 202

NOTE P.

The Baptismal Formula 204

NOTE Q.

The Mission of Jesus 206

NOTE R.

The Ministry 213

INDIRECT TESTIMONY OF HISTORY

TO THE

GENUINENESS OF THE GOSPELS.

CHAPTER I.
CONTROVERSIAL WANTS OF THE EARLY CHRISTIANS.

§ 1. *These called for Jewish or Heathen Records of Jesus.*

CHRISTIANS, in spreading their Master's religion, alleged that he had been divinely commissioned. In proving this to an inquiring and candid mind they could in most cases use our Gospel narratives, because the internal evidence of their truthfulness would suffice.

In dealing with opponents, or with the indifferent, this evidence could not be used, since the Gospels were professedly written by Christians, and this very fact rendered them inadmissible as proof of Christian allegation. A heathen would naturally say: "Some of your own people wrote these books. If you wish me to credit your statements give me testimony from outside your ranks as to their correctness.[1] You must not expect me to believe

---

[1] "You distrust our writings and we distrust yours. We invent [you say] false accounts concerning Christ." — **Arnobius**, *Adv. Gentes*, 1, 57. **Tertullian** likewise, after stating that the rulers and chief men of the Jews had extorted from Pilate the crucifixion of Jesus, adds: "He himself had predicted that they would do so. This would be of small account if the prophets also had not previously done it." — *Apol.* 21; *Opp.* p. 22 A, edit. Rigault; **1**, p. 89, edit. Gersdorf. The prediction by Jesus rested on Christian testimony; that of the prophets did not. Yet Tertullian may have meant: If you can attribute the prediction by Jesus to human sagacity, that by the prophets was too early to permit such explanation.

your own testimony in behalf of your own assertions." Christians were thus debarred from appeal to their Master's history in evidence of his supernatural mission.[2] They could cite moral teachings from the Gospels as approving themselves to the judgment, but this was all. Had the Gospels been fabricated for controversial purposes, or with dishonest intent, or by persons subsequent to the Apostles, they would inevitably have been ascribed to heathen or Jewish, not to Christian, authors.

---

[2] Christians, by their inability to cite the Gospels as evidence, were, when dealing not with right-minded inquirers, but with opponents or with the captious, debarred almost entirely from appealing to their Master's miracles. The true cause for this seems to have been overlooked by all writers, many of whom have supposed that it was due to their underrating the argument from miracles. The following is a concise statement of the conclusion to which many modern scholars have arrived. "Of the evidence from miracles he (Justin) scarcely takes any notice. . . . Miracles were regarded as of no rare occurrence, and they were supposed to be wrought by magical arts. Christianity might, then, have the support of miracles ; but this support would be regarded as of trifling importance by those who were believers in the reality of charms and sorcery. The miracle might be admitted ; but the evidence derived from it could be invalidated by ascribing it to the effects of magic. That the early Fathers and Apologists really felt a difficulty of this kind, there can be no doubt." — **Lamson**, *Church of the First Three Centuries*, p. 39.

The insufficiency of this explanation is obvious from the following considerations.

1. In the Pseudo-Heathen and Pseudo-Jewish records concerning Jesus which Christians fabricated, an important place is given to miracles.
2. Such Christians as trusted to, or were willing to use, these records, or who thought by the aid of prophecy to prove the statements of the Gospels, show no hesitation in appealing either to their Master's miracles or to those connected with his history. **Justin Martyr** says: "As to the prediction that our Christ should heal all diseases and wake the dead, hear what was said. It is as follows. 'At his appearing the lame shall leap as a deer ; the tongue of the dumb shall speak distinctly ; the blind shall see ; the lepers be cleansed ; the dead shall rise and walk about.' And that he did these things you can learn from the Acts prepared under Pontius Pilate." — *Apol.* **1**, 48 ; *Opp.* **1**, 232 C. **Tertullian** mentions the darkness at the crucifixion as miraculous. He says that it

§ 2. They occasion Pseudo-Heathen and Pseudo-Jewish Documents.

The average morality of Christians much exceeded that of heathens.[a] Yet Christianity numbered among its adherents some who were unprincipled, or weak-principled. The number of these was comparatively small so long as Christians were in a decided minority, and could offer to converts neither place nor profit in a worldly sense. Yet a hundred and twenty years after Jesus taught, that is about A. D. 150, we find that some one had already supplied by fraud the want most annoying to their controversialists, namely, the lack of heathen testimony to the facts of their Master's life. At that date we find a document called the ACTS OF PILATE, and still later a professed LETTER FROM PILATE to Tiberius. Each of these documents is mentioned by but one writer during the first three centuries. Probably the chief use made of them and of subsequent forgeries was in the fourth century, when the two political parties which advocated

---

had been foretold, and tells the heathens, "You have, recorded in your archives, that accident to the world. . . . Pilate . . . announced at that time all those things concerning Christ to Tiberius."—*Apol.* 21; *Opp.* 22 B C, edit. Rigault; **1**, pp. 89, 90, edit. Gersdorf. Compare fuller statement in *Judaism*, p. 442. 3. Christians appealed to their own miracles. **Justin** says: "Many of our Christian men, adjuring in the name of Jesus Christ, who was crucified under Pontius Pilate, have healed and do now heal many possessed by demons throughout the world and in your city, [persons] who had not been healed by other exorcists and enchanters and physicians." —*Apol.* **2**, 6; *Opp.* **1**, 296 – 298. See also *Dial.* 11, cited in Note P, footnote 7, and compare in *Underworld Mission*, p. 78; 3d edit. pp. 74 – 75, the vehement challenge of Tertullian to the heathens, that they should test this power of the Christians. 4. Christian apologists, from the middle of the second to the middle of the third century, though in arguing with heathens they laid extravagant stress on predictions, yet laid none on those by their Master any more than on his miracles.

[a] By heathens must not be understood the large, though in the second century decreasing, class of Gentile Monotheists who adhered to Judaism rather than to Christianity.

Christianity and Heathenism were nearly equal in strength. Before this date Christians had fewer of the unprincipled in their ranks, and fewer opportunities, even when so disposed, to give currency to any forgery in their own favor. Subsequently to the fourth century, when Christianity had the upper hand, and when strife was solely or chiefly between sections of its own followers, the authority of saints and martyrs outweighed that of heathens. Later forgeries were in the name of Christian leaders, and even the forgeries which already existed were correspondingly altered; so that the "Acts of Pilate" became the "Gospel of Nicodemus," while the "Letters of ABGARUS and Christ" became the "Letters of CHRIST and Abgarus"; those of SENECA and Paul being headed "Letters of PAUL and Seneca."

The Pseudo-Heathen and Pseudo-Jewish documents fabricated by Christians may be classified under four heads.

CLASS 1. *Pseudo-Records concerning Jesus.*

The most important of these was entitled ACTS OF PILATE. It professed to record the trial of Jesus before Pilate. During this trial, the persons cured by Jesus are represented as testifying to their cure. These miracles were thus attested, not by Christian writers who could be suspected of partiality, but by the records of a Roman court. The varying localities in which this document was used, the various prejudices to which it needed accommodation, and the various objections which it had to parry, caused alteration and re-alteration of its heading, as can be seen by appended quotations from various MSS.[4] Copies of this document from two different texts will be found in the Appendix, Note A.

---

[4] In the *Codex Monacensis* CXCII. (designated by Thilo as Monac. A.) the title reads, "Record of the things done to our Lord Jesus Christ, under Pontius Pilate, governor of Judea, — committed to writing in Hebrew by Nicodemus, ruler of the Synagogue of the Jews." — **Thilo**, *Cod. Apoc.* p. CXXVIII.

The *Codex Venetus* bears for a heading, "Narrative concerning the

§ 2.]   PSEUDO-RECORDS CONCERNING JESUS.   5

Next after the above the most important fraud was a reputed LETTER or REPORT OF PILATE to Tiberius. This

estimable suffering of our Lord Jesus Christ and concerning his holy resurrection, written by a Jew named Ennæus, which Nicodemus the Roman Toparch translated from the Hebrew language into the Romaic [that is, the common Greek] dialect." — **Thilo**, *Cod. Apoc.* p. CXXVI, compared with statement on p. CXXIX, ll. 11, 12. The word *estimable* is doubtless a somewhat late addition to the title, not earlier probably than the fourth century.

The Latin manuscript *Codex Parisiensis*, 1652, has prefixed to it the following : " In the name of the Lord. [*Here*] begins the Book concerning the deeds of our Lord [*the*] Savior ; by Emaus, the Hebrew, *post*, after [*or*, according to] Nicodemus." — **Thilo**, *Cod. Apoc.* p. CXXXIX.

Paris A bears the simple heading, " Records concerning our Lord Jesus Christ, which were made under Pontius Pilate, governor of Judea." — **Thilo**, pp. CXXI, 489. A prologue to the same manuscript will be found further on in this note.

The preface to *Paris D* will be found in the Appendix, Note A, at the beginning of the document, and should be compared with the foregoing.

In the account of Christ's doings in the Underworld, which was subsequently added to the " ACTS," is a statement that, "Joseph and Nicodemus immediately announced to the governor all these things which were said by the Jews in their Synagogue ; and Pilate himself wrote all things which were done and said by the Jews concerning Jesus, and deposited all the words [thereof] in the public records of his Prætorium." — **Acts of Pilate**, *Lat. Vers.*, **Thilo**, *Cod. Apoc.* p. 788. This would fairly imply that the action of Pilate's court and the testimony given in it had been PREVIOUSLY recorded by himself.

The heading of *Codex B* of **Pilate's Epistle** blends that document with the Acts of Pilate, or implies that Pilate's letter merely accompanied the Memoirs. It reads as follows : "Memoirs [of what was done] touching our Lord Jesus Christ under Pontius Pilate . . . and also whatever Nicodemus narrated as done by the Jews and chief priests subsequently to the crucifixion and suffering of Jesus. This same Nicodemus wrote in Hebrew." — **Thilo**, *Cod. Apoc.* pp. 803 n – 804 n.

The headings of several manuscripts represent this document as found at a later date in the Prætorium. In one (Thilo, *Cod. Apoc.* pp. CXLI, CXLII) the person finding it is not mentioned. In another (Thilo, *Cod. Apoc.* p. CXXXV) he is said to be the Emperor Theodosius (A. D. 379 – 395). In some this emperor is said to have found the account in

seems to have been less used than the preceding. It will hereafter be given in three different forms and from four different texts. See Appendix, Note B.

Yet another, first mentioned in the fourth century, is the CORRESPONDENCE OF ABGARUS WITH CHRIST, given in the Appendix, Note C.

One more document attributed to a heathen is the LETTER OF LENTULUS, not mentioned by any ancient writer. It resembles the preceding documents in nothing save its alleged heathen origin. They were intended chiefly to reproduce the facts of the Gospels. This letter was an effort to counteract the results of defective judgment and interpretation among Christians. It will be found in the Appendix, Note D.

An INTERPOLATION OF JOSEPHUS testifying to facts in the life of Jesus will be given in the Appendix, Note E.

Hebrew (Thilo, *Cod. Apoc.* p. cxxxiv, note 133, and p. cxlvi, ll. 1, 2), which would imply that it had been written by another hand and merely deposited in the public archives by Pilate.

The prologue of *Paris A* says that, "I Ananias [now] prætorian prefect, learned in the Law, according to the divine Scriptures, recognized our Lord Jesus Christ, coming to him by faith and being deemed worthy of his holy baptism. Searching the records made at that time, in the days of our master Jesus Christ, which the Jews laid away in the time of Pilate, I found these records in the Hebrew language — translating them also by the grace of God into Greek, that they may be recognized by all who call on the name of our Lord Jesus Christ — in the seventeenth year of the reign of our master Flavius Theodosius [A. D. 395], the sixth of Flavius Valentinianus, the ninth of the Indiction [a treasury cycle, according to Pierer's *Universal Lexicon*, of fifteen years]. All you who read copy into other books." — **Thilo**, pp. 490, 492.

A Preface to the Latin MS. *Cod. Paris.* [No.] 1652 (Thilo, pp. 491, 493, 495) agrees in outline, though not in detail, with the foregoing Prologue. Its writer calls himself "Emaus, a Hebrew, a teacher of the law among the Hebrews," but does not claim official capacity as prefect or otherwise.

Additional variations in the heading or Prologue are cited by Thilo; but the foregoing will indicate the difficulties and perplexities which constantly presented themselves to those who were propagating a fraudulent narrative.

CLASS 2. *Pseudo-Records concerning Christians.*

In the fourth century Eusebius mentions a document of which, under the heading EDESSENE ARCHIVES OR PSEUDO-THADDEUS, an account will be found in the Appendix, Note F. It testifies to miracles of Thaddeus.

An alleged CORRESPONDENCE OF SENECA WITH PAUL, manifesting his respect for the latter, has come down to us, for which see Appendix, Note G.

An alleged LETTER OF MARCUS ANTONINUS testifying to the miraculous result of prayer by a Christian legion will be given in the Appendix, Note H.

CLASS 3. *Pseudo-Predictions.*

In the second century Christians had a mania for finding predictions concerning Jesus in the Old Testament.[5] Inability to make these plain to others prompted somewhat later a forgery called the ASCENSION OF ISAIAH, wherein the prophet is made to speak more plainly than in his genuine writings. It is described in Note I.

PREDICTIONS BY SIBYLLA concerning Jesus, quoted or mentioned in Note J, were also an effort to fabricate prophetic evidence. On HYSTASPES see *Judaism,* pp. 459, 460.

CLASS 4. *Pseudo-Teaching.*

Lactantius quotes views common among Christians from HERMES TRISMEGISTUS, "*Mercury Thrice Greatest,*" concerning which document see Note K.

§ 3. *Alleged Uncanonical Gospels in the Second Century.*

An erroneous supposition exists, that in the second century Gospels were afloat, out of which the four now in use were formed or selected. To avoid distracting the reader's attention this subject is deferred.[6]

---
[5] See Ch. III. § 12 and *Judaism at Rome,* pp. 344 – 348.
[6] See Appendix, Note L.

CHAPTER II.

CONTROVERSIES.

§ 1. *Between Jewish and Gentile Christians.*

IN the Apostolic Age, from the moment when Christianity numbered Gentiles among its converts, a controversy sprang up between these and their Judaizing brethren. The Gentile Christians were regarded by the latter as aspiring to the benefit of God's promises, while shrinking from the burden of his law. The difficulty must frequently have amounted to non-intercourse between the two schools of Christians, the separation being as sharp as' if they did not recognize a common master. Peter on one occasion visited a Gentile Monotheist of blameless and benevolent life, of whose benevolence the Jews received no small share. The object of the visit was to communicate Christian truth, yet Peter's Judaizing brethren took him sharply to task for so doing.[1]

Outside of Judea the dissension as to whether Gentile Christians must adopt Jewish customs caused the sending of a delegation to the Apostles at Jerusalem. Here the dispute was animated,[2] but resulted in a decision not to require of the Gentile brethren obedience to the laws of Moses, though it did require of them obedience to a precept in Genesis,[3] as also abstinence from meat offered to idols and adherence to Jewish and Christian views of the relation between the sexes.[4] The omission

---

[1] "Thou wentest in to men uncircumcised and didst eat with them." — **Acts 11**, 3.

[2] Acts **15**, 7.

[3] See Ch. IV. § 3.

[4] Among heathens the view seems to have prevailed, that where there was a mutual consent between a man and woman no wrong was done. This view can hardly have been universal among the better class of heathens, yet it evidently prevailed to an extent which required an

§ 1.] CONTROVERSIES: JEWISH WITH GENTILE CHRISTIANS.

of any requirement as to truthfulness, honesty, and other items of rectitude is due to the fact doubtless that no question was raised concerning these. Both parties were, in respect to them, of one mind.

Paul regarded the ceremonial law as not binding, and the eating of meat offered to an idol as a matter of indifference unless when it might mislead others, or in cases where the person who ate deemed it wrong.[5] He taught that Gentiles could become Christians without observing circumcision or the sabbath;[6] and it is possible that

---

express injunction on the subject, an injunction for which Paul would have been equally zealous as his more Judaizing brethren. Some of the Gentile Christians may have held laxer ideas of morality.

[5] "Now as touching things offered unto idols. ... Some with a conviction that the idol is a real being, eat even yet as of something sacrificed to this being, and their conscience being weak is polluted. ... We gain nothing by eating and lose nothing by not eating. ... If any one should see you who have [as you think] knowledge, reclining at an idol-feast, will not his conscience because of his weakness be emboldened to eat idol sacrifices, and your weak brother will be lost as the result of your knowledge." — **1 Cor. 8,** 1-11. "Whatever is sold in the market that eat without asking questions for the sake of conscience. ... And if one who is an unbeliever inviteth you to a feast and you choose to go, eat whatever is set before you without asking any questions for the sake of conscience. But if any one say to you, This has been offered in sacrifice to an idol, do not eat of it on account of him that showed you this." — **1 Cor. 10,** 25-28. *Noyes' trans.* "Let not him that eateth despise him who forbears eating; and let not him who forbears eating judge him that eateth : for God hath received him. ... I know, and am persuaded as a Christian, that there is nothing unclean of itself; but to him that esteemeth anything to be unclean, to him it is unclean. ... And he that doubteth is condemned if he eat, because he eateth not with conviction [of its lawfulness] : for whatsoever is not [done] with confidence [in its lawfulness] is sinful." — **Rom. 14,** 3, 14, 23.

[6] "For in Christianity neither circumcision availeth anything nor uncircumcision." — **Galat. 5,** 6; **6,** 15. "One man esteemeth one day above another : another ESTEEMETH EVERY DAY ALIKE. Let every man be fully persuaded in his own mind." — **Rom. 14,** 5. "I went up to Jerusalem with Barnabas [more than seventeen years after becoming a Christian], taking with me also Titus. I went up for the purpose of

some of his arguments, if rigidly carried out, might have seemed to absolve Jews also from these observances. A consequence was that on his last visit to Jerusalem his fellow Apostles and more liberal friends feared violence towards him at the hands of his Christian but Judaizing brethren.[7]

In periods of political disturbance which caused more than usual alienation between Jews and Gentiles, this controversy became very bitter, intensifying the antagonism between the two branches of the Christian community, and increasing the number of localities where this antagonism amounted to non-intercourse.[8]

The violent advocates of ritual observance may not even in Jerusalem have been conscientious observers of what they advocated,[9] yet the control which they exer-

---

a disclosure, and I communicated to them the Gospel which I preach among the Gentiles, — privately, however, to the more prominent, — that I might not run, or have run, in vain. Neither was Titus, a Gentile who was with me, compelled to be circumcised; though [an effort to that effect was made] because of false brethren privately introduced, that they might spy out our freedom in Christianity for the purpose of enslaving us, to whom I did not even for an hour give in." — **Galat. 2**, 1-5.

The words translated, "for the purpose of a disclosure," are frequently rendered, "in accordance with a revelation." A different translation is sometimes given also to the remarks concerning Titus; but the sharpness of collision is not affected by any translation.

[7] "You see, brother, how many myriads of Jewish believers there are, and they are all zealots for the Law. But they have been informed that you teach all Jews among the Gentiles to forsake Moses, telling them not to circumcise their children, nor to walk after the [Jewish] customs. What then is to be done? The multitude will assuredly come together; for they will hear that you have come. Do therefore what we advise you. We have four men who have a vow on them. Take these and purify yourself with them, and pay the expenses for them, that they may shave their heads; and all will know that those things of which they have been informed concerning you are nothing, but that you yourself also walk in observance of the Law." — **Acts 21**, 20-24.

[8] See *Judaism at Rome*, pp. 254, 255, and on 266 the text prefixed to note 30.

[9] "Now therefore why do you provoke the anger of God, by putting a

cised is evinced by the fact, that, in a locality outside of Judea, not only Peter was temporarily overborne by their vehemence, but also Barnabas, who, though a Jew, had been born and brought up in a Gentile locality.[10]

Of all this controversy and conflict, not a trace appears in the Gospels. Had they, instead of being honest histories of earlier events in Judea, been the fancy sketches which some have supposed, — had they originated in the midst of this struggle, or had they grown by accretion under the hands of those who were engaged in the dispute, or living among the disputants, it seems morally impossible that the Master should not have been made to say one word on the subject at issue.

§ 2. *Between Jews and Christians.*

This controversy may be divided into two parts: 1. Was the Ceremonial Law essential to salvation? 2. Was Jesus the Christ?

The first of these questions brought out essentially the same points and counterpoints as the discussion in the preceding section. Christians affirmed that Abel, Enoch, Noah, and others had been acceptable to God without being circumcised, and therefore that circumcision could not be essential to his approval; that Abraham had been acceptable without observing the sabbath, and that its observance therefore was not binding.[11]

---

yoke upon the neck of the disciples, which neither our fathers nor we were able to bear?" — **Acts 15,** 10, *Noyes' trans.*

[10] "When Peter came to Antioch, I withstood him to his face, because he was to be blamed. For, before the arrival from James of certain [Judaizers], he ate with the Gentiles: but when they were come, he withdrew, and separated himself, fearing those of the circumcision. And the other Jews dissembled likewise with him; insomuch that Barnabas also was carried away with their dissimulation." — **Galat. 2,** 11 – 13.

[11] "We say that faith was reckoned to Abraham as righteousness. At what date was it so reckoned? After he was circumcised? or when he was yet uncircumcised? It was . . . while he was uncircumcised." — **Rom. 4,** 9, 10. The intended inference is that if Abraham did not need circumcision as a means of becoming acceptable to God, neither do other

The most animated opponents of the Jews were the semi-Jewish Christians, who, because they shared largely

men. "Let no one then call you to account about food or drink, or a feast-day, or a new moon, or sabbaths; which are a shadow of the things to come." — **Coloss. 2**, 16, 17, *Noyes' trans.* "Why do you turn to the weak and beggarly rudiments whereunto you desire again to be in bondage? You observe DAYS and months." — **Gal. 4**, 9, 10. The meaning is made plain by the following. "The new moon and SABBATHS I cannot away with." — **Is. 1**, 13. Compare note 6.

Justin Martyr argues from the predecessors of Abraham against circumcision and from the predecessors of Moses against sabbath-keeping. "Have you any other blame to lay against us, my friends . . . except that we do not like your ancestors circumcise our flesh, nor like you keep sabbaths οὐδὲ ὡς ὑμεῖς σαββατίζωμεν. . . . This is what we wonder at, said Trypho . . . that you who profess εὐσεβεῖν to monotheize practically . . . differ IN NOTHING from the Gentiles as to your way of life in that you observe neither feasts nor sabbaths." — *Dial.* 10. "The law given in Horeb [Justin answers] is antiquated and concerned you only."— *Dial.* 11. Further on he argues, "It was on account of your wickedness and that of your fathers, as I before said, that God commanded you to observe the sabbath for a sign." — *Dial.* 21. "Observe the material universe, it is not idle, neither does it keep sabbaths. Remain as you were born; for if there was no need of circumcision before Abraham, nor of sabbath-keeping and feasts and offerings before Moses, neither is there now." — *Dial.* 23. "Trypho answered, Why do you select what you please from the prophetical writings and make no mention of the express injunctions to keep the sabbath? . . . Because [says Justin] I supposed that you did and do understand that if you are commanded throughout all the prophets to observe these same things which Moses commanded, it is on account of your hardness of heart and thanklessness. . . . Else as regards the Just Men, who were well pleasing to God, prior to the time of Moses and Abraham, and who neither observed circumcision nor the sabbath; why did he not teach THEM to observe these things?" — *Dial.* 27. Compare Ch. VII. § 6. "As therefore circumcision took its rise from Abraham, and the sabbath and the offerings and the feasts from Moses, and were instituted, as has been proved, because of the hardness of your people's heart; so it is necessary they should cease." — *Dial.* 43. "If any one should ask you, seeing that Enoch and Noah and their children and several others, who were neither circumcised nor observed sabbaths, did please God, what can be the reason why God after so many generations, by other leaders and the promulgation of other laws,

in Jewish views, were the more anxious to make prominent those points in which they differed from them.

Of all this acrimonious discussion nothing appears in the Gospels. None of the points made prominent by it are explained or enforced by the Master.

In behalf of the second position, that Jesus was the

---

did vouchsafe to justify the posterity of Abraham until Moses by circumcision and those that succeeded Moses by circumcision and other precepts, that is the sabbath and sacrifices and ashes and offerings . . . unless you can prove that it was as I said before, lest you should give yourselves up to idolatry and be unmindful of the true God . . . unless this be the case, God will be calumniated with not having the knowledge of future events, and with acting partially and inconsistently because he did not teach all men [compare Ch. VII. § 5] to know and practise the same just and righteous laws." — *Dial.* 92.

"But that God gave circumcision not as a fulfilment of righteousness, but for a sign that the race of Abraham might continue discernible, we learn from Scripture itself. . . . And that man was not justified by these, but that they were given to the people as a sign is evident, because Abraham himself, without circumcision and without observance of sabbaths, believed God; and it was reckoned to him for righteousness, and he was called the friend of God. But Lot also, without circumcision, was led out from Sodom obtaining the salvation which is from God. Also Noah, pleasing God when uncircumcised, received the world's expanse in its second age. But Enoch also, pleasing God without circumcision, performed, though only a man, a mission [see *Judaism*, p. 486, note 7] to angels. . . . But all the remaining multitude also of those who were just before Abraham, and of those patriarchs who were before Moses, were accounted just without the before-mentioned [observance of circumcision and sabbath] and without the Mosaic Law." — **Irenæus**, *cont. Hæres.* 4, 16, 1, 2.

The author of the **Epistle to Diognetus**, in the early part of the second century, says of the Jews: "But as to their horror of certain meats, and their superstition concerning sabbaths and their boasting about circumcision, and their pretended observance of fasts and new moons, which are all of them ridiculous and not worth speaking of, I [do not] deem that you need instruction from me. For what right has any one to accept some of the things created by God for man's use as if they were properly created, and to refuse others as useless and superfluous? and what IMPIETY is there not in falsely charging God with prohibiting the performance of good on the sabbath?" — c. 4.

Other quotations bearing on this subject will be found in Ch. IV. § 1.

Messiah, the arguments were almost exclusively based upon interpretations, or misinterpretations, or misapplications of passages in the Old Testament, a subject to which we shall hereafter return.[12]

§ 3. *Between Heathens and Christians.*

1. A prime point of this controversy was the question whether there were but one God,[13] or whether there were many. This was blended with the question whether the universe had been created, or at least formed into its present shape, by the Deity, or whether the deities were of subsequent origin to the universe. If the universe had been created or formed by Divine power, then the harmony of its design implied that it was the work of one mind, not of many. The question as to the existence of but one God had been fiercely debated before the appearance of Christianity, and it is plain, from the persecution of Monotheists and of Christians[14] subse-

---

[12] See Ch. III. § 12.

[13] " We Christians are simply adorers of the Highest King and Ruler with Christ as our *magistro*, teacher."— **Arnobius, 1,** 27. **Theophilus** argues that if a ship be seen steering steadily to its harbor, the presence of a pilot on board who guides her becomes obvious. "Thus we are compelled to perceive that God is a pilot of the universe." — *Ad Autol.* **1,** 5 ; *Opp.* p. 16 B, edit. Otto ; p. 340 D E, edit. Maran. Compare the application to God of the term Pilot by Jews and Stoics in *Judaism,* p. 51.

[14] Prosecutions for unbelief were a favorite resort of the Roman aristocracy against their opponents, subsequently at least to A. D. 14, if not earlier. A strong impetus was given to these accusations after the patrician rebellion of October 18, A. D. 31. During this rebellion the aristocracy had murdered many prominent men of the popular party. When prosecuted by relatives of the murdered individuals they defended themselves by counter charges of unbelief. See *Judaism at Rome,* pp. 8, 534. And the professional prosecutors whom they hired seem in many cases to have been paid, not by the individuals who employed them, but from the senatorial treasury (Dio Cass. **58,** 14, quoted in *Judaism,* p. 532), an indication that the remainder of the senatorial party were making com-

§ 3.] CONTROVERSIES: HEATHENS WITH CHRISTIANS. 15

quently, that this debate had lost none of its earnestness or of its acrimony.[16]

Connected with the question whether there were a Supreme Being, the creator and ruler of this world, came other queries. Was he corporeal or incorporeal?[16] What

---

mon cause with them. A Roman consul, wealthy and cultured, a near friend of the elder Pliny and relative of Caligula, was kept for seven years in his house by charges of unbelief. See *Judaism*, p. 211, note 85. At the date of this event (A. D. 31–37) Christianity can hardly have reached Rome, but its adherents equally with other Monotheists must have been exposed to these prosecutions from the moment that they obtained foothold in the imperial city.

[15] Already in B. C. 76, when a monotheistic document imposed on the Roman Senate had given a new impetus to discussion, Cicero represents himself as present where one friend ridicules and burlesques monotheism while another, who had under the guise of stoicism upheld it, insists on another discussion of the subject, since it is *pro aris et focis*, "for the dearest of human possessions." — **Cicero**, *de Nat. Deor.* **3**, (40), 94.

[16] Heathens believed in corporeal gods. **Tatian** says of the heathens, "Some hold God to be corporeal, but I deem him incorporeal." — *Orat.* 25; p. 104 C, edit. Otto; p. 265 B, edit. Maran. When monotheistic discussion in B. C. 76 received an impulse at Rome (see *Judaism*, p. 142), **Cicero** makes his speaker on the heathen side allege that the existence of a god without a body *intelligi non potest*, "cannot be understood, for he must NECESSARILY lack perception, understanding, pleasure." — *De Nat. Deorum*, **1**, (12), 30. "For you know no pleasure which does not originate from the body." — *De Nat. Deorum*, **1**, (39), 111. And so late as the tenth century we find the statement of one who had listened to an argument that God was a spirit. "It appears that God is nothing at all, since he has no head, no eyes." — **Mosheim**, *Ecc. Hist.* **2**, p. 137, note 6, by Murdock. If God pervaded the universe, as Monotheists and Stoics believed, the question whether he were corporeal involved the question whether two bodies could coexist in the same space. An opinion of the Stoics (Philosophumena, **1**, 21) quoted in *Judaism*, p. 44, may have had either the bearing there suggested on the resurrection, or may have been an affirmation that God, since he pervaded the universe, was not material but spiritual. Compare also (in Appendix, Note M, footnote 21) the argument of **Athenagoras** against the existence of two or more unoriginated gods, part of which seems based on an assumption of their corporeal character.

was his form?[17] Did he take interest in human morality?[18]

Of this debate nothing appears in the Gospels. The recognition of one God is assumed. The teacher of Christianity supplies his apostles with no arguments on the subject.

2. The second point to be proved was that Jesus had been authorized and commissioned by the Supreme Being. Christians, as already explained, could not on this point appeal to their Gospels except when dealing with right-minded inquirers. They had, however, in the character of their Master's religion a great advantage, for in the countries where monotheism had spread there was a large number of right-minded men, who, without being inquirers or opponents, were likely to side with morality and worthy conceptions of God, as against the follies and immoralities of heathenism. When the writer of the **Oratio ad Græcos** affirmed (c. 5), " Our commander does not wish strength of body, nor beauty of form, nor vaunting of noble birth, but a pure soul walled around with righteousness," he must have found many who would at least speak respectfully of such as aimed in this direction, and who would defend them with more or less decision against attacks by the unworthy.

In dealing with opponents, Christians appealed to the

---

[17] Cicero makes his heathen speaker argue (see *Judaism*, Ch. III. note 11) for the human form of gods as the most excellent with which we are acquainted. The Stoics held that he was spherical. The two positions on which this belief rested — namely, that the universe was spherical and that God pervaded it — were borrowed from Monotheists. It is possible also that some Monotheists believed that God was spherical in form, and that their anticipations of future likeness to God gave rise to a belief that the resurrection body would be spherical. See belief of Origenian monks mentioned in Huet's Origeniana, **2**, 2, 9; Origen's Works, edit. Lommatzsch, **23**, pp. 143 – 150 ; edit. de la Rue, **4**, (Appendix) pp. 200 – 215.

Heathens treated a spherical God as necessarily DEVOID OF HEAD, and therefore of intelligence. See *Judaism*, p. 42, note 4.

[18] See *Judaism*, Ch. II. note 3 ; Ch. X. note 53.

§ 3.] CONTROVERSIES: HEATHENS WITH CHRISTIANS. 17

Old Testament[19] for predictions of certain facts in their Master's life which heathens admitted, or which they were not in position to deny, and argued or assumed that, because these facts had been predicted, a Divine provision had been made for their Master's ministry, a provision which would not have been made unless he had been commissioned by God.[20]

In Rome, however, we find two appeals by Justin Martyr to the Acts of Pilate, and in Africa one by Tertullian to Pilate's Report, in proof of facts in the Master's life. Indirect evidence implies that both documents must have been more used in Syria and Asia Minor than at the West.[21] The letter of Abgarus to Christ containing similar spurious evidence must also have found some currency at the East.[22]

The discussion, like many others in which the feelings of disputants are excited, was largely diverted to side issues.

3. A third point, which perhaps occupied more space and excited more feeling than any other, was concerning the heathen deities or demons. Christians were brought into constant collision with the worship of these beings, and were tortured and put to death because of not worshipping them. Many, instead of discrediting their existence, seem to have been equally persuaded of it as the heathens themselves. They regarded them as super-

---

[19] The author of the **Cohortatio ad Græcos** (close of ch. 13) offers to take a copy from the Jewish synagogue, so that no suspicion of Christian interpolation could find place. **Theophilus** says: "All the prophets spoke things harmonious and accordant with each other, and proclaimed beforehand what should happen to the whole world. The issue of the predicted and now accomplished events can teach the lovers of learning, or rather the lovers of truth, that the things predicted through them [the prophets] concerning ages and times before the flood, from the time when the world was created until now, are true." — *Ad Autol.* **3**, 17; *Opp.* p. 230, edit. Otto; p. 390 - 391, edit. Maran.

[20] See Ch. III. § 12.

[21] See Appendix, Notes A and B.

[22] See Appendix, Note C.

natural, malicious beings who had got mankind into their power, and who were the authors of all the evil in the world.[23]

Heathens charged the Christians with having offended these gods, and having thereby prompted them to inflict miseries on mankind.[24]

4. Closely connected with the foregoing was the subject of idolatry, the views of which will be hereafter given.[25]

5. The comparative antiquity of Christianity and heathenism was not a little debated. The points involved in this part of the discussion were various and in some cases deserving of but little attention.[26] In other cases the question was handled with more judgment. Arnobius (*adv. Gent.* **2,** 72) takes ground that the antiquity of God was in no wise affected by the date at which men began to show him due homage. Theophilus alleges the superior antiquity of Christianity by treating Moses as a part of it.[27]

---

[23] See Ch. III. § 1.

[24] "I have found some who were very wise in their own opinion, who raved and raged and declared as if under the prompting of an oracle that since the Christians existed in the world the earth was perishing and the human race was attacked by evils of manifold kinds; that the gods themselves, the usual rites being neglected wherewith they were wont to inspect our affairs, had been driven away from the earth." — **Arnobius,** *adv. Gentes,* **1,** 1.

[25] See Ch. III. § 2.

[26] Thus we find a statement (Lactantius, **2,** 14; Vol. **1,** col. 327 A) that Bacchus cannot have invented the vine, since Noah's drunkenness (Gen. **9,** 21) implies that he, an older than Bacchus, was acquainted with wine. The fact that he and his family alone survived the flood was regarded as proving him to be older than the heathen deities.

[27] "Our prophet and servant of God, Moses, narrating concerning the origin of the world, related in what manner the flood took place over the earth." — Theophilus, *ad Autol.* **3** 18; *Opp.* pp. 230 – 232 A, edit. Otto; p. 391 B, edit. Maran. After giving the sequence of Egyptian kings after the time of Moses, **Theophilus** adds: "So that the Hebrews are shown to be older than the cities celebrated among the Egyptians,

§ 3.] CONTROVERSIES: HEATHENS WITH CHRISTIANS. 19

Again: Moses was recognized as older than Plato or Socrates, and from Moses the latter were by many (compare Ch. VIII. note 14) affirmed to have obtained their ideas. The Sibylline verses were alleged to be older than even Homer, and on this point the Christians had a controversial advantage; for the Roman Senate had deposited in its archives as an authoritative document the professed work of Sibylla, which predicted that Homer would copy from her, and which also predicted that Æneas, a Monotheist, would found the Latin kingdom, thus making monotheism the original religion of Italy and the gods of Rome a subsequent invention.

6. Heathens charged Christians that by their offences they caused the gods to inflict manifold plagues on mankind.[28] To this, the answers were various. Some, without denying the allegation, or at least without denying the whole of it, argued that this showed the contemptible character of the gods.[29] Others alleged that the earth was growing old, and could not be so fruitful in its old age as in its youth.[30] One writer evinced from history that the calamities to which heathens referred were equally

---

who [the Hebrews] are OUR FOREFATHERS, from whom also we have the sacred books, which are older than all [other] compositions, as we have previously said." — *Ad Autol.* **3,** 20; *Opp.* pp. 238 – 240 C D, edit. Otto; p. 392 D, edit. Maran.

[28] See note 24.

[29] "Although the whole host of demons and spirits of that class be subject to us, yet like wicked slaves they mingle contumacy with fear, and delight to injure those whom they otherwise fear, since fear inspires hatred; . . . those whom they war against at a distance, they beseech when near." — **Tertullian,** *Apol.* 27. See also views of Justin, as given by Kaye, in Ch. III. note 2.

[30] The belief that the earth was growing old and in various ways degenerate seems to have been held by Jews before the Christian era, from whom it was copied by the Stoics. See *Judaism at Rome,* p. 57, note 50. In a Jewish work of the second century we are told: "Since greater evils than those which thou hast now seen happen, shall happen hereafter. For in proportion as the world grows old and infirm, in the same proportion shall the calamities of those, who dwell therein, be multiplied." — **2 Esdras,** Laurence's Vers. **14,** 15, 16; cp. com. vers. 16, 17.

prevalent before as since the appearance of Christianity;[31] another appeals to the Sibylline Oracles (the authority which the Roman Senate had recognized) in proof that the Supreme God controls such matters;[32] another calls attention to the fact that the gods gave no law to men, and asks why, therefore, they should be angry at non-obedience.[33] The same writer tells the heathens that their own statements of Divine doings would be a much surer reason for Divine anger.[34]

7. Heathens did not regard man as created by any of their gods. Christians alleged that he had been made by the Supreme Being, or by his Logos, or wisdom, which they personified, or by the joint action of both. **Theophilus** says (*ad Autol.* 2, 18): "The circumstances attending man's creation exceed [any capacity of] narration." See also in Appendix, Note M, the text prefixed to footnote 17.

Of all the points raised and discussed in this controversy not one appears in the Gospels. Considering the prominence which they held during the contest, it seems impossible that the Gospels, if at that date in course of formation, should have borne no traces of them.

§ 4. *Between Catholics and Gnostics.*

The Gnostics were two bodies of Gentile Christians originating about A. D. 140, in localities widely distant from each other, and of whom each branch was in many respects intensely unlike the other. Both these branches

---

[31] Arnobius, **1**, 3, 4.
[32] Theophilus, *ad Autol.* **2**, 3.
[33] " By these [deities] nothing was ever appointed or sanctioned. . . . What justice, therefore, is there that the heavenly gods should for various causes become angry at those to whom they never deigned to show themselves, nor gave or laid down any laws?" — **Arnobius, 7**, 7. Compare the statement of **Commodianus** : " You pray to so many gods . . . from whom there is not in the [whole] earth a [single] law." — *Instruct.* **8**, ll. 8, 9.
[34] Arnobius, **3**, 11.

of Gnostics held that the Jewish God was a different being from the God who sent Christ.[35] With both branches the Catholic [36] Christians had for more than half a century a violent and imbittered contest.

Of this Gnostic controversy nothing appears in the Gospels. Jesus is not made to utter anything touching it.

CHAPTER III.

OPINIONS OF CHRISTIANS.

§ 1. *Concerning Heathen Deities.*

So soon as Christianity commenced spreading outside of Judea it came in contact with heathen belief and customs.[1] Heathens taught the existence of numerous deities, who even before the Christian era had by some Jews been regarded as devoid of existence, while others deemed them to be evil spirits. Some questions as to the light in which God was thought to view any worship of these deities will be considered in the next section.

---

[35] See *Judaism at Rome*, pp. 331 – 336 ; also the second and third volumes of Norton's *Genuineness*. The Gnostics originated during, or immediately after, a protracted and violent war between Jews and Romans. Their existence was due to the feelings engendered by this war.

[36] By Catholics must not be understood any particular denomination, but merely the main body of Christians, who regarded their God as identical with the Jewish one, but were variously divided on other points.

[1] At Lystra (Acts **14**, 11 – 18) we find heathens on the point of sacrificing to Paul and Barnabas, whom they termed Mercury and Jupiter. At Athens (Acts **17**, 16 – 18) Paul is stirred by the idolatry which he witnesses, and is charged with advocating foreign divinities. At Ephesus (Acts **19**, 24 – 41) the shrine-makers raise a tumult, and Paul in his letters to the Corinthians (1 Cor. **10**, 14, 20, 21 ; 2 Cor. **6**, 16) finds need of directions concerning meat offered to these beings. Compare citations in Ch. II. note 5.

In the second century many Christians, as already said, attributed nearly all evils to the rule of these deities. Part of their ideas may have been borrowed from Jews, and some may have been superadded by themselves, but their vehement expressions of feeling show that their minds were filled with thoughts of the contest waged by themselves against these enemies of God and man. The appended passages of Lamson and Kaye[2] give certainly no

---

[2] "God, he [Justin] very gravely tells us, having formed man, committed him, together with all sublunary things, to the care of angels, whose too susceptible natures caused them to trespass with the frail daughters of earth; and hence sprang the race of demons. These demons did not long remain idle. They mixed in all human affairs, and soon obtained universal sway in the world. They deceived men by arts of magic, frightened them with apparitions, caused them to see visions and dream dreams, perpetrated crimes, and performed numerous feats and prodigies, which the fabulous poets of antiquity, in their ignorance, transferred to the gods. They presided over the splendid mythology of the Heathen, instituted sacrifices, and regaled themselves with the blood of victims, of which they began to be in want after they became subject to passions and lusts. They were the authors of all heresies, fraud, and mischief. Their malice was chiefly directed against the Savior; whose success, they well knew, would be attended with their overthrow: and therefore, long before his appearance on earth, they tasked their ingenuity to defeat the purpose of his mission. They invented tales about the gods of the nations, corresponding to the descriptions of him given by the Hebrew prophets; hoping so to fill the minds of men with 'lying vanities,' that the writings which predicted his advent might be brought into discredit, and all that related to him pass for fable. For example, when they heard the prophecy of Moses, **Gen. 49**, 10, 11, — 'The sceptre shall not depart from Judah, nor a lawgiver from between his feet, until Shiloh come; and he shall be the expectation of the nations, binding his foal to the vine, and washing his garment in the blood of the grape,' — they got up, as a counterpart, the story of Bacchus, the son of Jupiter and inventor of the grape, and introduced wine into the celebration of his mysteries, and represented him as finally ascending into heaven. They were exceedingly sagacious, but, with all their astuteness, found some difficulty in interpreting parts of the above-mentioned prediction of Jacob. The prophet had not expressly said whether he who should come was to be the son of God, or the son of man; nor whether he was to make use of

§ 1.]   OPINIONS CONCERNING HEATHEN DEITIES.   23

exaggerated picture of the position assigned by Justin to these supposed malevolent beings. The same holds true of a statement by the latter concerning Tatian.[3] The

---

the foal spoken of while he remained on earth, or only during his ascent into heaven. To get over this difficulty, these crafty demons, in addition to the story of Bacchus, trumped up that of Bellerophon, who was a man born of men ; and who, as they tell us, mounted on his Pegasus, ascended into heaven. The prediction of Isaiah relating to the virgin (7, 14), they said, was fulfilled in Perseus ; that in **Ps. 19**, 5, ' strong as a giant to run a race' (which Justin seems to have applied to the Messiah), in Hercules, who was a man of strength, and traversed the whole earth. Again : when they found it predicted that he should cure diseases and raise the dead, they appealed to the case of Æsculapius, who also recalled the dead to life, and was taken up into heaven. . . . They ' hover about the beds of the dying, on the watch to receive the departing soul.' The spirits of just men, and prophets equally with others, he assures us, fall under their power ; of which we have an instance in the case of Samuel, whose soul was evoked by the witch of Endor. Hence, he continues, we pray, in the hour of death, that we may be preserved from the power of demons." — **Lamson**, *Church of the First Three Centuries*, pp. 43–45.

" Actuated [**Justin** says] by a spirit of unremitting hostility against God and against goodness, the demons instigated all the persecutions to which not only the Christians, but the virtuous among the heathen were exposed. They also excited the Jews to put Christ to death. They were the authors of the calumnious accusations brought against the Christians. To their suggestions were to be traced the different heresies which had arisen in the Church ; the unjust and wicked laws which had been enacted in different states ; in short, they were the authors of all evil existing in the world. Among these evil Angels the serpent who deceived Eve, called also in Scripture Satan, and the Devil, was pre-eminent ; who, together with the other apostate Angels, and with wicked men, will be consigned to eternal flames at the consummation of all things.

" With respect to demoniacal possessions, Justin says, that the Christians, by abjuring demons in the name of Christ, were enabled to work cures which the Jewish and heathen exorcists had in vain attempted."
— **John** [**Kaye**] Bishop of Lincoln, *Writings and Opinions of Justin Martyr*, pp. 109, 110.

[3] " The sole object of the Demons [**Tatian** holds] is to lead men away from the truth. With this view they invented the Arts of Divination,

author of the Clementines is equally unmistakable in treating them as the source of almost all evil.[4] The views of Tertullian as given by Kaye[5] are not exagger-

---

and set up the Oracles. They employ every artifice to prevent the soul from rising upwards, and pursuing its way to heaven. . . . One great object of the demons is, to persuade man that whatever happens to him, either of good or evil, whether he falls sick or recovers from sickness, is owing to their agency. To this end they invented amulets, philters, and charms, in order that man might be induced to trust to them, or, at least, to the properties of matter, rather than to his Creator." — **John** [**Kaye**] Bishop of Lincoln, *Writings and Opinions of Justin Martyr*, pp. 203, 204. The demons " do not heal, but by artifice lead mortals captive." — **Tatian,** *Orat.* 18 ; *Opp.* p. 82 C, edit. Otto ; p. 259 D E, edit. Maran.

[4] In the **Clementine Homilies (8**, 12 - 19) it is said that the angels who inhabited the region nearest the earth took to themselves earthly brides. Their children were the giants, by whose misdeeds the earth was polluted ; they were swept away by the flood. To mankind, after the flood, who no longer retained the pristine excellence of the race, a law became necessary, and it was given through an angel. "But you as yet ignore the law ; for any one doing homage to demons, or sacrificing, or partaking of their table, becoming [thus] their bondsman, partakes — like [others] under wicked masters — of all the punishment which they inflict. . . . You ought to know that demons have no authority over any one unless he first becomes a participant at their table." — **8**, 20. See also *Judaism at Rome*, p. 362, note 12.

[5] **Tertullian** "asserts, in the first place, that there are spiritual substances, or material spirits : this is not denied even by the philosophers. These spiritual or angelic substances were originally created to be the ministers of the Divine will ; but some were betrayed into transgression. Smitten with the beauty of the daughters of men, they descended from heaven [compare Book of Enoch, c. 7, and *Judaism at Rome*, p. 484], and imparted many branches of knowledge, revealed to themselves, but hitherto hidden from mankind : the properties of metals — the virtues of herbs — the powers of enchantment — and the arts of divination and astrology. Out of complaisance also to their earthly brides, they communicated the arts which administer to female vanity : of polishing and setting precious stones — of dyeing wool — of preparing cosmetics. [Compare Book of Enoch, c. 8.]

"From these corrupt angels sprang demons ; a still more corrupt race

ated, though they may need slight correction from other passages.[6] He has also given the views of Clement of

---

of spirits, whose actuating principle is hostility against man, and whose sole object is to accomplish his destruction. This they attempt in various ways; but as they are invisible to the eye, their mischievous activity is known only by its effects. They nip the fruit in the bud; they blight the corn; and, as through the tenuity and subtlety of their substance they can operate on the soul as well as the body, while they inflict diseases on the one, they agitate the other with furious passions and ungovernable lust. By the same property of their substance they cause men to dream. But their favorite employment is, to draw men off from the worship of the true God to idolatry. For this purpose they lurk within the statues of deceased mortals; practising illusions upon weak minds, and seducing them into a belief in the divinity of an idol. In their attempts to deceive mankind, they derive great assistance from the rapidity with which they transport themselves from one part of the globe to another. They are thus enabled to know and to declare what is passing in the most distant countries; so that they gain the credit of being the authors of events of which they are only the reporters. It was this peculiarity in the nature of demons which enabled them to communicate to the Pythian priestess what Crœsus was at that very moment doing in Lydia. In like manner, as they are continually passing to and fro through the region of the air, they can foretell the changes of the weather; and thus procure for the idol the reputation of possessing an insight into futurity. When by their delusions they have induced men to offer sacrifice, they hover about the victim; snuffing up with delight the savory steam, which is their proper food. The demons employed other artifices in order to effect the destruction of man. As during their abode in heaven they were enabled to obtain some insight into the nature of the Divine dispensations, they endeavored to preoccupy the minds of men, and to prevent them from embracing Christianity, by inventing fables bearing some resemblance to the truths which were to become the objects of faith under the Gospel. Thus they invented the tales of the tribunal of Minos and Rhadamanthus in the infernal regions; of the river Pyriphlegethon, and the Elysian Fields; in order that when the doctrines of a future judgment, and of the eternal happiness and misery prepared for the good and wicked in another life, should be revealed, the common people might think the former equally credible, the philosopher equally incredible, with the latter." — **John [Kaye]** Bishop of Lincoln, *Ecc. Hist. Illust. from Tertullian*, 3d edit. pp. 200 – 204.

[6] Tertullian evidently identifies in some passages the demon with the

Alexandria,[7] to whose opinions an additional reference is subjoined.[8]

Origen and Minucius Felix believed, equally with others of their time, in the active agency of demons. Even the agony in the garden and on the cross seem, in the eyes of the former, to have resulted from anticipations of conflict with them.[9]

---

heathen deity. See his *Apology*, 12, cited in *Underworld Mission*, p. 78; 3d edit. pp. 74, 75. Kaye has not made sufficient allowance for the fact that Tertullian's views were somewhat inconsistent with each other.

[7] "Clement speaks of apostate angels, who, smitten by the beauty of women, and giving themselves up to their lusts, were cast down from heaven. They revealed to women the Divine mysteries which had come to their knowledge, and which it was intended to keep secret until the advent of the Lord. Thus men received the doctrine of Providence and the knowledge of sublime things (τῶν μετεώρων). Demons, according to Clement, are hateful and impure Spirits, always tending downwards to the earth, hovering about tombs and monuments, where they are obscurely seen, like shadowy phantasms. He couples them with bad angels, and says that the name of angels or demons was given to the souls of men. In some places he applies the name δαίμονες [demons] to the heathen gods; in others he alludes to the Platonic distinction between gods and demons.

"With respect to the worship of demons, Clement doubts who first erected altars and offered sacrifices to them; but says expressly that the first altar to Love was erected by Charmus (qu. Charinus) in the academy. He speaks of a demon to whom gluttons are subject; but says that men cannot truly ascribe their sins to the agency of demons; since, if they can, they will themselves be free from guilt. He defines the passions, impressions made upon the soft and yielding soul by the spiritual powers, against whom we have to wrestle. The object of these malevolent powers is on every occasion to produce something of their own habits or dispositions, and thus to bring again under their subjection those who have renounced them (in baptism). In the case of demoniacal possessions, the demon entered into the possessed person, who in consequence did not speak his own language, but that of the demon. The magicians, however, pretended that they could at all times command the services of the demons." — **John [Kaye]** Bishop of Lincoln, *Writings and Opinions of Clement of Alexandria*, pp. 359 – 361.

[8] See *Underworld Mission*, p. 97; 3d edit. p. 93, note 1.

[9] See *Underworld Mission*, § XV. Origen, however, believed equally

The overthrow of these demons was sometimes held up as the object of Christ's mission. **Justin Martyr** says (*Apol.* **2,** 6): "He became man . . . that he might overthrow the demons."

If we now turn to the Gospels we find not one word concerning the heathen deities. The Teacher of teachers does not even allude, as there represented, to this fearful conflict which his followers were to wage at every step through life. Any demons mentioned in the Gospels are simply depicted as authors of some physical disease, but are nowhere identified with the heathen deities, nor represented as objects of worship. It is morally impossible, if the early Christians had tampered with their Master's history, that this — to them all absorbing — subject should have been totally overlooked, and no teachings in regard to it have been ascribed to the Master.

§ 2. *Concerning Idolatry.*

Distinct from any question as to the origin and character of these beings was their identification with the wooden or metallic or earthenware images which were supposed to represent them. This treatment of an image as a god was heartily ridiculed by Christians, as it had been (Wisdom of Solomon, **13,** 11 - 19) by Jews before them. When the image was of wood, or of cheap metal, or of pottery, they took satisfaction in pointing out its defects, or the base uses to which chance only prevented it from being applied. If it were of costly metal, Christians pointed out that the god needed a guard to prevent him from being stolen. The Epistle to Diognetus (§ 2) condenses these arguments.

---

in the ministry of good angels ; see Lamson, *Church of the First Three Centuries,* pp. 195, 196, and Huet, *Origeniana,* **2,** 2, 5 ; pp. 272 - 350 in Vol. **22** of Lommatzsch's Origen.

"By these and similar fables the same demons have filled the ears of the inexperienced that they might excite an execrating horror against us." — **Minucius Felix,** *Octavius,* 28, pp. 142, 143, edit. Davis. Minucius had previously given a list of crimes charged against Christians, among which (p. 142, compare p. 49) was the eating of infants.

Another question concerning Idolatry was ethical: Did, or did not, God regard it as a crime the most serious which his children could commit?

Before attending to this, it may be well to say that, even prior to the Christian era, Idolatry was by the ruling classes kept up for political reasons. (Compare *Judaism*, p. 155 n.) In the reign of Claudius, A. D. 41 – 54, it had died out at Rome and needed to be revived. The effort to revive it was merely a political one, yet the privileged classes, who labored for its restoration, seem to have found a moderate degree of belief among the weak-minded and superstitious. Honest belief in Idolatry was the exception, yet the exception was frequent enough to deserve attention. Let us set aside the credulity of the dishonest, who thought that by paying a god sufficiently, he would aid them in misdeeds, and let us take a case of honest belief.

Let us suppose that a heathen had sacrificed to a heathen divinity either because of his own escape from peril, or because some member of his family had been restored to health. If he did it in good faith, believing in aid received from the deity, was he committing a crime which the Supreme Being would not forgive?

Let us suppose that a monotheistic brother or relative were invited by the heathen to join in the feast of thankfulness. Would such guest, by tasting ignorantly or knowingly the meat which had been offered to an idol, commit a crime the most serious in the eye of God?

Some Liberalist Jews would, equally with Paul, have taken ground that eating the meat[10] was indifferent, save when it caused risk of misleading others into what they believed wrong. The mass, however, of Jews and Jewish Christians would have deemed it a gross delinquency under any circumstances to taste such meat. The Council of Christians held at Jerusalem expressly forbade

---

[10] "Do not for the sake of food undo the work of God. All things indeed are clean ; but that which is pure is evil for that man who eateth so as to be an occasion of sin." — **Rom. 14**, 20. See also 1 Cor. **8**, 8 – 10, quoted in Ch. II. note 5, and Coloss. **2**, 16, quoted in Ch. II. note 11.

it. Even the heathen, who with a good motive, or at least with nothing wrong in his purpose, had spread such a feast, would, by many Jews and by a large proportion of Jewish Christians, have been deemed guilty of an offence for which he could not deeply enough bow himself in penitence.

The Christians, in their conflict with heathenism, came to regard Idolatry as the chief of all sins.[11]

Of this question, which caused great trouble even in Apostolic times, — and by which the mentally weak may have been perplexed even to agony, — nothing appears in the Gospels. The Teacher of teachers is not represented as uttering one word for the guidance of his followers.

§ 3. *Christ's Mission to the Underworld.*

Among early Christians a belief prevailed, which began probably in the first century, that Christ at his death entered on a Mission to the Underworld. This belief permeated every branch of the Christian community, and seems to have taken deep hold in each and every one of them.[12] It was a favorite explanation of the object for which Christ died.[13] The vicarious atonement does not at the present day occupy a more prominent place in the theology of those denominations which attach most importance to it, than did the Underworld Mission in the theology of the early Christians.

The Gospels make no mention of Christ's Mission to the Underworld. Had the early Christians fabricated them from their own views, this omission would be unac-

---

[11] "The principal crime of the human race, the chief indictment against the world, the sole cause of the judgment, is Idolatry." — **Tertullian**, *de Idololat.* 1.

"Others say: We more than others practically recognize the Divine nature, recognizing it and [its] images. . . . How do you pronounce yourself more than others practical recognizers [of the Divine nature, you] who recognize it least of all, meriting destruction of your souls by this one and unequalled sin, if truly you persevere in it?" — **Clementine Homilies, 11,** 12.

[12] *Underworld Mission,* §§ 1 - 24.   [13] *Underworld Mission,* § 6.

countable. Jesus is not even made in the Gospels to tell his disciples, after returning to life, the important work which he was supposed to have performed.

§ 4. *Resurrection of the Flesh.*

Prior to the Christian era a belief prevailed among Jews in a future *anastasis*, that is, a resurrection or replacement. In some cases a replacement of mankind alone may have been intended, but in others a replacement of the world, of mankind, and of the animal creation may have been included in the term. In this latter shape the Stoics seem to have borrowed the view.[14]

Christians adopted the Jewish term, but differed among themselves as to what they should understand by it. Some understood a physical resurrection of mankind, while others held that at death we permanently left our present physical bodies. Between these two divisions of Christians there was sharp discussion. The believers in a physical resurrection regarded the opposite party as heretical. The opposite party regarded adherents of the physical resurrection as weak-minded or stupid.

In a former work[15] an outline has been given of the two parties. Even in Apostolic times we find that the

---

[14] *Judaism at Rome*, p. 44, note 12, and p. 57, note 50.

[15] *Underworld Mission*, Appendix, Note E. To the citations there given should be added the following. **Tatian**, after telling the heathens that they held a medley of conflicting opinions, adds: "Some say . . . that the soul only is rendered immortal, but I, that the flesh [is rendered immortal] with it." — *Orat.* 25; *Opp.* p. 104 C D, edit. Otto; p. 265 C, edit. Maran. "Since the Lord . . . arose bodily . . . it is manifest that his disciples, . . . receiving their bodies and rising perfectly, that is, bodily as the Lord arose, will thus come into the presence of God." — **Irenæus, 5,** 31, 2.

Tertullian, in a work devoted to this question, argues (*de Resurrect. Carnis*, 7, 8) that the body ministers to the privileges of the soul and in martyrdom suffers imprisonment or torment, and would not be fairly treated unless gifted equally as the soul with future reward. Compare a similar idea in Athenagoras, *de Resurrect.* 18, p. 264 D A, edit. Otto.

discussion touching the resurrection and the future body must have been animated.[16]

If we now turn to the Gospels, we find nothing taught by the Master, nor any question raised, concerning man's future body, or as to whether he should have a body. An argument of our Savior in one passage implies that those who had passed away were yet in existence.[17] In another passage a FUTURE resurrection might seem to be implied,[18] but in neither case is there an argument or distinct statement as to the character of the future body.

§ 5. *The Millennium.*

Among Jews a belief existed in a Millennium, a period of one thousand years, during which the good were to live on earth untroubled by the presence of the bad.[19] Among Christians this belief reappears already in Apostolic times,[20] and must have been largely held by Jewish and semi-Jewish Christians.[21] Among Liberalist Catholics, however,

---

[16] 1 Cor. **15**, 12-44.

[17] Jesus quotes (**Matt. 22**, 32; **Mark 12**, 26, 27; **Luke 20**, 37, 38) from the Old Testament the words : " I am the God of Abraham, and the God of Isaac, and the God of Jacob," and appends the remark, " God is not a God of the dead, but of the living," implying that at the date when God uttered these words Abraham, Isaac, and Jacob were alive.

[18] Jesus speaks of those who were in their graves (John **5**, 28, 29) as hereafter to hear his voice and to come forth. The passage, though it affirms nothing concerning a physical resurrection, might suggest it to those who already believed in it.

[19] Trypho the Jew is represented by Justin as saying : " Tell me truly, do you confess that this place, Jerusalem, is to be rebuilt, and do you expect your People to be assembled and rejoice with the Messiah, together with the patriarchs and prophets and those [either] of our race, or who became proselytes [to our views] before the advent of your Christ ? " — **Justin Martyr**, *Dial.* 80, *Opp.* **2**, 272 C, edit. Otto ; p. 177 C, edit. Maran. The answer (see note 21) implies that the rejoicing would be for a thousand years.

[20] Rev. **20**, 2-7.

[21] **Papias** "said that after the resurrection of the [just ?] dead there would be a special thousand years, the reign of Christ being understood

we find it so sharply ridiculed as to imply that its opponents were anxious to avoid any appearance of holding it. Its advocates looked upon those who rejected it as swerving from the true faith.

On this disputed point not a word appears in the Gospels. The Teacher gives his followers no instruction on the subject.

§ 6. *Restoration of Jerusalem.*

From the date when the Jewish Temple was destroyed, or surrounded by Roman armies, which threatened its destruction, a belief gained currency among the Jews, that

---

as a physical one upon this earth."— **Eusebius,** *Ecc. Hist.* **3,** 39 ; *Opp.* **1,** p. 284, edit. Heinich.; **1,** 112 C, edit. Vales. To this Eusebius appends the remark that Papias was a man of exceedingly little mind.

Justin Martyr says : "I and any other Christians who think correctly on all points, understand that there is to be a resurrection of the flesh and a [residence of a] thousand years in Jerusalem rebuilt and adorned and enlarged, as the prophets Ezekiel [**37,** 12 sqq.] and Isaiah [**65,** 17-25] and the others acknowledge."— *Dial.* 80, *Opp.* **2,** 276 B, edit. Otto ; p. 178 B C, edit. Maran.

" These things [promised by Jesus] are [to be received] in the times of the kingdom, that is, in the seventh day . . . which is the true sabbath of the just . . . all animals — using the kinds of food which are derived from the earth — will be made pacific and mutually harmonious." — **Irenæus,** *cont. Hæres.* **5,** 33, 2-3.

"God made the work of his hands in six days and finished on the seventh day and rested on it. . . . This means that God will finish all things in six thousand years, for a day with him is as one thousand years. . . . He rested on the seventh day. This means, when his son, coming, shall do away the time of the Law-less One and shall condemn unbelievers, and shall change the sun and moon and stars, then he shall rest gloriously on the seventh day." — **Barnabas,** *Epist.* 15 ; (*al.* **13,** 3-6.)

"Papias . . . is said to have enunciated the Jewish Millennium — a duplicate of it ; whom Irenæus and Apollinarius and others followed, saying that after the resurrection the Lord will reign bodily with his saints. Tertullian also, in a book *On the Hope of the Faithful*, and Victorinus of Pettaw and Lactantius followed this view."— **Jerome,** *de Viris Illust.* 18, *Opp.* **2,** col. 859, 860.

Jerusalem would be rebuilt and enlarged by Divine power.[22] The belief must have appeared equally early among Jewish Christians, who regarded it as the locality where their Master was to reign.[23] It was held by semi-Jewish Christians in the second century.[24] Even Liberalist Catholics retained Jewish phraseology whilst essentially modifying Jewish views.[25]

Of these expectations nothing whatever appears in the Gospels, although these Gospels were obviously written by persons of Jewish education.

§ 7. *Rome's Destruction.*

Sixty-three years before the Christian era, a Roman general had shocked Jewish feeling by entering the Holy of Holies, and had wounded Jewish pride by conquering their nation. From that time we find a belief among Jews, that God had doomed Rome to destruction, and that this destruction would be the precursor of the new or Messianic era.[26]

Christians adopted this belief in apostolic times,[27] and it retained its hold on the Jewish and semi-Jewish portions of them for centuries.[28]

No word concerning this belief appears in the Gospels.

---

[22] Sympathy with Jewish feeling and opinion is the only source whence Christians can have obtained this view. **Irenæus** quotes (**5**, 35, 1, 2) various passages from the Old Testament in support of it, using, among others, a passage of **Baruch** (**4**, 36, 37) in which is the statement, "Arise, Jerusalem, and stand on high . . . and see thy children collected from the rising of the sun even to his setting." — The extant Latin differs slightly from the Septuagint.

[23] Rev. **21**, 9 - **22**, 5.

[24] See note 21, and compare *Judaism*, pp. 256, 268.

[25] According to Origen, the holy city (Matt. **27**, 53) into which the saints entered was the "Heavenly Jerusalem," the "TRULY holy city, the Jerusalem over which Jesus had not wept." — **Origen**, *Comment. in Matt.* Lib. **12**, 43, *Opp.* edit. de la Rue, **3**, 566 A; edit. Lommatzsch, **3**, 203.

[26] See *Judaism at Rome*, pp. 116 - 134.

[27] *Judaism*, pp. 265 - 268.   [28] *Judaism*, pp. 135, 136.

§ 8. *Beliar, or Antichrist.*

As early as A. D. 52, in which year the Jews were expelled from Rome, or else in the succeeding year, we find, both among them and Christians, a belief that the Roman emperor, as chief opponent of the religion which God had introduced, would be overthrown, and that his destruction would introduce the new era. In Jewish documents [29] he is called Beliar. In a Christian document he is termed the LAWLESS ONE,[30] that is, THE HEATHEN.

In the year 52 or 53 an effort must have been made by some of the aristocracy to place the statue of Claudius in the Temple at Jerusalem.[31] The expulsion of the Jews and the current of anti-Jewish feeling may have prompted some of them to suppose that it would be a happy political stroke. The effort seems to have been made from Samaria, where its designers may have secured co-operation from some of the less religious Samaritans.[32]

---

[29] *Judaism*, pp. 138 – 140, 239 n.

[30] *Judaism*, pp. 235, 236. **Irenæus** mentions "the resurrection of the Just . . . which takes place after the advent of Antichrist." — *Cont. Hæres.* **5**, 35, 1.

[31] Tacitus tells us *indirectly* (*An.* **12**, 54) that the Jews were expecting Claudius to attempt putting his statue in the Temple. Josephus mentions (*Wars*, **2**, 12, 1) a difficulty at the Temple in which, according to his — no doubt exaggerated — account, ten thousand Jews were killed; and attributes the commotion, as also some subsequent ones, to causes so trifling as to imply that for some reason he has avoided telling the truth. We find, moreover, in the same writer (*Wars*, **2**, 12, 7) that the younger King Agrippa, who visited Rome perhaps with special reference to this difficulty, confronted there the Roman governor and THE SAMARITANS; and in the writings of Paul (see *Judaism*, p. 236 n) we find a passage scarcely explicable, unless some effort had been made which was parried by Agrippa. Josephus would willingly pervert the truth if it suited his interest, which at Rome may have been the case.

[32] Justin Martyr mentions (*Apol.* **1**, 26, 56) that in the time of Claudius a statue had been voted to a Samaritan named Simon, whom Justin identifies with Simon Magus. A statue to a Sabine deity, which has been dug up on an island in the Tiber, may have misled Justin, who was

Whether the Roman emperor, at a yet earlier date, had been regarded as the aspiring opponent whom God was to crush, may admit question. Between A. D. 41, when Caligula was murdered, and A. D. 52 or 53, whose occurrences we have just narrated, the Jewish aristocracy had been inventing falsehoods against Caligula.[33] Whether the charge against him, of intending to put his statue in the Temple, had any existence before A. D. 52 or 53, is a matter of inference. The Jewish aristocracy, who in exculpation of their own crimes had been maligning him, may not have invented this particular charge until the action of their political associates, the Roman aristocracy, had rendered it necessary.

Of Beliar, or Antichrist, or of any questions connected with such a being, not a trace appears in the Gospels.

§ 9. *Nero's Return.*

Blended with the preceding head, was the belief held by many Jews and Christians, subsequently to Nero's death, in A. D. 68, that Nero would return as Beliar, or Antichrist.

Among heathens the belief that he would return had nothing supernatural connected with it, being based on the supposition that he was not dead. In the course of a lifetime it died out.

Among Jews and Christians an anticipation existed that he was to come back from the Underworld, or from some locality outside of this life, and that his return was to precede the new era.[34] Of this belief not a word appears in the Gospels.

---

not critically gifted, and who may have known only at second-hand concerning the statue there. That any co-operation with the patricians should have been rewarded by them with a statue, or at least with the voted promise of one, is natural enough. The death of Claudius may have prevented its erection. Compare preceding note.

[33] See *Judaism at Rome,* pp. 137–140.

[34] See *Judaism at Rome,* Appendix, Note F.

§ 10. *Conflagration of the World.*

A belief which originated among Jews, and had been adopted by Stoics, before the Christian era, was that the world would undergo a renovation by fire, from which it would emerge in pristine excellence and beauty.[35]

Christians adopted, even in Apostolic times, the belief in such a conflagration.[36] In the second and subsequent centuries [37] it prevailed to no small extent.

No allusion appears in the Gospels to this expectation, one of the most vivid which prevailed among Christians.

§ 11. *God Devoid of Name.*

In the controversy between Christians and heathens no little stress was laid by the former on an assertion that the Supreme and Uncreated God must necessarily be devoid of name.[38] In heathen lands, where the Gentile gods had names, this view of the Christians originated naturally and acquired prominence.

---

[35] See *Judaism*, pp. 44, 45, 55–57.

[36] "The heavens and the earth, which are now, by the same word are kept in store, reserved unto fire against the day of judgment and perdition of ungodly men. . . . The heavens being on fire shall be dissolved, and the elements shall melt with fervent heat. Nevertheless, we, according to his promise, look for new heavens and a new earth, wherein dwelleth righteousness." — **2 Pet. 3**, 7, 12, 13. Compare *Judaism*, pp. 485, 486.

[37] "Sibylla and Hystaspes say that there will be a dissolution of corruptible things by fire." — **Justin Martyr**, *Apol.* **1**, 20. "The prophetic spirit fore-indicated through Moses, that there will be a conflagration." — *Apol.* **1**, 60. "We affirm that the conflagration will take place thus." — *Apol.* **2**, 7. "The wicked demons strive to persuade you that there will be no conflagration for the punishment of heathens." — *Apol.* **1**, 57. Compare a conjectural emendation of editors, *Apol.* **1**, 45; in Otto's edit. p. 228, note 3. "Some one [among Stoics? or heathens?] will say . . . that the conflagration will take place at stated times, but I [that it will take place] only once." — **Tatian**, *Orat.* 25; *Opp.* p. 104 C, edit. Otto; p. 265 B, edit. Maran. See also *Judaism at Rome*, p. 45, note 15.

[38] See *Underworld Mission*, p. 152 n, 3d edit. p. 146 n, and compare in the present work a citation from Eusebius in Ch. VIII. note 4.

No allusion to it appears in the Gospels. The term God appears in them as having a well-settled meaning, which permitted no questions concerning it.

§ 12. *Old Testament Predictions.*

In Apostolic times we find quotations made from the Old Testament, and arguments based upon these quotations, in proof that Jesus was the Christ.[39]

In the second century, after the Jewish rebellion under Hadrian, Christians, or at least a large portion of them, had a mania for arguments of this class.[40] Passages from the Old Testament, which often needed laborious and improbable explanations, as a means of forcing them to predict circumstances in the life of Jesus, were quoted at length and treated as conclusively plain. The Jews were treated as wilfully blind and obstinate in their refusal to accept these interpretations. The professed discussions with, or arguments against, them were probably intended for circulation among Gentiles, and passages therein quoted as arguments were urged on Gentiles, as if they admitted no other explanation.

The inability of Christians to use their own records in behalf of their assertions predisposed them to stretch other arguments to their utmost. The author of the **Cohortatio ad Græcos** calls attention to the preservation of these Old Testament predictions by the Jews, as a work of Providence, since the Christians, by quoting from writings preserved in the synagogues of their enemies, would be free from suspicion of having tampered with them.[41]

The stress laid on prophecy may be inferred from an objection to the heathen deities, made by Commodianus, that they had not been predicted.[42] He meant, probably,

---

[39] Acts **2**, 25-36; **13**, 32-37; **18**, 28.
[40] *Judaism at Rome*, pp. 344-346.
[41] Ch. 13, Justin, *Opp.* p. 48 E.
[42] "No one prophesied beforehand that he (Saturn) would be born." — **Commodianus**, *Instruct.* **6**, line 13. "You pray to so many gods . . . nor were they themselves predicted." — *Instruct.* **8**, ll. 8, 9.

that beings who came into existence without having been foretold had nothing divine about them.

In the Gospels there is no quotation from the Old Testament extant, on which Jesus is represented as basing an argument for his Divine mission. Two passages [43] might raise the question whether he believed the Old Testament to contain such predictions, but no quotation of them, with an argument from them by Jesus, is to be found in the Gospels.[44] This certainly would not have been the fact, if Christians of the second century, or even of Apostolic times, had fabricated or interpolated them with reference to their own conceptions of truth.

§ 13. *Jesus as Deity of the Old Testament.*

A little after A. D. 150 [45] the opinion was broached among Christians that Jesus was the God who had spoken to the Patriarchs, had shut the door of the Ark after

---

[43] One of these passages (**John 5**, 39, 46, 47), though frequently understood as an appeal to predictions, favors by its connection the supposition that Jesus had in view the moral and religious instructions of Moses, written with reference to himself, that is (see *Judaism*, p. 394), to prepare the way for his mission. The impediment specified by Jesus as preventing belief on him is not an inability to decipher predictions, but that, "you have not the love of God in you. . . . How can you believe who accept honor from each other and seek not that honor which is from the Only God ? . . . Had you believed Moses you would have believed me, for it was with reference to me that he wrote."

The other passage (**Luke 24**, 25-27) admits either supposition, that Jesus referred to predictions or to moral instructions, yet the latter is favored by a subsequent remark of the disciples (**24**, 32): "Did not our hearts burn within us . . . as he opened to us the Scriptures?" An explanation of predictions would have exercised the mind rather than warmed the heart.

[44] Jesus appeals (John **5**, 32-34) to the testimony of John, though alleging that it ought to be needless; he appeals (John **5**, 36) to his miracles and (John **7**, 17) to the character of his teaching, but in no instance does the record contain an explanation by him of the manner in which an Old Testament prediction is applicable to himself.

[45] See Appendix, Note M.

Noah, and whose presence was in various ways recorded in the Old Testament. This view had in the third century gained considerable foothold, but it is difficult to say whether within a quarter of a century after its origin it found adherents enough to create any strong probability of its ingress into the Gospels, if at that date they had been in process of formation. The probability will seem stronger or weaker, according to the hold on the minds of Christians which the reader supposes the above view to have taken.

The view of course does not exist in the Gospels.

§ 14. *Personal Appearance of Jesus.*

In the latter half of the second century, and the first half of the third, a mania, as already said (see § 12), existed among many Christians for misapplying to their Master passages from the Old Testament, which they had deluded themselves into regarding as predictions.[46] They treated the words of **Isaiah,** "He had no form, nor comeliness, that we should look upon him, nor beauty, that we should take pleasure in him,"[47] as spoken of Jesus, and put into their Master's mouth the twenty-second **Psalm,** of which verse 6 reads, "I am a worm, and not a man; the reproach of men, and the scorn of the people."[48]

Justin repeatedly mentions "the first coming of Christ,

---

[46] See *Judaism,* pp. 344-346, with the explanation there given as to what strengthened this mania.

[47] Ch. **53,** 2, *Noyes' trans.*

[48] Justin, though treating the Psalm (*Dial.* 98-106) as spoken by Christ, interprets verse 7 (*Dial.* 101) as indicating merely Jewish contempt for Jesus. Origen, though understanding the passage as spoken by Jesus, and giving two widely divergent interpretations of the verse (*In Exod. Hom.* **7,** 8, *Opp.* **2,** p. 156 A; *In Lucam, Hom.* **14,** *Opp.* **3,** p. 948 F), does not in either of them apply it to the personal appearance of Jesus. Tertullian, however (*adv. Judæos,* 14, p. 228 B), quotes it separately from the rest of the Psalm, and in a connection which indicates that he so applied it. Probably Justin and Origen shrank from an interpretation which their heathen opponents were over-willing to see and use even without Christian aid.

in which it was foretold that he should appear without honor, and UNSIGHTLY and mortal." [49]

The **Pseudo-Thaddeus** is represented as telling Abgarus, "To-morrow gather together all the citizens, and then in their hearing I will . . . inform them of the coming of Christ, . . . and about the MEANNESS and DESPICABLENESS of his outward appearance." [50]

A passage in the **Sibylline Oracles** says of Christ: "Not in glory, but as a mortal [on the way] to his trial he will come, pitiable, dishonored, DEVOID OF FORM, that he may give hope to the miserable." [51]

Whether Irenæus meant to affirm the same unsightliness, may be a question. His language favors it.[52]

Statements and quotations such as the foregoing were admirably adapted to furnish material for heathen humorists and controversialists who wished to caricature the Founder of Christianity. Nor were they slow to avail themselves of the offered material. **Celsus** says: "Since the Divine spirit was in the body [of Jesus], it ought entirely to surpass those of others in size, or beauty, or strength, or voice, or majesty, or persuasiveness, for it is impossible that he, in whom the divinity is present more than in others, should in no wise differ from another; but this [body] differed nothing from another, but, as they say, was SMALL and UNSIGHTLY and IGNOBLE." [53]

Origen replies that Celsus ignores opposite delinea-

---

[49] *Dial.* 14. Compare similar statements in cc. 49, 85, 100, 110; pp. 52 D, 158 B, 288 A, 336 E, 364 E. Justin evidently lays emphasis on these statements.

[50] See fuller quotation in Appendix, Note F.

[51] Book **8**, 256, 257, quoted more fully in Appendix, Note J.

[52] "They who say . . . '*He will take on himself our infirmities, and will bear our weaknesses*' [Is. 53, 4], announced the cures which were performed by him. Some also predicted that 'he would come to Jerusalem as a man INFIRM and INGLORIOUS, and knowing how to bear infirmity' [**Is. 53**, 3] and sitting on the foal of an ass."— **Irenæus**, *cont. Hæres.* **4**, 33, 11 - 12.

[53] Celsus quoted by **Origen**, *cont. Cels.* **6**, 75 (requoted **6**, 77) ; *Opp.* edit. de la Rue, **1**, pp. 688, 689; edit. Lommatzsch, **19**, p. 425.

tions of Jesus in the Scriptures. He says: "Confessedly there is written the things [said] concerning the body of Jesus having been unsightly; but not as set forth, that it was ignoble, nor is it clearly manifested that it was small." [54] He then quotes, as equally apposite to Jesus, the words of **Psalm 45**, 3, "Gird thy sword upon thy thigh, mighty in thy stateliness and beauty," [55] and asks, "How does (Celsus) not see the superiority of the body of Jesus (and its consequent usefulness) in its ability to appear to beholders as it ought to be seen by each one?" [56]

Origen had already mentioned that Jesus had not merely the unsightly body, but also the glorified one, in which he appeared with Moses and Elijah; [57] yet it is evident that besides these two forms of unsightliness and glory, he assumed a changeability in the personal appearance of Jesus. In at least one other instance he utters the same view.[58] Whether this were a conviction, or a temporary mental expedient for meeting an opponent's

---

[54] *Cont. Cels.* **6**, 75; edit. de la Rue, **1**, 689 B; edit. Lommatzsch, **19**, 426.

[55] *Cont. Cels.* **6**, 75; edit. de la Rue, **1**, pp. 689–690; edit. Lommatzsch, **19**, 427.

[56] *Cont. Cels.* **6**, 77; edit. de la Rue, **1**, p. 690 D; edit. Lommatzsch, **19**, 429.

[57] *Cont. Cels.* **6**, 76.

[58] The following translation is from **Norton's** *Genuineness*, Vol. **3**, p. 174, and is, he says, "considerably abridged" from the original. "'A tradition has come down to us, that Jesus had not only two forms, that in which he was seen by all, and that in which he was seen by his disciples at his transfiguration; but that he appeared to every one in the form of which he was worthy; and that (at times) when present, he appeared to all like another person. Thus he resembled the manna, which had a different taste for different individuals, accommodated to every man's liking. And this tradition does not seem to me incredible. But if it were so, we may explain why the multitude which accompanied Judas, though they had often seen Jesus, nevertheless needed some one familiar with him to point him out to them, on account of the changes of his form.'"— Origen, *Series Comment. in Matt.* § 100; *Opp.* **3**, p. 906, edit. de la Rue; Vol. **4**, p. 446, edit. Lommatzsch.

argument, is not obvious, though the latter is the more probable.

Possibly some Christians may, even during the mania above mentioned, have revolted at the thought of attributing to their Master, without historical evidence, an unsightly appearance. Clement of Alexandria, by his general tone of reference to Jesus, renders improbable that he can have shared the disposition to treat him as personally repulsive. A forged letter in the name of Lentulus,[59] an assumed heathen, has come down to us, which must have been an effort by some Christian to counteract the foregoing folly. It ascribes to Jesus personal stateliness and beauty. This — though the miracles receive a passing mention — is the chief object of the letter, and places it in marked contrast to other pseudo-heathen or pseudo-Jewish records of Jesus, which testify mainly to his ministry and miracles.

Concerning the personal appearance of Jesus not a word appears in the Gospels; neither unsightliness nor beauty is attributed to him.

CHAPTER IV.

CHRISTIAN CUSTOMS.

In some respects customs are more likely than mere opinions to cause collision or friction between those who observe different ones. In so far as we can feel assured of this having been the case touching Christian usages, they afford a strong and independent argument for integrity of the Gospels.

§ 1. *Concerning the Sabbath.*

Jewish Christians continued in most cases, equally with non-Christian Jews, to rest from labor on the seventh day,

---

[59] See the letter in Appendix, Note D.

and to assemble on it for religious services. Gentile Christians found difficulties in the way of observing any day of rest, especially in times of political excitement. In such times a man of standing would have risked prosecution for observance of Foreign Rites, had he kept the seventh day as one of rest, while many slaves and many free laborers would not have been allowed control of their time.

We find in the Apostolic Age that Paul treats the sabbath as not binding on Gentile Christians,[1] and his tone indicates that there was no little feeling on the subject. He urges that those who deemed one day more holy than another, and that those who deemed ALL DAYS alike, should not interfere with or condemn each other. His own views are plainly expressed that the Gentile Christians should not keep the sabbath.

In the second century, after the imbittered war between Jews and heathens under Hadrian, we find intense feeling in discussions concerning the sabbath. A portion of the Christians treat the Jews as utterly foolish for observing any day of rest, and speak of the sabbath as a temporary institution, imposed upon the Jews because of their hard-heartedness.[2]

---

[1] See Ch. II. note 11.

[2] Portions of this discussion from Paul (Galat. **4,** 9, 10 ; Coloss. **2,** 16, 17), Justin Martyr, Irenæus, and the Epistle to Diognetus have already been given in Ch. II. note 11 ; see also Rom. **14,** 5, quoted in Ch. II. note 6.

Irenæus, equally with some other writers, takes ground that the sabbath was a temporary institution for the Jews, intended as a *sign*, or reminder, of an agreement between them and God. He argues : " The prophet **Ezekiel** [20, 12] says the same concerning sabbaths : ' I have given them my sabbaths that they may be for a sign between me and them,'. . . and in **Exodus** [31, 16, 17] God says to Moses, 'and you shall observe my sabbaths, for it will be a sign to you with me, as regards your race.' These things, therefore [circumcision and the sabbath], were given for a sign." — Irenæus, **4,** 16, 1.

Tertullian says : " Finally, whoever contends that the sabbath is to be observed until the present time as a means of salvation . . . let

Of this discussion and of the acrimonious feeling occasioned by it not a word appears in the Gospels. The sabbath is there recognized (Mark **2**, 27) as made for man, not man for the sabbath. Nowhere do we find a word implying that it had come to an end.

§ 2. *Sunday as a Day of Religious Gatherings.*

Concerning the origin of Sunday service, no historical statement has been left us. Circumstances render probable that it originated towards the close of A. D. 52 or in A. D. 53. At that date a political condition of things rendered it dangerous for Gentiles to observe even in a limited degree the Jewish sabbath.[3] Paul, on separating from the Jewish synagogue at Corinth, seems to have commenced holding services on the first day of the week.[4]

In the second century Sunday was regarded as a day of religious joy. Christians on that day were not allowed either to fast or kneel, and, when called to pray, were told, "Stand perfectly straight."[5]

The custom of meeting on Sunday for religious service

---

him teach that the JUST MEN of former time [that is, those before Abraham or Moses] kept sabbaths . . . and were thus rendered friends of God. . . . He (God) commended his (Adam's) offspring, Abel, when offering sacrifices to himself, though . . . keeping no sabbath." — *Adv. Judæos*, 2.

"Those who were conversant with the old order of things have come to a new hope, no longer sabbatizing but living a life agreeably to the Lord's Day." — **Ignatius**, *Magnes.* 9 ; *al.* **3**, 3. See citation from the epistle ascribed to Barnabas in Ch. III. note 21.

[3] See *Judaism*, pp. 228 – 229.

[4] See *Judaism*, pp. 234, 239, 240. On the different terms "First Day," "Eighth Day," "Lord's Day," and "Sunday," see *Judaism*, pp. 68 – 70.

[5] See *Underworld Mission*, pp. 80, 81 ; 3d edit. pp. 77, 78. The term sabbath as a designation for Sunday had no existence for centuries after the Christian era. Christians of the second and of several succeeding centuries would have spurned any one as recreant to the Master who had dared to treat the day of that Master's victory over Death and the Underworld as the Jewish sabbath.

§ 2.] SUNDAY AS A DAY OF RELIGIOUS GATHERINGS. 45

led gradually to abstinence from any occupations which might distract attention from, or mar the effect of, these services. This doubtless was the chief reason for renouncing ordinary business, although Tertullian, the earliest writer who mentions such Sunday rest, attributes it to a different cause.[6]

Eastern Christians, though equally attentive as Western ones to an erect position on Sunday, differed from them by showing a similar respect for the seventh day or sabbath,[7] a respect which sometimes awakened ire in their western and more anti-Jewish brethren.[8]

---

[6] **Tertullian** says : "On the day of the Lord's resurrection we ought not only to abstain from it [kneeling] but from every anxiety . . . deferring even business, lest we should afford opportunity to the Devil [of rendering us anxious]." — *De Orat.* 18. An anxious or clouded face would have been deemed derogatory to the Master's triumphal day. The Christians individually, and in legislative enactments, designated Sunday as a festival, and subsequently needed perhaps on this account to guard the more against its devotion to public amusements. An extract or two are here added. Others can be found in Rheinwald's *Archæology*, § 61. In A. D. 321 an edict of **Constantine** (*Cod. Justin.* 3, 12, *de feriis*, 3), after forbidding lawsuits and mechanical arts on Sunday, permits harvesting. Somewhat later another edict (*Cod. Theod.* 2, 8, *de feriis*, 1) determines "all should have liberty of emancipating on [our] FESTAL day." The connection implies that Sunday is the day meant. The edicts will be found in the CORPUS JURIS CIVILIS, Vol. 2, col. 250.

Those who favored resting on Sunday are careful to guard against any supposition that it is the sabbath. The **Council of Laodicea** says (c. 29) "that it is not proper for any Christians . . . to avoid work on THE SABBATH, but . . . to show higher honor to the Lord's Day IF they can avoid work."

[7] The observance of both days is advocated in the **Apostolic Constitutions, 7,** 23 : "We make festival days of the sabbath AND the Lord's Day. The one as a remembrance of the creation, the other of the resurrection."

[8] "As concerns kneeling also [our habits of] prayer suffer diversity through a certain few who on the sabbath [seventh day] abstain from kneeling. . . . The Lord will favorably grant either that they [the dissentients] give up, or that they practise their opinions without scandal-

If we turn to the Gospels we find no direction uttered by the Savior as to the manner in which Sunday should be observed, or as to whether it should be observed at all. We find, also, no such terms as "Lord's Day," "Eighth Day," or "Sunday," but merely the Jewish term "First Day."

§ 3. *Eating of Blood.*

Among Jews a belief prevailed that the life or soul was in the blood, so that if the blood remained in cooked meat the life or soul would be eaten equally as the body. This gave rise doubtless to the prohibition in Genesis,[9] — a prohibition which is deemed binding by Jews even at the present day,[10] and has been adopted in the Greek Church,[11] a Church more influenced than the Latin one by Jewish views.

Jewish Christians retained the belief or prejudice in which they had been brought up. The favorite argument [12] against the obligation of Gentiles to obey what were deemed Mosaic institutions did not apply to the present prohibition. When the Apostles and elders at Jerusalem debated this with other matters, there was (**Acts 15,** 7) "much disputing." Peter's statement seems to have effected a decision that the Mosaic ritual law was not binding on Gentiles, but to this the following answer was obvious. If we assume that the Mosaic law is not binding, how does that justify us in releasing Gentile Chris-

---

izing others." — **Tertullian,** *De Orat.* 18; *al.* 23. Compare, however, (in Rheinwald, p. 160, note 2) views of Tertullian, *De Jejun.* 14, after he became a Montanist.

[9] "But flesh with the life thereof, which is the blood thereof, shall ye not eat." — **Gen. 9,** 4.

[10] If it be true that needless suffering is caused to slaughtered animals for the sake of freeing them from all blood, it could be wished that Jews might learn to regard the eating of blood in a different light.

[11] "The Eastern Church has continually preserved this abstinence [from blood], and preserves it even now." — **Routh,** *Reliquiæ Sacræ,* **1,** note on p. 343.

[12] See note 2, and in Ch. II. note 11.

tians from an obligation which existed before the Mosaic law? The present precept was given before the time of Moses, and cannot therefore have been intended for Jews only.

The Apostles and elders evidently did not see their way clear to meet this objection, and, in writing to the Gentile Christians, they include abstinence "from blood and from things strangled" as among necessary observances.[13]

The question caused sharp disputing among the early Christians, but in the Gospels we find no word concerning it. The statement of Jesus (Matt. 15, 11; Mark 7, 15), that a man is not defiled by what enters his mouth but by what proceeds from it, does not accord with the view that

---

[13] "It seemed good to the Holy Spirit and to us to lay upon you no greater burden than these NECESSARY things. That you abstain from meats offered to idols, and from blood, and from things strangled, and from fornication." — **Acts 15**, 28, 29. The allusion to the Holy Spirit means probably that they INTERPRETED Peter's vision as a communication from God which justified them in NOT requiring from Gentiles an observance of the Mosaic ceremonial law, though they did not infer from it any exemption from other obligations, or supposed obligations, which they specify.

In the Letter from the **Churches of Lyons and Vienne** it is said: "How should they [the Christians] — for whom it is not lawful to eat the blood of unreasoning animals — eat children?" — **Routh**, *Reliq. Sacræ*, **1**, 304. **Tertullian** says: "Your error [concerning] Christians should cause a blush, since we do not have even the blood of animals among our articles of food, since we abstain, moreover, from things strangled . . . lest we should be contaminated by any blood." — *Apol.* 9; *Opp.* pp. 10 D, 11 A. **Clement of Alexandria** says: "To human beings it is not lawful to touch blood, since to them the body is merely flesh, operated [vivified?] by blood. Human blood participates in the logos [reason?] and shares with the spirit the [Divine] favor." — *Pædag.* 3, 25, *al.* 3; *Opp.* p. 267, edit. Potter. **Minucius Felix** also states (*Octavius*, 30, p. 154) that Christians do not reckon blood in their list of eatables. These writers, except Clement of Alexandria, belong to the semi-Jewish school of Christians. **Origen** mentions (*cont. Cels.* **8**, 29) the letter of the Apostles and elders above cited, but prefixes to it the words of Jesus (Matt. **15**, 11) that not the things which enter the mouth but those which come out defile us, and the remark of Paul (1 Cor. **8**, 8)

blood in the food must be avoided, nor is it so specific on this point as it would have been made by the opposite party of Christians.

§ 4. *Baptism.*

The date when baptism originated is unknown. A question addressed to John the Baptist implies that it existed before his time.[14] Probably Jewish belief in the uncleanliness of heathens had prompted the ablution of converts to Judaism, and this ablution came thus to be considered as an initiatory rite.

Subsequently to the Savior's ministry, when the Apostles were diffusing their Master's religion, baptism seems to have been commonly administered to those who accepted their teachings. Whether it were the universal form of admission may be open to question, though admissions without it cannot have been numerous. We even find mention in one locality of vicarious baptism,[15] which implies that those who practised it must have imagined the rite a necessary one.

In the second century baptism seems to have been the generally accepted form of admission. Great importance and efficacy were attached to it. None but the baptized were, if we may credit Justin Martyr, admitted[16] to the

---

that food does not determine our acceptability to God. **Augustine** states (*cont. Faustum*, **32**, 13 ; *Opp.* **6**, p. 200, col. 2 C) that the avoidance of things strangled and of blood had about died out in Gentile churches where there was no admixture of Jews. He may have referred specially to Latin ones.

[14] The question addressed to John (**John 1**, 25) is not concerning the meaning of baptism, but "WHY baptizest thou ?" The questioners seem to have been acquainted with baptism and to have wished information merely as to why John practised it.

[15] Baptism for the dead (1 Cor. **15**, 29) indicates that some had been baptized for their departed relatives or friends.

[16] "In what manner we have dedicated ourselves to God, being created anew through Christ, we will now relate. . . . As many as are persuaded . . . are led by us where there is water . . . are born again, for they perform this bathing . . . in the name of the Father of all things and

§ 4.] BAPTISM. 49

Lord's Supper, which had already become something mysterious; yet we find dissentients.
"Those wretches excite questionings. They say, 'baptism is therefore unnecessary [for those] to whom faith is sufficient.'"[17]

If we now turn to the Gospels we find that although Jesus was baptized, yet the only baptism of those who followed him was performed by his disciples, not by himself (John 4, 2), and there is no statement that this baptism was by his direction. Some dispute on the subject took place between John's disciples and a Jew or Jews,[18] the former of whom seem to have felt sore on the subject.[19] Thereupon Jesus left that section of country[20] and during the rest of his ministry not the slightest allusion is made in three of the Gospels to baptism[21] and but one mention of it in the remaining Gospel. That mention occurs in the following direction of Jesus:—"Go and make disciples of all nations [*baptizing them into the name of the Father, and of the Son, and of the Holy Spirit*] teaching them to observe all things which I have commanded you."[22]

Master-God, and of our Savior Jesus Christ, and of the Holy Spirit." — **Justin Martyr**, *Apol.* **1,** 61.
"This nourishment is called among us the Eucharist, of which it is not permissible for any one to partake unless . . . bathed with the bathing for remission of sins and for regeneration." — **Justin Martyr**, *Apol.* **1,** 66. Compare views of Hermas quoted in *Underworld Mission*, pp. 58, 59; 3d edit. pp. 55-57.

[17] **Tertullian**, *de Baptismo*, 13. Tertullian's opponents (*de Baptismo,* 11) call attention to the fact that Jesus did not baptize.

[18] "Then there arose a question between some of John's disciples and the Jews, about purifying." — **John 3**, 25.

[19] "And they came unto John, and said unto him, Rabbi, he that was with you beyond Jordan, to whom you bore testimony, behold, the same baptizeth, and all men come to him." — **John 3,** 26.

[20] "He left Judea, and departed again into Galilee." — **John 4**, 3.

[21] The concluding verses appended to Mark's Gospel (**16,** 9-20) are known to be spurious. Compare on this subject Ch. XI. note 10. The Gospel as written by Mark ends with verse 8.

[22] **Matt. 28,** 19, 20. Compare Appendix, Note A, § 15. The bap-

In this instance, and in this only, we have in one of the Gospels a custom of the second century unknown to the Apostolic Age.[23] The question may arise whether the passage in brackets be not due to some marginal comment which has crept into the text; whether it be supposable that if Jesus had given such a direction the Apostles would have omitted to comply with, and teach obedience to it.

The formula, whether it belongs or not to the text, originated earlier than the doctrine of the Trinity. We find it in Justin Martyr, who wrote half a century before any deification of the Spirit as a person.[24] He treats the formula as common at a date when, as may be inferred from his writings, the deification of Jesus was barely incipient. On its origin see Appendix, Note P.

§ 5. *The Lord's Supper.*

Jesus at the close of his ministry, when partaking for the last time of a meal with those who had been companions of his ministry, asked them that when subse-

---

tismal formula however, as it exists in Matthew, is not found in the Acts of Pilate. Did it originate later than that document?

[23] The formula in the Apostolic Age appears in the following passages: "They were baptized in THE NAME OF THE LORD JESUS." — Acts 8, 16. "He [Peter] commanded them to be baptized in THE NAME OF THE LORD." — Acts 10, 48. "They were baptized in THE NAME OF THE LORD JESUS." — Acts 19, 5. "Be baptized and wash away thy sins, calling on THE NAME OF THE LORD." — Acts 22, 16.

[24] At an earlier date than the one mentioned above, the Alexandrine Gnostics (concerning whom see *Judaism*, pp. 331-336) personified the Holy Spirit as an æon. Whether they regarded these æons as real beings may be doubted, but according to their statements Christ and the Holy Spirit were developed subsequently to Man and the Assembly. No thought, therefore, of deifying either can have had place in their minds. Neither Christ nor the Holy Spirit in their system belonged to the first or higher Ogdoad of the æons. See Norton's *Genuineness*, 1st edit. Vol. 3, pp. 113-130, and compare, in *Judaism*, a note on pp. 353, 354.

quently they were at any time together, they should, in remembrance of him, break bread and drink a cup of wine.

In the second century we find that Christians, in copying this custom, had mingled with it conceptions to which the Master nowhere alludes. Had they originated the Gospel narrative the simple request of Jesus would have worn a much more marvellous appearance.

CHAPTER V.

DESIGNATIONS FOR GOD.

AMONG heathens the term god, equally as the term man, was a common noun, designating any or every god, but specifying no one in particular.[1] If they wished to specify some one god they did so by using his name.

Christians alleged, as already stated (see p. 36), that the Supreme Being was devoid of name: that he had no need of a name, since he had no equals from whom he needed to be distinguished. They said that he could not have a name because there was no one older than himself who could have named him.[2]

In addressing heathens, however, the Christians found constant need of using some designation for the Supreme Being, which should prevent their words from being misapplied to any other. Sometimes they termed him "the God without a name."[3] In other instances they used

---

[1] See *Judaism at Rome*, pp. 2–4.

[2] See quotations in *Underworld Mission*, p. 152, note †; 3d edit. p. 146, note 5. Compare in the present work Ch. VIII. note 4.

[3] Ἀνωνόμαστος, Tatian, *Orat.* 4; Just. Mart. *Apol.* 1, 63, p. 262 C. On this and other designations by Christians compare *Judaism*, p. 352, note 46. For designations used by Jews among heathens see *Judaism*, p. 4, note 4.

designations, several of which are subjoined with a slight attempt at classification.

"The true God"; "Him who is really God"; "the sole God"; "the unborn" or "unoriginated God"; "the first God"; "the ineffable God" or "the God not to be conversed with."[4]

"The Father of Justice"; "the Just Overseer"; "the God not to be swayed" nor "bribed."[5]

"The God free from suffering"; "the imperishable God"; "the ever-existing God"; "the eternal God."[6]

"The God of all things"; "the Master-God"; "The All-Ruler"; "King of the Heavens"; "God over the world."[7]

"The Creator"; "God the Maker"; "God, Maker of

---

[4] Θεὸς ἀληθινός, Justin Martyr, *Apol.* 1, 53, p. 242 C. ὁ ὄντως θεός, or θεὸς ὄντως ὤν, Just. *Apol.* 1, 13, p. 164 E; Clem. Alex. *Protrept.* 23, *Paed.* 1, 88, pp. 20, 150. ὄντως μόνος ὤν, Clem. Alex. *Paed.* 1, 71, p. 140. Θεὸς ἀγέννητος, Cohort. ad Græcos, 22, p. 66 A; Just. Mart. *Apol.* 1, 14, 25, 49, 53, 2, 6, 12, 13, pp. 66 A, 164 B, 190 B, 234 B, 240 A, 296 D, 310 C, 312 D; ἀγένητος, Athenagoras, *Legat.* 4, 8, 22, pp. 20 B, 38 D, 108 B. ὁ πρῶτος θεός, Just. *Apol.* 1, 60, p. 256 B. θεὸς ἄρρητος, Just. *Apol.* 1, 9, 61, 2, 12, 13, pp. 154, D, 260 D, 310 C, 312 D.

[5] Πατὴρ δικαιοσύνης, Just. *Apol.* 1, 6, p. 148 C. τῶν πάντων ἐπόπτης δίκαιος, Just. *Apol.* 2, 12, p. 310 A. θεὸς ἄτρεπτος, Just. *Apol.* 1, 13, p. 164 A. οὐδὲ δωροδοκητέος, Tatian, *Orat.* 4.

[6] Θεὸς ἀπαθής, Just. *Apol.* 1, 25, p. 190 B; Athenag. *Legat.* 8, p. 38 D; Clem. Alex. *Strom.* 2, 40, p. 450. θεὸς ἄφθαρτος, Just. *Dial.* 5, p. 28 D. θεὸς ἀεὶ ὤν, Cohort. ad Græc. 22; Just. *Apol.* 1, 14, pp. 66 E, 164 A. ἀΐδιος, Cohort. ad Græc. 22, p. 66 A (comp. 25, 26, pp. 74 A B, 76 D); Athenag. *Legat.* 22. p. 108 B.

[7] Τῶν πάντων θεός, Just. *Apol.* 1, 58, p. 252 A. θεὸς συμπάντων, Clem. Alex. *Paed.* 1, 74, p. 142. τῶν ὅλων θεός, *Strom.* 2, 45, p. 453. δεσπότης or δεσπόζων θεός, Just. *Apol.* 1, 12, 14, 32, 36, 40, 44, 46, 61 [bis], 2, 6, pp. 162 A, 166 D, 206 C, 212 E, 218 A, 224 C, 230 D, 258 A D, 296 D. δεσπότης τῶν ὅλων, Clem. Alex. *Protrept.* 10, 96, p. 77; Tatian, *Orat.* 5. παντοκράτωρ, Just. *Dial.* 16, 96, 139, 142, pp. 56 B, 328 A, 456 A, 462 D; Clem. Alex. *Paed.* 1, 81; *Strom.* 4, 172, pp. 148, 641. Theophilus, *ad Autol.* 1, 4, p. 14 D. Βασιλεὺς τῶν οὐρανῶν, Just. *Apol.* 2, 2, p. 288 C. ὑπὲρ κόσμον θεός, Just. *Dial.* 60, p. 200 A.

the world"; "Maker of the universe"; "Architect [of the world]."[8]

"Parent of all things"; "Father of the universe"; "Father of things visible and invisible"; "Father of the Heavens" or simply "the Father," meaning "the Originator" or sometimes, in accordance with Jewish usage, "the watchful Parent."[9]

Possibly some heathen may have treated these epithets as equivalent to names, since a Christian writer parries any such view.[10]

If we turn to the Gospels we find that the appellatives for the Deity are simply those which had been common among Jews in their intercourse with each other. They show no traces of Christian effort to prevent heathen misconception.

---

[8] Κτιστής, Just. *Apol.* **2**, 6, p. 296 D. θεὸς ὁ ποιήσας, Just. *Apol.* **1**, 58, p. 252 B. θεὸς τὸν πάντα κόσμον ποιήσας, Just. *Apol.* **2**, 5, p. 294 A. τοῦ κόσμου ποιητής, Athenag. *Legat.* 8 [bis], 10, pp. 38 D, 42 C, 48–50. ὁ ποιητὴς τῶν πάντων, Just. *Apol.* **1**, 20, 58, 67, pp. 180 C, 252 A, 268 D. ποιητὴς τοῦδε τοῦ παντός, Just. *Apol.* **1**, 26, p. 194 B, Athenag. *Legat.* 4, 30, pp. 22 C, 160 D; *De Resurrect.* 18, p. 262 D. θεὸς δημιουργός, Just. *Apol.* **1**, 8, 13, 23, 26, 58, 63, pp. 152 A, 162 C, 186 C, 192 A, 252 A, 264 B; Athenag. *Legat.* 10, 13, pp. 48–50, 58 B; Clem. Alex. *Paed.* **1**, 73, p. 141.

[9] Θεὸς ἀπάντων γεννήτωρ, Just. *Apol.* **1**, 13, p. 164 A. πατὴρ τῶν πάντων, Just. *Apol.* **1**, 8, 12, 32, 40, 45, 46, **2**, 6, pp. 152 A, 162 A, 206 B, 218 A, 228 D, 230 D, 296 D. πατὴρ τοῦ παντός, Athenag. *Legat.* 13, p. 58 B. πατὴρ τῶν ὅλων, Just. *Apol.* **1**, 44, 61 [bis] 63 [ter], 65, pp. 224 C, 258 A D, 264 B C [bis], 266 D; Clem. Alex. *Paed.* **1**, 35, 68, **3**, 40, pp. 129, 138, 278. πατὴρ αἰσθητῶν καὶ ἀοράτων, Tatian, *Orat.* 4. πατὴρ τῶν οὐρανῶν, Just. *Apol.* **2**, 2, p. 288 C.

[10] "The terms Father, and God, and Creator, and Lord, and Master, are not names, but appellations [derived from] his benefits and actions."—Just. Mart. *Apol.* **2**, 6; *Opp.* **1**, p. 296 D.

CHAPTER VI.

TERMS APPLIED TO CHRISTIANS.

§ 1. *Ἀσεβεῖς, Unbelievers.*

IN the contest between Judaism and heathenism, and subsequently in that of Judaism and Christianity against heathenism, certain terms came into existence as designations for those who had given up heathenism. During political embitterment the active use of these terms was such that we find them frequently occurring in historic literature. Had the Gospels been in process of formation during such times, it is hardly possible that some of these epithets should not have been mentioned, and that those deemed unjust should not have been condemned.

One of these terms was "Unbelievers." We find it in active use at Rome when Jesus was yet teaching in Judea, though then it can have applied only to monotheists, or their allies in the popular party. The aristocracy had endeavored by conspiracy and open revolt to overthrow Tiberius and crush the popular party. They had murdered many of its leaders and prominent members. When order was restored and the murderers were prosecuted for their crimes, they retorted with charges of Unbelief.[1] If the prosecutor alleged: You murdered my brother or my relative, the answer was: You do not believe in the Gods; or, You do not believe in the divinity of Augustus. A notable instance of this has been given in the latter half of note 14 in Ch. II. The aristocracy subsequently resorted to the same charge against others, whenever they deemed it for their political interest so to do.[2] Against Christians it was a common charge.

---

[1] For a fuller account see *Judaism,* p. 211, note 85, and for the political condition under which it occurred see the same work, pp. 531–534.

[2] See *Judaism,* pp. 7–10, 473–474, and 534, note 114.

The term Unbeliever, or Unbelievers, does not occur in the Gospels. This would have been very improbable if they or any of them had been fabricated in Europe, or perhaps even in Asia, at a later date.

§ 2. *Atheists.*

Towards the close of the first century the term ATHEISTS came into use as a designation for Christians. The use of this term was not confined to Italy or to Europe, for we find it used by the Jewish aristocracy in Judea. A relative of the Emperor Domitian was put to death on a charge of Atheism; and Polycarp was asked to save his life by saying, "Destroy the Atheists." The term must from the close of the first century have been actively in use as a designation for Christians, who of course earnestly denied the propriety of such usage.[3] The term is not found in the Gospels.

§ 3. *Christians.*

The term CHRISTIANS[4] came into use already in Apostolic times, as a designation for the followers of Jesus. It must have been widely current both in Europe and Asia before the last quarter of the first century.

Heathens sometimes altered the word *Christos* or *Christus*, Christ, to *Chrestos* and *Chrestus*, a term to which Clement of Alexandria gives an ethical meaning of his own and to which others objected.[5]

Neither of these terms occurs in the Gospels; their absence would be very remarkable were the Gospels fabricated in the second century, or even at the close of the first.

---

[3] See citations from different writers in *Judaism*, pp. 473, 474, footnotes 52-57.

[4] "The disciples were called Christians first in Antioch." — **Acts 11**, 26. "Then Agrippa said to Paul: You almost persuade me to become a Christian." — **Acts 26**, 28. "Yet if any man suffer as a Christian, let him not be ashamed." — **1 Peter 4**, 16.

[5] See *Judaism*, Ch. VIII. note 136.

§ 4. *Third Race.*

Christians occasionally spoke of themselves as a new, or distinct race,[6] meaning to distinguish themselves from Jews and heathens. This prompted heathens to designate and persecute them as a "Third Race." No such term or allusion to it occurs in the Gospels.

CHAPTER VII.

TERMS USED BY CHRISTIANS.

§ 1. Ἀσεβής, ἀσέβεια, ἄνομος, ἀνομία.

CHRISTIANS equally with Jews, when brought into contact with Gentiles, needed terms to express the various classes of the latter. They designated a heathen as ἀσεβής, an Unbeliever. Heathenism they termed ἀσέβεια, Unbelief, or non-recognition of God. By ἄνομος, LAW-less, they understood a heathen, or a Monotheist who did not accept the ceremonial law; and by ἀνομία, LAW-lessness, the non-acceptance of this law. This special sense of the words law-less and law-lessness did not of course prevent their being used in their common signification of a transgressor and transgression.

These terms were in use, the first two in common use,

---

[6] Peter uses it (1 Pet. **2,** 9) in connection with nation and people, as one of several designations for Christians. See other uses of it in *Judaism*, p. 474. **Tertullian** stoutly objects to it. "Have Christians a different kind of teeth, or a different opening for their jaws? ... We are called a third race, — dog-tailed, perhaps, or shadow-footed, or it may be Antipodes from below the earth. ... Ridiculous madness. ... But we are deemed a third race because of our religion not of our national origin as Romans or Jews." — *Ad Nat.* **1,** 7, 8; p. 53 A D, edit. Rigault. Elsewhere he speaks of the heathen with their circus : " Where they can readily cry out, how long to the third race ? " — *Scorpiace,* 10, p. 628 B.

among Christians outside of Judea, and are not infrequent in the Apostolic writings. In the Gospels the first two do not occur, nor in the sense above mentioned is either of the latter to be found.² This would be difficult to account for, at least as regards the first two, if the Gospels were anything different from what they profess to be, honest records of events in Judea.

§ 2. Σεβόμενος, φοβούμενος.

These terms were common ones among Jews and Christians, resident in heathen communities, to designate a CONVERT to the belief in one God.³ The former of them does not occur in the Gospels, and the latter, though occurring twice in Luke (1, 50; 18, 2), is nowhere in the Gospels used in this peculiar sense.

§ 3. Εὐσέβεια, εὐσεβής.

Jews and Christians used the above terms to designate practical-monotheism and a practical Monotheist,⁴ one who lived in accordance with his obligation to God. These terms were common outside of Judea, and appear several times in the Apostolic writings,⁵ but are unknown to the Gospels.

---

¹ Ἀσεβής, Rom. **4**, 5, **5**, 6; 1 Tim. **1**, 9; 1 Peter **4**, 18; 2 Peter **2**, 5, **3**, 7; Jude, 4, 15. Ἀσέβεια, Rom. **1**, 18, **11**, 26; 2 Tim. **2**, 16; Tit. **2**, 12; Jude, 15, 18. Ἄνομος, Acts **2**, 23; 1 Cor. **9**, 21; 2 Thess. **2**, 8; 1 Tim. **1**, 9; 2 Peter **2**, 8. Ἀνομία, Rom. **4**, 7. On the use of this word see *Judaism*, pp. 467, 468.

² In Mark **15**, 28, and Luke **22**, 37, is the quotation from Isaiah (53, 12) "He was reckoned with the LAW-less," meaning apparently with transgressors, a use of the word different from that above noted. Ἀνομία occurs four times in Matthew, but nowhere in the specific sense above mentioned.

³ See quotations in *Judaism*, p. 471.

⁴ See quotations in *Judaism*, pp. 465–467.

⁵ Εὐσέβεια, Acts **3**, 12; 1 Tim. **2**, 2; **3**, 16; **4**, 7, 8; **6**, 3, 5, 6, 11; 2 Tim. **3**, 5; Tit. **1**, 1; 2 Pet. **1**, 3, 6, 7, **3**, 11. Εὐσεβής, Acts **10**, 2, 7; **22**, 12; 2 Pet. **2**, 9.

Closely related to the foregoing is the verb εὐσεβεῖν, to monotheize-practically, and the adverb εὐσεβῶς, practically monotheistic, which occur with sufficient frequency in Christian writers to strengthen the argument somewhat by their non-appearance in the Gospels.

§ 4. Θεοσέβεια, θεοσεβής.

These words with some of their cognates appear frequently in Christian writings of the second and third centuries,[6] so that their absence from the Gospels, with the one exception noted below,[7] would have been unlikely if they had been written or in course of accretion during the second century. The argument is less applicable to the Apostolic Age, because at that date the question of εὐσέβεια, practical-monotheism, that is, the question whether a man could PRACTICALLY recognize God without becoming a Jew, overlaid, as a subject of discussion, any question of mere conversion to monotheism.

§ 5. Ἀδελφοί, ξένοι, πάντες.

The first of these words, *Brethren*, came into use, at least among Jewish Christians, in the Apostolic Age to denote their fellow-Christians of Jewish origin.[8] The second, *Foreigners*, was used to denote Christians of Gentile descent.[9] The third term, *All Men*, was a designation for both classes, namely, Jews and Gentiles.[10] In some

---

[6] See *Judaism*, pp. 460–465.

[7] In the Gospel of John (9, 31) θεοσεβής is represented as used by one who had been cured of blindness. Jesus is nowhere said to have uttered a word concerning θεοσεβεῖς, large as was this class of believers in God.

[8] See *Judaism*, p. 255, note 211.

[9] *Ibid.*

[10] Rom. **3**, 22, 23 ; **5**, 12, 18 ; Gal. **3**, 28 ; 3 John, 12. The Cohortatio ad Græcos (c. 14) contrasts the words Monotheists and *All Men*. Under the latter term its author intended to include reputed heathens. He may have had in mind Stoics, but more probably referred to the writers of certain Jewish documents temporarily in circulation with a professedly heathen authorship. On these documents, see *Judaism*, pp. 336–342.

cases it meant only such of these as had become Christians, though it is also used to designate non-Christians, whether Jew or Gentile.

In the peculiar sense above mentioned these words do not occur in the Gospels.

§ 6. Δίκαιοι, *Just Men.*

This was a term for those who, prior to the time of Moses, or else prior to the time of Abraham, were said to have been acceptable to God.[11] Two ages, or eras, of Just Men were recognized. In Irenæus these ages may have been from Adam to Noah and from Noah to Abraham. He uses the word patriarchs for those acceptable to God during the period from Abraham to Moses,[12] and the term prophets for subsequent teachers in the old dispensation.

In Justin Martyr[13] and in Hermas[14] the first age of Just Men must mean those from Adam to Abraham, who were deemed just without circumcision, and the second age those from Abraham to Moses who, though circumcised, did not observe the Mosaic Law.

---

[11] See *Underworld Mission*, 3d edit., pp. 5, 9, 11, 12, 21.

[12] "The whole remaining multitude of those who prior to Abraham were Just, and of those patriarchs who lived prior to Moses, were justified without the things already mentioned and without the Mosaic Law." — **Irenæus**, *cont. Hæres.* **4**, 16, 2. Compare citation in Ch. II. note 11, where the second age of the world commences with Noah.

The "things already mentioned" mean circumcision and the sabbath, yet **Irenæus** inconsistently identifies (**4**, 15, 1) the *Decalogue* (which commands observance of the sabbath) with the "natural precepts which from the beginning God implanted in men," and speaks of precepts or a covenant (**3**, 11, 8) given through Noah. Compare **4**, 16, 3. The covenant through Noah was, according to his Greek text, the first of four; the second being through Abraham, the third through Moses, and the fourth through Jesus.

[13] The distinction of Just Men into two ages seems distinctly implied in Justin's *Dialogue*, 27, cited in Ch. II. note 11, though I believe that he nowhere uses the phrase "two ages of Just Men."

[14] Compare *Similitude*, **9**, 3, with its explanation in **9**, 15, both cited in *Underworld Mission*, p. 58 ; 3d edit. p. 56.

In the Gospels the term Just Men occurs once (Matt. 13, 17), but without being used in a controversial sense. Not only is it there unopposed to those under the Law, but it is grouped with them as if they were parts of one whole.

§ 7. *Jesus Christ.*

While Jesus taught in Judea the question was debated whether he were the Christ. This term had not yet been conjoined to the word Jesus as part of one name. In the Gospels the Master is almost universally called Jesus, a term which occurs more than six hundred times.[15] If the word Christ be at any time employed it is as an official title, usually with the prefix THE,[16] and we also find Jesus THE Christ.[17] The exceptions[18] confirm, rather than militate against, the inference to be drawn from this usage.

---

[15] In the Glasgow edition of Schmidt's *Concordance* the word Jesus, as quoted from the Gospels, occupies more than eleven and one half columns, and occurs about fifty-four times in each column.

[16] Matt. **1,** 17 ; **2,** 4 ; **11,** 2 ; **16,** 16 ; **22,** 42 ; **23,** 8, 10 ; **24,** 5, 23 ; **26,** 63. Mark **8,** 29 ; **12,** 35 ; **13,** 21 ; **14,** 61 ; **15,** 32. Luke **2,** 26 ; **3,** 15 ; **4,** 41 (bis) ; **9,** 20 ; **22,** 67 ; **23,** 35, 39. John **1,** 20, 25, 41 ; **3,** 28 ; **4,** 25, 29, 42 ; **6,** 69 ; **7,** 26, 27, 31, 41 (bis), 42 ; **10,** 24 ; **11,** 27 ; **12,** 34 ; **20,** 31. In all these passages the article is in the Greek text prefixed.

In the following four instances the article is omitted, but the word Christ is nevertheless used as an official title. "A Savior who is [the] Christ, [the] Lord." — **Luke 2,** 11. "We found this man . . . alleging himself to be [the] Christ, [who is a] king." — **Luke 23,** 2. "If any one should acknowledge him [as the] Christ." — **John 9,** 22. "That they know Thee [as] the only true God, and thine envoy Jesus [as the] Christ." — **John 17,** 3.

[17] Matt. **16,** 20.

[18] The exceptions will be better understood by classification under two heads, those which pertain to the ministry of Jesus and those which do not. To the former class belong two passages.

Mark 9, 41 : "Whoever shall give you a drink of water in my name [*because you are Christ's*] I say to you in truth he shall not lose his reward." The question may be raised whether the bracketed words have been added in after times as an explanation. If so, they have in some authorities displaced part of those which precede them.

Had the Gospels been written, either in Apostolic or post-Apostolic times, by persons not conversant closely with the history of Jesus, the phraseology of these times would inevitably have been applied to the Master. Jesus Christ would have been a customary term.

CHAPTER VIII.

MISCELLANEOUS QUESTIONS.

§ 1. *Public Games.*

IN those provinces of the Roman Empire which were under control, not of the prince, but of the senate, public games were a common occurrence. In the western portion of the Empire, that is, in Italy, Gaul, North Africa (which must not be understood as including North Egypt), and perhaps in Greece and Spain, these barbarous amusements involved frequent destruction of human life, and were in some cases the means by which a political party in power wreaked its malignity on some of its opponents. Probably in Asia Minor and Syria the strong influence which the Jews exercised may have mitigated these barbarities. Public opinion may there and in North Egypt have condemned sacrifice of life for human amusement, and have rendered the Games comparatively harmless. Yet even these countries, or such of them as were under immediate control of the senate, were at times heavily taxed to furnish the pecuniary means for perpetrating

---

John 1, 17 : "Favor and truth came through Jesus Christ." John speaks this in his own person. He wrote when old, and when the term Jesus Christ had become familiar as a name.

To the second class belong three passages, only one of which probably proceeded from an evangelist. They are Matt. **1**, 1, 18 (concerning which see Appendix, Note N) and the heading of Mark's Gospel, **1**, 1. These show how prone Christians would have been to use Christ as a name when not recording his actual history.

these barbarities on a grand scale elsewhere.[1] We find that such games, in a milder form perhaps, were being exhibited at Ephesus when Paul was there.[2]

At a later date in letters from Rome during Paul's first and second imprisonment, we find allusions to these games, prompted perhaps by some of them which had taken place in Italy.[3]

In post-Apostolic writers we not infrequently find men-

---

[1] See in *Judaism*, p. 72, mention of the Ædilitian tribute from which Cicero's brother had relieved the provincials.

[2] The Asiarchs mentioned (Acts **19**, 31) were officers from different localities who superintended, or gave at their own expense, these games. Their presence at Ephesus renders it highly probable that the games were in course of exhibition when Paul was there. We find in a letter which he wrote at this date three or four allusions to, or illustrations taken from, the public games. Paley might have added to his *Horæ Paulinæ* this coincidence between the Acts and Paul's epistles. Asiarchs is in the common version not very expressively rendered by chief of Asia.

Paul's allusions to the public games are as follows : " Know ye not, that of those who run in the race-course all run, but one receiveth the prize ? Thus run, that ye may obtain. And every one who contendeth in the games is temperate in all things ; they, however, to obtain a perishable crown, but we an imperishable. I therefore so run, not as one uncertain ; I so fight, not as one striking the air." — **1 Cor. 9**, 24-26 ; *Noyes' trans.* " If after the manner of men I have fought with beasts at Ephesus, what advantageth it me, if the dead rise not ? let us eat and drink ; for to-morrow we die." — **1 Cor. 15**, 32. " I think that God has exhibited us apostles last as [those in the public games] condemned to death." — **1 Cor. 4**, 9.

[3] The Epistle to the Ephesians was written during Paul's first imprisonment at Rome. In it is the statement, " We wrestle not against flesh and blood, but against principalities, against powers, against the world-rulers of this darkness." — **Ephes. 6**, 12. Again : In the Epistle to the **Philippians**: " Forgetting the things behind, and straining towards those before, I press toward the goal — the prize of the upward call from God through Christ Jesus." — **3**, 13, 14.

The **Writer to the Hebrews** borrows also a simile from these games. " Seeing we also are encompassed by so great a cloud of witnesses, let us lay aside every weight, and the sin which [like a cloak] might so easily entangle us, and let us run with endurance the race lying before us." — **12**, 1.

tion of, or illustrations taken from, these games.⁴ Christians were often sacrificed in them either by being pitted against wild beasts or in some other way. It would even seem that in the time of Claudius and Marc Antonine lions had been taught to slowly mangle their victims. At least the historian's language presents no intelligible meaning except this.⁵

In the Gospels we find from the Teacher of teachers no word on the subject of these games; no condemnation of them as barbarities; no answer put into the mouth of his followers, which might aid them in escaping; no word of encouragement to assist them in enduring these atrocities.

The second Epistle to Timothy was written during Paul's second imprisonment. In it he says, "If a man contend in the games, he is not crowned, unless he contend lawfully." — **2 Tim. 2,** 5.

⁴ See Clem. Alex. *Strom.* **2,** 110, cited in *Underworld Mission*, p. 97 ; 3d edit. p. 93. The Letter from the **Churches of Lyons and Vienne** (in Eusebius, *Ecc. Hist.* **5,** 1) is mainly devoted to an account of barbarities practised against Christians in that neighborhood during the public games. Among other atrocities mention is made (Euseb. *Ecc. Hist.*, Vol. **2,** p. 32, edit. Heinichen) of a Christian woman enclosed in a net and exposed for a bull to toss as an amusement to the brutal spectators. Compare mention from the same letter of another victim, cited in *Judaism*, p. 335, note 10. The question whether God (compare Ch. III. § 11) were devoid of name seems to have been among test questions addressed to Christians. "Attalus, . . . being asked what name God has, answered : God has not a name like a human being." — **Eusebius**, *Ecc. Hist.* **5,** 1 ; Vol. **2,** p. 29, edit. Heinichen.

Tertullian devotes a treatise, *de Spectaculis*, to the subject of public games.

⁵ See Dio Cass. **60,** 13, **71,** 29, quoted in *Judaism*, pp. 75, 361. During the reign of Tiberius public butcheries in the games were not allowed. Under Caligula, probably during his illness, one such occurrence took place which caused him to abolish the games and to utter an earnest reproof to those who had been willing witnesses of such doings. It must have been the public opinion cultivated during these two reigns, which compelled Claudius to have the lion killed. Marc Antonine was a better man than Claudius, so that his permission for the torture and murder of human beings by a trained lion implies a degeneracy and growth of barbarism at Rome between A. D. 41 and A. D. 161.

§ 2. *Slavery.*

Slavery among the Jews must have been confined to the households of a few among their princes or rulers. In heathen or semi-heathen lands it was common, and at Rome it existed in an aggravated form so as to force itself constantly on public attention.[6]

In the Epistles we find references to slavery,[7] though perhaps fewer than would have occurred had not Apostolic teaching found its chief supply of converts among the partly monotheized Greeks, rather than among the Latins.

In the Gospels Jesus is nowhere represented as lay-

---

[6] See *Judaism*, pp. 86–89, 172 note 86, 315 note 109, 320 note 124, 455 note 130. A Roman law required, in case of a master being murdered, that all his slaves, innocent or guilty, should be executed. Such an atrocity took place in A. D. 61 (see *Judaism*, p. 88), though not without effort by the people to prevent it. Plutarch in the next century mentions (see *Judaism*, p. 306) a law probably by Domitian, that a slave, by giving up claim to freedom, could demand sale and thus change his master.

[7] "Are you called being a bondman, do not feel concerned, but, moreover, if you can become free prefer to serve." — **1 Cor. 7,** 21. The conclusion admits an opposite translation, — "Avail yourself of the opportunity." "Bondmen, be obedient to them that are your masters according to the flesh, with fear and trembling, in singleness of your heart, as unto Christ." — **Ephes. 6,** 5. "Bondmen, obey in all things your masters according to the flesh ; not with eye-service, as men-pleasers ; but in singleness of heart, fearing God." — **Coloss. 3,** 22. "Masters, give unto your bondmen that which is just and equal ; knowing that you also have a Master in heaven." — **Coloss. 4,** 1. "Let as many bondmen as are under the yoke count their own masters worthy of all honor, that the name of God and his doctrine be not blasphemed." — **1 Tim. 6,** 1. "Exhort bondmen to be obedient unto their own masters, and to please them well in all things ; not answering again." — **Titus 2,** 9. The Epistle to Philemon was specially written with reference (see verses 10–21) to the bondman who carried it. "Slaves of the household, be subject to your masters with all fear ; not only to the good and gentle, but also to the froward." — **1 Peter 2,** 18.

In the foregoing the word translated bondman usually designates one who is so born.

ing down rules for the relation between master and slave, or as teaching specially either the permissibility or the wrongfulness of slavery. Three times in them we find the recorded mention of a born bondman or bondmen, δοῦλος, δοῦλοι,[8] but no mention of, or allusion to, ἀνδράποδον, one who has been made a slave, large as was this unhappy class among heathens.

§ 3. *Two Wars.*

In the history of Judea during the first and second centuries we find two wars, one beginning in the reign of Nero, and the other in that of Hadrian, which could scarcely have escaped mention in the Gospels if these had been fabrications or accretions during this period. No gift was more lauded by public opinion than the capacity of foretelling future events, and persons in preparing a fictitious narrative would almost assuredly have put into the mouth of Jesus predictions as to the course and termination of both contests. In the former of these wars the temple was destroyed.[9] Immediately before, or during, the latter a temple of Jupiter Capitolinus was placed on its site.[10]

---

[8] Jesus is represented as curing the bondman of a centurion. Matt. 8, 5 – 13. Compare Luke 7, 2 – 10. A nobleman is represented as being told by his bondmen that his son had recovered. John 4, 51. Two bondmen of the high priest are also mentioned. John 18, 10, 26. Compare Matt. 26, 51, Mark 14, 47, Luke 22, 50.

[9] According to Josephus (*Wars,* 6, 4, 5), it was burned, the burning being due to the unauthorized act of an individual soldier contrary to the will of Titus. According to Orosius, 7, 9 (cited in Ch. IX. note 2), Titus had it destroyed AFTER BEING DECLARED EMPEROR by the army. Any such declaration — placing him in antagonism to his father — must have come from the patrician element, which was to be found more among the officers than among the soldiers. A statement by Josephus (*Wars,* 6, 4, 7) that Titus with his officers entered the Holy of Holies, accords best with the last-mentioned narrative. Titus, even if reluctant to destroy the temple, was easily swayed by patricians, so as usually to become their tool. Compare Sibyl. Orac. 1, 393, 394, quoted in Appendix, Note J.

[10] See *Judaism,* pp. 325, 326.

§ 4. *Philosophy.*

In the Greek-speaking countries where Judaism had preceded Christianity, the term Philosophy frequently designated love of moral wisdom, a use of the term which was carried by the Stoics and their disciples into Europe.[11] The same term was used for mental speculations of various kinds.

In the former of these significations Clement of Alexandria doubtless uses it when he speaks of Philosophy as a schoolmaster,[12] preparing the Greeks as the Law did the Jews for Christianity. The different senses of the word were often confused by undiscriminating minds.

Christians were divided in their views as to the origin of Philosophy. Some thought that it came from the Devil; others that it came from the Deity.[13] The respec-

---

[11] See *Judaism*, p. 49 n.

[12] "We should not err in saying that Philosophy was given to the Greeks, especially as a 'Testament' [or 'covenant'] of their own, it being a basis of the philosophy which is according to Christ." — **Clem. Alex.** *Strom.* **6**, 67 ; *Opp.* **3**, 138. **Clement** quotes as words of the Deity the passage (**Jer. 31**, 31, 32 ; **Heb. 8**, 8, 9) : "'*I appoint you a new covenant* [*testament*], *not as I appointed to your fathers in Mount Horeb.*' He appointed a new one to you [Christians], since those of the Greeks and Jews were antiquated." — *Strom.* **6**, 41 ; *Opp.* **3**, 122. "Justly therefore the Law [was given] to the Jews but Philosophy to the Greeks until the coming [of Christ]." — *Strom.* **6**, 159 ; *Opp.* **3**, 198.

"Those who proclaim the atheism of Epicurus and pleasure [as life's object], and whatever else contrary to true teaching has been sowed in Grecian philosophy, are spurious fruits of an agriculture divinely given to the Greeks." — *Strom.* **6**, 67, (*al.* 8) ; *Opp.* p. 774.

[13] "Let those who say that Philosophy proceeds from the Devil understand what the Scripture says, that the Devil transforms himself into an angel of light. . . . But if he teaches as an angel of light, he speaks what is true." — **Clem. Alex.** *Strom.* **6**, 66 ; *Opp.* p. 773. "Those who say that Philosophy is not from God incur danger." — *Strom.* **6**, 156 ; *Opp.* p. 321. "Greek Philosophy, as some [think], is accidentally, somehow, possessed of the truth faintly and imperfectly, and as others will have it, is prompted by the Devil." — *Strom.* **1**, 80 ; *Opp.* p. 366. "Some think that from an evil man [or the evil one] Philosophy has crept into life for the ruin of men." — *Strom.* **1**, 18 ; *Opp.* p. 326, Potter's edition.

§ 4.] PHILOSOPHY.

tive antiquity of Jewish and heathen views mingled with this debate. Greek Philosophy was alleged to have been pirated from Judaism.[14] Much of the dispute as to whether this Philosophy came from God or the Devil may have been due to difference in the disputants as to the kind of teaching which they intended to designate.

We find allusions to philosophy in the Apostolic [15] and early Christian writings,[16] but not in the Gospels. Jesus

---

[14] "All things concerning immortality of the soul or punishment after death ... which Philosophers and poets spoke they were enabled to understand by taking their leading ideas from the Prophets." — **Justin Martyr**, *Apol.* **1**, 44. "The poets and philosophers stole from the Sacred Scriptures." — **Theophilus**, *ad Autol.* **1**, 14. "They [the heathen writers] uttered what accords with the Prophets, though they were much later and stole these things from the Law and the Prophets." — *Ad Autol.* **2**, 37. "Moses is manifestly older than the aforesaid old heroes, wars, demons, and we should trust the older rather than those Greeks who have from his fountain unintelligently drawn his teachings." — **Tatian**, *Orat.* 40. "For they [your teachers] were necessitated by the divine foreknowledge of the [prophetic] men to speak though unwillingly concerning us, especially those who had been in Egypt and been profited by the monotheism of Moses and his ancestors." — **Cohort. ad Græcos**, 14. **Clement** says: "We may show that the Hebrew Philosophy is older by many generations [than the Greek]." — *Strom.* **1**, 64; *Opp.* p. 353. "Philo, the Pythagorean, shows that of all these [previously mentioned] the Jewish race is by much the oldest, and written Philosophy among them much preceded that of the Greeks." — *Strom.* **1**, 72; *Opp.* p. 360. "Of these things the Greek Philosophers were the stealers and plunderers, taking before the Lord's coming from the Hebrew Prophets part of the truth, not intelligently." — *Strom.* **1**, 87; *Opp.* p. 369. "Concerning the tenets of Philosophers having been cunningly put together from those of the Hebrews, we shall, after a little, treat in detail, but now must speak of the times after Moses, through which will be shown beyond question that of all wisdom the Hebrew Philosophy is the oldest." — *Strom.* **1**, 101; *Opp.* p. 378, Potter's edition.

[15] "The Greeks seek after wisdom." — **1 Cor. 1**, 22. "Then certain philosophers of the Epicureans, and of the Stoics, encountered him." — **Acts 17**, 18.

[16] **Justin Martyr** wore a philosopher's cloak, and, on the title-page of his writings, the term "philosopher" is appended to his name. He tells us: "Philosophy is in reality the greatest acquirement and most

is nowhere represented as saying a word for or against it. He neither commends it to his disciples as coming from God nor cautions them against it as an invention of the Devil.

Two different sects of philosophers are mentioned by name once in the Apostolic,[17] and, with others, frequently in early Christian, writings,[18] but no mention of them by Jesus is found in the Gospels.

---

honored by God, to whom it alone leads and unites us." — *Dial.* 2; *Opp.* 2, p. 8 C. "This [predicted Christian] Philosophy alone I found safe and profitable." — *Dial.* 8; *Opp.* 2, p. 32 C. edit. Otto.

"Plato thinks that there are Philosophers among Barbarians [i. e. non-Grecians], but Epicurus conceives that only Greeks can philosophize." — **Clem. Alex.** *Strom.* 1, 67; *Opp.* p. 355. "As children dread hobgoblins, thus the multitude dread Grecian Philosophy, fearing lest it should carry them off." — *Strom.* 6, 80; *Opp.* p. 780.

"The authority of Physical Philosophers gives protection as being a possession of wisdom. Truly the wisdom of philosophers is unadulterated, whose weakness is in the first place attested by the variety of their opinions proceeding from their ignorance of the truth. But who can be wise if devoid of truth, if he does not know God, the Father and Lord of wisdom and truth?" — **Tertullian,** *ad Nat.* 2, 2; *Opp.* p. 65 A. These citations, and those which have been given in notes 12, 13, 14, are but a small portion of what appear in the early Christian writers.

[17] See note 15.

[18] The names of one or more of the Philosophic sects, Stoics, Epicureans, Eleatics, Platonics, Peripatetics, Pythagoreans, and others appear in Cohort. ad Græcos, 4; Just. Mart. *Apol.* 1, 20 (twice), 2, 7 (twice), *Dial.* 2 (five times), *Opp.* 1, pp. 22 A, 180 C, 298 D E, 300 A B, 310 E, 2, 8 C E A, 10 B D; Tatian, *Orat.* 9; Athenagoras, *Supplicat.* 6, 19, 22 (twice); Theophilus, *ad Autol.* 2, 4, 3, 5, 6; Clem. Alex. *Protrept.* 66 (*al.* 5 twice); *Strom.* 1, 51, 62, 63, 64 (*al.* 11, 14 three times), 2, 19, 34, 54, 101, 129, 138 twice (*al.* 4, 7, 12, 19, 21, 23 twice), 3, 24 (*al.* 3), 4, 19, 28, 123 twice (*al.* 5, 6, 19 twice), 5, 9, 58, 59, 60, 90, 93, 94, 96, 98, 101, 106, 140 (*al.* 1, 9 three times, 14 eight times), 6, 27, 139 (*al.* 2, 16), 7, 37, 88 (*al.* 7, 14), 8, 4, 10 twice (*al.* 2, 4 twice), *Opp.* pp. 58 bis, 346, 352, 353 bis, 438, 447, 458, 482, 497, 503 bis, 521, 572, 575, 618, 619, 649, 680 bis, 681, 699, 701, 702, 703, 705, 708, 712, 732, 752, 811, 852, 886, 915, 920; Potter's edition. In Origen, there are, according to the Index of de la Rue, thirty-five references to the Stoics, six to the Epicureans, fifteen to the Platonists, and sixteen to the Pythagoreans. The works of

§ 5. *Dress.*

When Christianity spread outside of Judea it came in contact with Greek and Roman society equally as with the Jewish. Wealthy heathens were often addicted to outside display,[19] and this tendency was not held in check among them, as among Jews, by a sense of responsibility to God, or by correct views as to the object of life.[20] We find in the Apostolic times that a word of caution is given on the subject of Dress, both by Paul[21] and by Peter,[22] and fuller attention is given to it by Christian authors of a subsequent date.[23]

Tertullian, according to Semler's Index, mention the Stoics five times and the Epicureans five times.

Besides the foregoing the leaders or disciples of the different philosophical sects are mentioned, or in some writers quoted, even more frequently than the sects themselves. Compare note 53.

[19] See in *Judaism* (p. 455, note 130) the remarks of Dio Chrysostom. The remarks of Dio Cassius (**57**, 11) cited in *Judaism*, p. 509, imply that the absence of display commended in Tiberius was something unusual.

Pliny *Senior* mentions (*Nat. Hist.* **33**, 19, 5) that he stood near Agrippina when she wore a cape woven of gold without admixture of other material. This was during the naval battle on Lake Fucinus (Tacitus, *An.* **12**, 56), where persons obnoxious to the party in power were compelled to murder each other for the gratification of their enemies. It is little to Pliny's credit, considering his earlier friendships (see remarks on Pomponius in *Judaism*, pp. 209-211), that he should have been present at the scene.

[20] The term heathens must not be understood as including a large class of Gentile monotheists, whose sense of responsibility to God and whose views of life may sometimes have compared favorably with those of their Jewish brethren.

[21] "In like manner also, that women, in seemly attire, adorn themselves with modesty and sobriety, not with braided hair, and gold, or pearls, or costly apparel; but, as becometh women professing monotheism, with good works." — **1 Tim. 2**, 9, 10, *Noyes' trans. altered.*

[22] "Whose adorning, let it not be the outward adorning of braiding the hair, and of wearing golden ornaments, or of putting on apparel; but the hidden being of the heart in the imperishable [adornment] of a meek and quiet spirit which is in the sight of God a costly [adornment]." — **1 Peter 3**, 2, 4, *Noyes' trans. altered.*

[23] **Tertullian** wrote two works concerning woman's dress, and one on

Had Christians outside of Judea composed the Gospels from their own conceptions of what a teacher should say, the subject of Dress would scarcely have been omitted.

§ 6. *Origin of Evil.*

This subject has been partly anticipated under the head of Controversies. An opinion among Jews outside of Judea was that the world had grown old,[24] and that the diseases of age were upon it. This view was adopted by the Stoics.[25] The Gnostics laid stress upon two points as

---

the wearing of veils by virgins. **Clement of Alexandria** "takes occasion to speak of the proprieties of dress, and particularly female dress; and enters minutely into a description of a lady's toilet. He condemns all extravagance, and a disposition to seek 'the rare and expensive in preference to that which is at hand and of low price.' He will not allow ladies to wear 'dyed garments'; but he insists on the use of veils, which must not be purple to attract the gaze of men. A chapter follows on covering for the feet, as sandals, and slippers on which it was customary to bestow great expense, and another, on ornaments of gold and precious stones. On this subject, it seems, the ladies of Alexandria did not unresistingly submit. They ventured to argue the case with the holy father. 'Why,' say they, 'should we not use what God has given? Why should we not take pleasure in that we have? For whom were precious stones intended, if not for us?' This was bringing the argument home: but Clement found means to reply, by pointing out the distinction between what is necessary, as water and air, and lies open to all; and what is not necessary, as gold and pearls, which lie concealed beneath the earth and water, and are brought up by criminals, who are 'set to dig for them.' Other arguments he employs. But the advocates for the use of ornaments rejoin, 'If all are to select the common and frugal, who is to possess the more expensive and magnificent?' To this Clement replies, somewhat obscurely and clumsily, by a reference to what it may be proper for men to use, if they avoid setting too high a value on it, and contracting too great a fondness for it. He concludes the discussion by objecting to particular articles of female ornament, or ornaments of a particular form; that of the serpent, for example, which was the form under which Satan tempted Eve, and therefore to be abjured."—**Lamson**, *Church of the First Three Centuries*, pp. 137, 138.

[24] See Ch. II. note 30.

[25] See *Judaism*, note on pp. 56, 57.

causing imperfection in the world, namely, that self-existent matter, from which it was made, was imperfect, and that the Jewish God who made the world was but an imperfect being.[26] The mass of Christians held that the heathen deities, who had in some way obtained control of the world, were (see Ch. III. § 1) chief authors of its evils. Several other explanations had more or less currency.[27]

In the Gospels Jesus is not represented as trying to solve this problem for his followers.

§ 7. *Sibylla, Bacis, Hystaspes.*

Before the Christian era a document in the name of Sibylla had been fabricated by a Jew.[28] It and subsequent documents under the same name were used by the popular party at Rome in their contests with the aristocracy. Some Christians also used them very freely, so as to bring on themselves the epithet "Sibyllists."[29]

---

[26] "Of this problem [the existence of evil] the solution peculiar to the Gnostics was twofold. . . . They taught, on the one hand, that the Creator was an inferior and imperfect being, and, on the other, that evil was inherent in matter."— **Norton**, *Genuineness*, Vol. **3**, p. 5, 1st edit. On the subject of evil as inherent in matter, a passage of Paul may be compared: "I keep under my body, and bring it into subjection: lest that by any means when I have preached to others, I myself should be a castaway." — **1 Cor. 9,** 27.

[27] **Theophilus** (*ad Autol.* **2,** 17; *Opp.* p. 106 B) maintains that beasts originally were not destructive. "For nothing evil originated from God, but all things were excellent, exceedingly so." He argues that if the head of a household do right or wrong, his domestics will imitate him; that when man, the lord of the earth, sinned, his slaves (that is, the animal creation) followed his example. "When, therefore, man shall ascend to what befits his nature, no longer doing evil, they also will be restored to their original mildness."

[28] See *Judaism*, Appendix, Note A, § 2, and compare in the present work p. 19.

[29] This epithet is used by **Celsus** (**Origen,** *cont. Cels.* **5,** 61) and complained of by Origen, who says that Christians making such use of the Sibylline writings were blamed by some of their fellow-Christians for so doing.

A composition frequently mentioned with Sibylla was named Bacis. It was probably moral rather than theological.[30]

Another document also mentioned usually in connection with Sibylla was Hystaspes.[31] It may have been of Stoic origin, interpolated by a Christian. It was predictive in character.

The Gospels contain no allusion to, or use of, these documents.

§ 8. *Prediction and Inspiration.*

The Jewish view of Inspiration, though not excluding the idea of Prediction, gave prominence to the idea of moral teaching under the influence of or by authorization from God, a view transmitted to not a few Christians.[32]

The heathen view had no connection with moral teaching. It regarded the inspired person as for the time being insane,[33] and unguided by any operation of his or her mind, but controlled wholly by a divine power. The only object of this inspiration was in heathen eyes the prediction of future events.

Some Christians seem to have taken in large degree the heathen view of Inspiration [34]

This view nowhere appears in the Gospels.

---

[30] See *Judaism*, pp. 454 – 459.
[31] See *Judaism*, pp. 459, 460.
[32] "The men of God filled with holy spirit and becoming προφῆτα, public teachers, being inspired by God himself and rendered wise, became God-instructed and holy and just. Wherefore they were thought worthy to receive in return this reward, [namely,] that of becoming instruments of God, and possessed of the wisdom which is from him, through which wisdom they uttered what pertained to the creation of the world and all other things, for they predicted pestilence and famines and wars. Not one [merely] or two, but several existed at different times and seasons among the Hebrews, but also Sibylla among the Greeks. . . . And first they taught with one accord that [God] made all things out of nothing." — **Theophilus**, *ad Autol.* 2, 9, 10.
[33] See *Judaism*, p. 415, note 52.
[34] **Athenagoras**, addressing the Emperor Marcus Aurelius Antoninus

§ 9. *Spurious Converts.*

In Apostolic times we find allusion to converts who did little credit to the Christianity which they professed.[35]

---

and his son, says: "You, who exceed others in understanding and piety as regards what is truly divine (*or* the true divinity), would pronounce it unreasonable [that we], giving up belief in the spirit of God which moved the MOUTHS of the prophets as its instruments, should attend to human teaching." — *Supplicat.* 7. "I think that you, being especial lovers of learning and highly gifted with understanding, are not unacquainted with the [writings] of Moses, or of Isaiah, or of Jeremiah, or of the other prophets, who, being OUT OF THEIR SENSES, under impulse of the Divine Spirit uttered what was instilled into them, the Divine Spirit using [them] as a flute-player a flute." — *Supplicat.* 9.

Justin at an earlier date seems to teach the same view in his *Dialogue*, ch. 115; *Opp.* **2**, p. 382 B, edit. Otto.

"A man who is in the spirit, especially when he sees the glory of God or speaks with God, must of necessity be out of his senses, being overshadowed by Divine power, concerning which [point] is the dispute between us and the *psychicos* non-spiritual." — **Tertullian**, *adv. Marcion.* **4**, 22. He had in the preceding sentence identified ecstasy (the condition of the prophet) with *amentia*, which, as used by him, meant temporary insanity.

[35] See 1 Cor. **5**, 1, 11, 13; **6**, 8. 2 Peter **2**, 13-15. I also understand Paul as referring in the following passage to morally unworthy converts, who for their own purposes misapplied his doctrine of exemption from the Mosaic (ritual) Law. "A pillar and basis of the truth and confessedly grand is the secret of practical-monotheism, — which has been manifested in human lives, attested by miraculous power in the most public manner" (more literally, in the sight of angels, or, to use a modern expression, in the sight of heaven), "has been proclaimed among the Gentiles, has found credence in the world and been honorably accepted, — but the Spirit expressly says that in the last times some will fall away from the faith, adhering to deceitful spirits, and to teachings of heathenized men, hypocritically false, cauterized in their conscience." — **1 Tim. 3**, 15; **4**, 2. On the persons whom Paul had specially in view compare *Judaism*, p. 250.

A Jew, or Judaizer, could boast that he carried in his flesh the evidence of his practical-monotheism. Paul probably had this in mind when he speaks of his practical-monotheism as manifested in the flesh, that is, in the lives of those who professed it.

In the second century we find that persons deemed unworthy were debarred from the Lord's Supper.[36] At a later date church discipline became more systematic, and had numerous details for those subjected to it.

In the Gospels the Master gives no specific direction for dealing with nominal though unworthy followers.

§ 10. *Chronology and Divisions of Time.*

The Romans counted time by the annual consulships. The Greeks, scattered in different localities, counted it in a variety of ways. We find that Josephus uses the Macedonian months[37] in giving the date at which various events happened.

Had the Gospels been partly or wholly fictitious and grown up outside of Judea, it seems morally impossible that their composers should not have inserted some Greek or Roman divisions of time, as a means for increasing credence for their work. We find, however, no allusion to the Greek divisions of time, though Christianity during the first two centuries found the larger part of its converts from among Greeks; nor do we find the most accustomed Roman chronology. Luke, a physician of Syria, mentions a taxation as commencing when Cyrenius was governor of that province,[38] and states that John began to preach in the fifteenth year of Tiberius.[39]

---

[36] See citations from Justin Martyr, *Apol.* **1**, 66, in Ch. IV. note 16.

[37] See *Judaism*, p. 555.

[38] Luke **2**, 2. The mention of Cyrenius seems natural enough in a Syrian who had either lived under the administration of that governor or else associated with others who had. Such mention would have been unlikely a century later, for at that date it would have conveyed a fixed idea of time to no one outside of Syria, and to very few inside of it.

[39] Luke **3**, 1, 2. In the divisions of provinces between emperor and senate (see *Judaism*, pp. 83 – 85) Syria was one of the provinces under control of the emperor. It was natural that those who were, as the inhabitants of Syria, more immediately subject to the emperor than to the senate, should sometimes fix dates by the year of the emperor under whom they had lived. Had the Gospels grown up in Asia Minor or in any senatorial province, such record of time would be unlikely.

§ 11.] DISUSE OF WORDS JESUS AND CHRIST. 75

§ 11. *Temporary Disuse of the Words* JESUS *and* CHRIST *in Controversy with Heathens.*

About the time of Marcus Antoninus works were written in defence of Christianity by Tatian, Athenagoras, and Theophilus. In these defences of Christianity neither the name Jesus nor the word Christ can be found. Any decision as to the cause of this should be preceded by attention to at least three different circumstances.

The word Logos had been used by some Jews [40] centuries before the Christian era, somewhat as we at the present day use the term Providence. It designated the agency of the Deity even when he was not specially named. Sometimes this agency was vividly personified. Stoics borrowed the term,[41] and there may have been in the Stoic emperor, Marcus Antoninus, or in his surroundings, something which stimulated its use as a dignified title for Jesus.[42]

Again: It is possible that Celsus or some other heathen may have already ridiculed the personal appearance of Jesus,[43] and on this account Christian controversialists may have sought a term not associated with the human body.

Again: The party in power, during the reign in question, was strongly reactionary and laid great stress on ancient usage. In meeting this tendency Christians may have wished to represent the teacher of their religion as more ancient than anything which heathenism could boast. In doing this they were tempted to ignore him who had lived less than two centuries previously, and to personify a teacher older than mankind.

If we now turn to the Gospels we find in one of them

---

[40] See *Judaism*, p. 358.

[41] See *Judaism*, p. 50.

[42] The term Logos was introduced by Justin at a somewhat earlier date. One of his objects must have been to dignify Jesus. He, however, did not carry it to the extent of shunning to use the word Jesus or the word Christ.

[43] See Ch. III. § 14.

a preliminary statement [44] concerning the Logos which has been understood in opposite senses, as affirming or as denying the separate existence of the Logos. There is, however, in John's Gospel equally as in the others, no effort to avoid using the word Jesus or the word Christ. Had any of the Gospels been in process of formation during this period, the word Logos would have replaced the more usual terms for the Savior. The argument applies only to a limited period of time.

§ 12. *Natural Science.*

European heathens, in discussing theological questions, such as the nature or character of the Divine Being and the future life, mingled into their discussions matters of natural science. The probable explanation of this is that they found in the Greek teaching of partly monotheized lands views of theology and natural science which were new to them and which they associated. In Plato's treatise on the immortality of the soul the earth is mentioned as a sphere;[45] an explanation of volcanoes is given, and a statement is made touching water, which implies that the doctrine of gravitation had been dimly if not clearly reached.[46]

In Cicero's work on *Divination* we find mentioned the order of the planets. It is stated that Venus and Mercury were between the earth and the sun, while the others were more remote.[47]

---

[44] John **1**, 1.

[45] *Phædo*, 132; *Opp.* edit. Ast. 1, p. 596 E. The spherical form of the earth seems to have been inferred (see Dio Cass. **60**, 26) from the shadow which it cast on the moon during eclipses of the latter. Dio speaks of the shadow as conical. He probably deemed the sun the base of said cone, and therefore much larger than the earth.

[46] *Phædo*, 139–141; *Opp.* edit. Ast. **1**, pp. 602 606. Plato alleges that the waters flow down into the earth on either [every?] side as far as the middle, but that the opposite side (606 E) would be "uphill." He talks, however, like a man retailing ideas to which he had listened and which he but imperfectly comprehended.

[47] *De Divinat.* **2**, 91, *al.* 43. Compare **2**, 10, *al.* 3, and 146, *al.* 71.

Seneca, the Stoic, belonged to a sect whose views were borrowed almost entirely from these monotheized lands. In his writings the revolution of the earth on its axis is stated as a theory held by several.[48]

Marcion, the Gnostic, interwove with his system the belief in three heavens,[49] which seems to have prevailed in Asia Minor.

In the Ascension of Isaiah we find mention of seven heavens, the system adopted by the Greeks in Egypt.[50] Clement of Alexandria seems to have shared this view.[51]

The Valentinian Gnostics interwove into their system the seven heavens already mentioned, and superadded a Pleroma, which was doubtless the supposed sphere of the fixed stars, — a sphere which we find mentioned in Cicero.[52]

The Gospels put into the mouth of Jesus no word on the subject of natural science. It is at least probable, if they had been fabricated from the fancy of his followers, that some one would have endeavored to make him seem wise in the pathway of natural science.

---

[48] **Seneca** raises the question "whether the universe revolves, the earth being quiescent, or whether the earth revolves, the universe being quiescent. For there have been those who said that we [on earth] were the ones whom, unconsciously to ourselves, the order of nature carries around, and that rising and setting is not caused by motion of the heaven." — *Nat. Quæst.* **7**, 2.

[49] Tertullian, *adv. Marcion*, **1**, 14, cited in *Underworld Mission*, § XXI. note 12. I surmise that one heaven was assigned to the moon, one to the sun, and a third to the stars.

[50] The sun, moon, and five then known planets were each regarded as occupying a distinct heaven.

[51] See *Underworld Mission*, § XXI. 3.

[52] *De Repub.* **6**, 10 ; *Somn. Scip.* 4. The latter of these documents is in Greek, the former in Latin. One, however, is a mere duplicate or translation of the other. The document in Greek contains (see *Judaism*, Ch. VII. note 23) a number of expressions technical in Jewish theology and obviously borrowed from Judaism.

§ 13. *Literary Heathens.*

Certain literary characters among the heathens, such as Plato, Homer, and others, are discussed, some of them copiously, by Christians [53] in the second and third quarters of the second century. Had the Gospels been at that date in process of formation, some criticism upon these heathen writers would almost inevitably have been put into the Master's mouth.

§ 14. *Persecutions.*

Any remarks of Jesus [54] on the subject of persecution are far less full than they would have been made by his followers in the second century.

---

[53] The references to Plato in the Indexes of various authors are as follows: In Justin Martyr, forty-five; in Clement of Alexandria, ninety-three; in Tatian, three; in Athenagoras, ten; in Theophilus, thirteen; in Vol. 1 of de la Rue's Origen, sixty-three, and in Vol. 4, twenty-five; in Irenæus, four.

The references to Homer are: In Justin Martyr, eighteen; in Tatian, five; in Athenagoras, five; in Theophilus, six; in Irenæus, nine; in Clement of Alexandria, fifty-six; in Vol. 1 of de la Rue's Origen, eleven, and in Vol. 4, one.

[54] "You will be hated by all men for my sake.... When they persecute you in one town, fly to another; and if they drive you from that town, fly to yet another." — **Matt. 10**, 22, 23. "They will lay hands on you and persecute you; they will deliver you over to synagogues, and put you in prison, and bring you before kings and governors for my sake." — **Luke 21**, 12. "If they have persecuted me, they will persecute you also." — **John 15**, 20. "They will put you out of their synagogues; nay, the hour is coming, when he who kills you will think that he is offering a sacrifice to God." — **John 16**, 2, *Norton's trans.* The disciples would as yet have failed to comprehend a mission to the Gentiles had it been foretold to them.

CHAPTER IX.

ROMAN POLITICS.

§ 1. *Emperors.*

HAD the Gospels undergone accretion in Italy it is almost impossible that they should have contained no allusions to the emperors who influenced the external history of monotheism. No allusion, however, is made in them to any emperor whose reign began later than the ministry of Jesus. In respect to some of the emperors this would be a remarkable fact if the Gospels were not honest efforts to record the life of Jesus by persons conversant with what they narrated. Two of the emperors who became prominent in Christian theology have already been mentioned.[1] Others became prominent in the history of monotheism.

Under Titus, who had been left by his father in command of the army, the temple at Jerusalem was destroyed. This must have been done by advice of the patrician faction, who were prompting him to rebellion against his father. While hesitating to rebel, he hesitated to destroy the temple; when he decided on rebellion, the temple fell.[2] He afterwards assumed a crown at Alexandria, but his father must have found means to reclaim him.

---

[1] See Ch. III. §§ 8, 9.

[2] Titus "deliberated long whether he should burn [the temple] as being an incitement to enemies, or whether he should preserve it as a testimonial of victory. . . . Titus, [on] being proclaimed emperor by the army, burned and pulled down the temple in Jerusalem." — **Orosius**, **7**, 9; *Opp.* pp. 479, 480. Josephus states (*Wars*, **6**, 4, 5) that a private soldier set the building on fire, contrary to the will of Titus. This statement was probably an effort to shield that emperor from any odium incurred by the transaction. Josephus sometimes accommodates himself to patrician likings (compare *Judaism*, Ch. V. note 126, with Ch. II. note 26), and they not infrequently, after carrying their point, liked to throw the odium of it upon others.

The only allusion in the Gospels to destruction of the temple[3] is accompanied by the remark, "Of that day and hour knoweth no man ... NEITHER THE SON, but the Father.[4]" This cannot have come from a Christian anxious to magnify his Master's foreknowledge.

The reign of Domitian, under whom, though perhaps contrary to his will, Monotheists were murdered and expelled,[5] would, if the Gospels were fictions, have probably been foretold.

Hadrian would hardly have escaped mention. He executed some of the aristocracy, and, as a matter of course, was deemed unfaithful to heathenism and to its deities. In order to regain standing as an orthodox heathen, he thought it necessary to commit the folly of stripping himself to nudity, and in this condition, in a public place, tugged an unfortunate lamb to an altar on which he sacrificed it. A medal is still extant commemorating the procedure.[6] He carried on war against the Jews, but gave some protection at least to Christians.

Trajan, the warrior, who preceded Hadrian, and the Antonines who followed him, would scarcely have escaped mention.

In the Sibylline Oracles we find all these emperors foretold. In Book **5**, ll. 12–51, they are described *seriatim*. In Book **8**, ll. 50–58, mention is made that fifteen of them should reign, and a description is there given of Hadrian. In Book **12**, ll. 13–223, a much fuller account of the emperors from Augustus to Commodus is predicted, with a designation of Julius Cæsar as dictator prior to Augustus.

---

[3] Matt. **24**, 2; Mark **13**, 2; Luke **21**, 6. These passages make no allusion to any destruction by fire.

[4] **Mark 13**, 32. In **Matt. 24**, 36, it reads: "Of that day and hour knoweth no man, no, not the angels of heaven, but my Father only." Compare Sibyl. Orac. **1**, 393–395, quoted in Appendix, Note J.

[5] See *Judaism*, pp. 279–282.

[6] Orosius, p. 489, Leyden edit. Compare *Judaism*, Ch. VI. note 34.

§ 2. *Political Personages.*

We find depicted in a monotheistic writing [7] Agrippina, sister of one emperor, wife of another, and mother of another, who for a time ruled her husband and the Roman world.[8] We also find in a Christian writer [9] mention of Capito, the most prominent of patrician lawyers, the head of a legal school, who is contrasted with the lawgiver from Judea.

Had any accretion to the Gospels taken place in Italy, these and other political personages would scarcely have been overlooked.

§ 3. *Contest with Greek Culture.*

In Italy Greek Culture was regarded as nearly allied in many ways to monotheism and popular rights, and therefore antagonistic to patrician privileges.[10] The belief in an incorporeal God, common among Jews and Christians, is treated by Cicero as a not uncommon opinion among Greeks.[11] Jewish and Christian views on morality were largely held by Greeks in the lands where monotheism had spread, and when Greeks from these lands came into Italy they brought their views with them.

---

[7] See Sibylline Oracles, **3**, 75–80, cited in *Judaism*, pp. 139–140.

[8] Agrippina, when first she became a mother, consulted her brother Caligula touching a name for her son. He jocosely suggested the name of their half-witted uncle Claudius, to which of course she showed becoming repugnance. In later life she, for the sake of power, married this weak-minded uncle. She has been more permanently known as the mother of Nero. Her father and mother had each of them headed a rebellion against Tiberius. See *Judaism*, pp. 186, 523.

[9] **Clement of Alexandria** quotes **Isaiah 2**, 3 : "*Out of Zion shall go forth a law*. . . . This my upright law chants . . . not the law of Capito . . . but the eternal law of the new harmony named from God." — *Protrept.* § 2 ; *Opp.* p. 3, ll. 15–22, edit. Potter.

[10] See *Judaism*, pp. 11–14, 367–371, 382–386.

[11] "*Deum . . . ut Græci dicunt,* ἀσώματον." — **Cicero**, *de Nat. Deorum*, **1**, (12), 30. The passage is a criticism on Plato, but treats other Greeks as using this phraseology.

It is plain that these views clashed with what patricians deemed to be their interest. Some mention of this collision has been elsewhere made.[12]

When Augustus, surrounded by the aristocracy, was condemning one after another to death, his surrounders gave the leader of Greek Culture no chance of speaking to him. Mæcenas, unable to break through them, wrote on a card, " Up at length, Butcher !"[13] and threw it to him. It is obvious from this and other circumstances that Mæcenas was the opponent of patricianism.

When **Virgil** wrote to please the leader of Greek Culture, he selected a peaceful topic, Georgics or agriculture,[14] but when he wrote for Augustus and the aristocracy, his first words were, " I sing of arms ";[15] and he makes Æneas, the *practical-monotheist*,[15a] superintend (*Æneid*, 5, 418, 461) a prize fight.

When Domitian spoke for the anti-patrician party, he gave point to his condemnation by quoting from the *Georgics* (2, 537) : " Before an impious race feasted on slaughtered bullocks."[16] When Augustus, under patrician influence, was striving to hinder Greek Culture, and wished to punish such Romans as wore a Greek dress, he quoted the *Æneid* (1, 282) : *Romanos rerum dominos gentemque togatam*, — " Romans, masters of the world, and a togaed nation."[17]

The efforts to drive Greek Culture from Rome took place always in the reign of patricianism.

---

[12] See *Judaism*, Ch. 1. § 4.

[13] **Dio Cass. 55,** 7. Augustus thereupon quitted his judicial seat.

[14] *Georgics*, **3,** 41, 42. The article on Virgil in Smith's *Biographical Dictionary* treats (p. 1264) the *Georgics* as " the most finished work of Virgil," adding " that his fame rests in a great degree on this work." — Possibly any extra finish given to it may have been aided by suggestions of Mæcenas.

[15] *Æneid*, **1,** 1.   [15a] See *Judaism*, pp. 417, 419.

[16] **Suetonius,** *Domit.* 9. I have little doubt that Virgil was copying, as in many other instances, from a Jewish document, and that the word impious was an intended translation of ἀσεβής, a word which in Jewish Greek means unbeliever, or heathen. See *Judaism*, p. 468.

[17] **Suetonius,** *August.* 40.

Had the Gospels grown by additions in Italy, there is at least a probability that the political conflict would in some way have become apparent. They make no allusion, however, to the writings, leaders, or arguments on either side.

CHAPTER X.

SUMMARY OF ARGUMENT.

IF we now summarize the argument, we find it as follows : —

1. Christian authorship of the Gospels was contrary to the controversial wants of the early Christians, and so embarrassed them in their arguments with heathens that it is morally impossible they could have fictitiously assigned such authorship to them.

2. Of all the controversies in which Christians were engaged, whether between themselves or against Jews or heathens, not a trace appears in the Gospels.

3. Of the opinions prominently asserted and defended by the early Christians, or by particular schools among them, and which they rode as hobbies, not one appears in the Gospels. The argument is strong as regards any of their cherished opinions, and is intensely strong as regards their views of the heathen deities and Idolatry. The very object which early controversialists assigned to the Master's ministry, namely, the overthrow of these deities, is utterly ignored in the Gospels.

4. Of the customs to which the early Christians attached importance, or to which they were wedded, we find nothing in the Gospels, except the baptismal formula of the second century.

5. The peculiar designations for God used by Christians in heathen lands are absent from the Gospels.

6. So are the terms by which Christians were designated.

7. So are the terms which we have mentioned as coming into use among them. That the phrase Jesus Christ, or that the latter portion of it without the article, should not be found in the Gospels beyond what has been pointed out, is a remarkable fact.

8. We find various questions about public games, slavery, and other things, in which the Christians were deeply interested, but on which the Gospels attribute no remark to the Master.

9. The absence of allusion to Italian politics renders very improbable that any of the Gospels underwent accretion in Italy, and adds somewhat, at least, to the probability that they were not unhistorically fabricated or reworked outside of that country.

It is morally impossible if the Gospels had been fictitious, or were slowly growing under the hands of Christians, that they should have omitted all the topics of chief interest to those who wrote them.

If we now turn to the spurious records which Christians forged, we can to some extent test the truth of the preceding remarks. The test is imperfect, because these spurious records were not strictly original compositions, but (setting aside the Letter of Lentulus) simply an effort to reproduce facts concerning Jesus — especially the miracles — as recorded in the Gospels, basing them, however, on non-Christian evidence. Had these documents aimed to originate a life of the Master rather than to substantiate one which already existed, they would have had a much wider field for introducing the peculiarities of other countries or later times. In these records we find Jesus charged with destroying the sabbath,[1] and effecting cures by magic.[2] Articles of clothing, belonging to official position, are mentioned by their heathen names;[3] the terms Lord's Day and Palm Sunday are introduced as if in use during the ministry of Jesus;[4] we find the

---

[1] See Appendix, Note A, §§ 1, 7 ; Note B, § 3.
[2] See Note A, §§ 1, 6, 7 ; Note B, § 1.
[3] See Note A, §§ 2, 4, 11.
[4] See Note A, §§ 2, 13, 14.

SUMMARY OF ARGUMENT.

Roman standards doing homage to Jesus;[5] we find twelve persons in Judea charged with being proselytes[6] and maintaining that they are born Jews, — a subject of dispute natural in localities outside of Judea, but unlikely to affect simultaneously twelve witnesses in Jerusalem; we find crucifixion treated as a Jewish form of punishment;[7] the results of Christ's mission to the underworld are plainly stated;[8] a description of his personal appearance is given at length;[9] the appeal to the Old Testament as having foretold the crucifixion and resurrection of Jesus admits but one interpretation;[10] and the pseudo-predictions foretell the destruction of the temple with a sufficient description of those who were to destroy it.[11]

There is yet an indirect argument to be drawn from a condition of things nineteen or twenty years after the ministry of Jesus.[12] Six different writers — heathen, Jewish, and Christian — concur in implying or referring to a wide-spread excitement at that date among Jews, the blame of which was thrown to some extent on Christians. The writers are Tacitus, Suetonius, the author of a Jewish Sibylline production, Paul, Luke, and Eusebius. There can hardly be a question that these writers, with the exception perhaps of Paul and Luke, wrote independently of each other. Their concurrence implies that at the date mentioned Christianity had taken considerable hold in Italy. The allusions, moreover, to the excitement and to some circumstances connected with it are, in the Acts of the Apostles and in Paul's letters to the Thessalonians, so incidental that they can only have been written by

---

[5] See Note A, § 4; compare Phil. **2, 10**.
[6] See Note A, § 6.
[7] See Note A, near close of § 7, col. 2, and Note B, § 3.
[8] See Note A, § 13, Note B, § 3, and speech of Thaddeus in Note F. Compare Note I, footnote 5.
[9] See Note D, and speech of Thaddeus in Note F.
[10] See Note A, § 7, Note E, § 1, and compare Note I, footnote 5.
[11] See Note J, No. 1.
[12] See *Judaism*, Ch. VIII. § 5.

persons who lived through it, and whose readers were familiar with it. Writers of a later date would not have expected such allusions to be understood. These allusions establish the fact that the documents were written by persons then living, and each of these documents implies a then accepted history of Jesus, essentially such as we find in the Gospels.

CHAPTER XI.

DID PSEUDO-RECORDS REACT ON THE GOSPELS?

If the genuineness of the Gospels be assumed, the question may be asked, whether any of them have suffered by interpolation from the pseudo-records concerning Jesus. If these records were independent of the Gospels; if they were not, with one exception, as already said, a mere effort to reproduce facts mentioned in the Gospels, but substantiated by other evidence, — the question would be more important. Still the question may be asked whether anything whatever has been interpolated from them. The answer as regards all of them save the Acts of Pilate is, No. There is not the slightest ground to suspect such interpolation.

If we now examine the Acts of Pilate, there is no reason to surmise interpolation from it into the Gospels of Mark (as corrected from the manuscripts) or Luke or John. In the case of Matthew there are passages in the last two chapters which seem to require a different answer. His Gospel was written in what was then called Hebrew, — a language not extensively spoken, and whose book-markets, therefore, could scarcely pay for that rigid revision of manuscripts which existed in the Greek ones. Judea, moreover, even before the destruction of the temple and to a far greater extent afterwards, must have been more poorly supplied with trained copyists than were the centres of Jewish thought and influence in other lands. The Jewish Christians became in Judea an obscure sect whose copyists cannot have exceeded others in that locality. The Acts of Pilate were originally written in this Hebrew, or Syro-Chaldaic, dialect,[1] and there are five, or perhaps six, instances in the last two chapters[2] of Matthew where the question may be fairly raised whether an addition has not been made from the Acts of Pilate. None of these passages pertain to the life or teaching of Jesus. They are here subjoined for the reader's study. The first two and the fifth contain nothing inherently improbable; yet they are more apposite to the Acts of Pilate, where the object is to "make out a case," than in the Gospels, which are elsewhere remarkably free from any such aim.

1. *Dream of Pilate's Wife.*

"Now at that feast, the governor was wont to release unto the people a prisoner, whom they would. And they had then a notable prisoner, called Barabbas. Therefore, when they were gathered together, Pilate said unto them, Whom will ye that I release unto you? Barabbas, or Jesus, which is called Christ? (For he knew that for envy they had delivered him.)

["When he was set down on the judgment-seat his wife sent unto him, saying, Have thou nothing to do with that just man: for I have suffered many things this day in a dream, because of him.]

"But the chief priests and elders persuaded the multitude that they should ask for Barabbas, and destroy Jesus."[3]

---

[1] See extracts in Ch. I. note 4, from the headings of various manuscripts of said document.

[2] The Acts of Pilate begin with the measures for the arrest of Jesus during his last visit to Jerusalem, and are parallel only with the last two chapters.

[3] **Matt. 27,** 15–18 [19], 20. Compare Appendix, Note A, § 5 at the beginning and § 7 near its close.

2. *Pilate washes his Hands.*

"And the governor said, Why! what evil hath he done? But they cried out the more, saying, Let him be crucified.

["When Pilate saw that he could prevail nothing, but that rather a tumult was made, he took water, and washed his hands before the multitude, saying, I am innocent of the blood of this just person: see ye to it. Then answered all the people, and said, His blood be on us and on our children.]

"Then released he Barabbas unto them: and having scourged Jesus, gave him up to be crucified."[4]

3. *The Dead of former Times arise.*

"And behold, the veil of the temple was rent in two from the top to the bottom: and the earth did quake and the rocks were rent: and the tombs were opened.

["And many bodies of the holy which slept arose, and came out of the tombs AFTER his resurrection, and went into the holy city, and appeared unto many.]

"Now, when the centurion, and they that were with him, watching Jesus, saw the earthquake, and those things that were done, they feared greatly, saying, Truly this was the Son of God."[5]

4. *The Tomb sealed and guarded.*

"And when Joseph had taken the body, ... and laid it in his own new tomb, ... he rolled a great stone to the door, ... and departed. And Mary Magdalene was there, and the other Mary, sitting opposite the tomb.

["Now, the next day that followed the day of the preparation, the chief priests and Pharisees came together unto Pilate, saying, Sir, we remember that that deceiver said, while he was yet alive, After three days I will rise again. Command therefore that the tomb be made sure until the third day, lest his disciples come by night, and steal him away, and say unto the people, He is risen

---

[4] Matt. 27, 23 [24, 25], 26. Compare Note A, § 10.
[5] Matt. 27, 51 [52, 53], 54. See Note A, close of § 13.

from the dead: so the last error shall be worse than the first. Pilate said unto them, You have a watch: go your way, make it as sure as you can. So they went and made the tomb sure, sealing the stone, and setting a watch.]

"With the week's close, as it dawned on the first day of the week, came Mary Magdalene, and the other Mary, to see the tomb. And behold [*a great earthquake took place for*] an angel of the Lord, descending from heaven, rolled away the stone, . . . and sat upon it.

["His appearance was as lightning, and his raiment white as snow, and from fear of him those watching quaked and became as dead.]

But the angel addressing, said to the women, Do not fear, I know that you seek Jesus who was crucified."[6]

5. *The Soldiers bribed.*

"Then said Jesus unto them, Be not afraid: go tell my brethren, that they go into Galilee, and there they shall see me.

["Now, when they were going, behold, some of the watch came into the city, and showed unto the chief priests all that had taken place. And when they were assembled with the elders, and had taken counsel, they gave much money unto the soldiers, saying: Say, 'His disciples came by night, and stole him away while we slept.' And if this come to the governor's ears, we will persuade him, and secure you. So they took the money, and did as they were taught: and this saying is commonly reported among the Jews UNTIL THIS DAY.]

"Then the eleven disciples went into Galilee, into a mountain where Jesus had appointed them."[7]

6. *Account of Judas.*

In the order of Matthew's Gospel the account of Judas precedes any of the five passages already cited. It is here placed last because, though it must be an interpolation, the evidence is unsatisfactory for its existence in the Acts of Pilate earlier than in the Gospel.

"When morning came, all the chief priests and elders

---

[6] **Matt. 27,** 59–61 [62–66]; **28,** 1, 2 [3, 4], 5. See Note A, pp. 137, 138.
[7] **Matt. 28,** 10 [11–15], 16. See Note A, § 14.

of the people took counsel against Jesus to put him to death. And having bound him, they led him away, and delivered him to Pontius Pilate the governor.

["Then Judas, ... when he saw that he was condemned,[8] repented, and brought again the thirty pieces of silver to the chief priests and elders, saying, I have sinned in that I have betrayed innocent blood. ... And he cast down the pieces of silver in the temple, and departed, and went and hanged himself. And the chief priests took the silver pieces, and said, It is not lawful to put them into the treasury, because it is the price of blood. And they took counsel, and bought with them the potter's field, to bury strangers in. Wherefore that field has been called, The field of blood, UNTO THIS DAY. Then was fulfilled what was spoken by Jeremiah the prophet, saying, And they took the thirty pieces of silver, the price of him that was valued, whom they of the children of Israel valued; and gave them for the potter's field, as the Lord commanded me.]

"And Jesus stood before the governor: and the governor asked him, saying, Art thou the King of the Jews? And Jesus said unto him, I am."[9]

Besides the foregoing there is in the Epitome of events after the resurrection,[10] subjoined to Mark's Gospel by a

---

[8] Jesus had not at this date been condemned nor even tried. In the pseudo Acts of Pilate (§ 3) the wording is, "Judas, seeing how they LED JESUS BEFORE PILATE, ... repenting," etc.

[9] **Matt. 27**, 1, 2 [3-10], 11. Compare Acts **1**, 18, where Judas is not said to have returned the money, but to have used it for buying a field. The statement there is part of a parenthesis (verses 18, 19) which Luke, speaking in his own person, has interjected into Peter's speech.

In the Acts of Pilate the account of Judas appears only in two cognate manuscripts which Thilo (*Cod. Apoc.* p. cxxix.) designates as *Cod. Venet.* and *Paris D.* This renders uncertain whether it existed in that document before Matthew's Gospel was translated into Greek.

[10] On this Epitome see Appendix, Note O, footnote 2. It is here given with the sources from which it seems to have been compiled.

"And having risen early, on the first day of the week, he appeared first to Mary of Magdala out of whom he had cast seven demons.

"She went and told those who had been with him, who were mourning and weeping. And they, when they heard that he was alive, and had been seen by her, did not believe.

"After this, he manifested himself

"Mary of Magdala cometh early ... to the tomb, ... and beheld Jesus standing." — **John 20**, 1, 14.

"Mary of Magdala cometh, bringing word to the disciples that she had seen the Lord." — **John 20**, 18.

"Two of them were going the same

later hand, a passage (verse 16) which may have been copied from the Acts of Pilate. The subsequent passage also (verses 17, 18) appears in two or more manuscripts of the same pseudo Acts. Yet in this latter document it is less supported by manuscript authority than the preceding verse, and may, therefore, have been copied INTO said document, not FROM it.

in another form to two of them as they walked, going into the country. And they went and reported it to the rest; and even them they did not believe.
"Afterward he manifested himself to the eleven themselves, as they were reclining at table, and upbraided them with their unbelief and hardness of heart, because they did not believe those who had seen him after he had risen.
"And he said to them, Go into all the world, and preach the glad tidings to the whole creation. He that believeth and is baptized will be saved; but he that doth not believe will be condemned.
"And these signs will accompany believers: In my name they will cast out demons; will speak languages new [to them]; will take up serpents; and if they drink any deadly thing, it will not hurt them; they will lay their hands on the sick, and they will recover.
"So then, the Lord, after he had spoken to them, was taken up into heaven, and sat down on the right hand of God.
"And they went forth, and preached everywhere, the Lord working with them, and confirming the word by the signs which followed it." — Mark 16, 9-20.

day to a village called Emmaus . . . Jesus himself drew near, and went with them." — Luke 24, 13, 15.

"He himself stood in the midst of them." — Luke 24, 36. "Jesus came and stood in the midst, and said . . . Be not faithless, but believing." — John 20, 19, 27.

"Go, and make all nations my disciples." — Matt. 28, 19.
"Whoever believes and is baptized will be saved, but the unbeliever will be condemned." — Acts of Pilate, § 15; Thilo, p. 622.
"You will receive power when the Holy Spirit hath come upon you; and you will be my witnesses." — Acts 1, 8. Compare Heb. 2, 4, cited below.
[In Acts of Pilate, § 15, of *Paris A*, the adjacent passage is perhaps an interpolation.]
"When he had spoken . . . he was taken up." — Acts 1, 9. "Sit on my right hand." — Heb. 1, 13.

"God also bearing them witness, both with signs and wonders, and divers miracles, and gifts of the Holy Spirit." — Heb. 2, 4.

The Epitomist seems to have understood the words of Jesus (Acts 1, 8) as a promise of miraculous powers, rather than of a divine influence, which should fit them for their work, and of which any miraculous powers were merely an accompaniment.

The taking up of serpents may have been based upon Paul's experience (Acts 28, 3), with which, however, compare Luke 10, 19.

CHAPTER XII.

TWO QUESTIONS FURTHER.

§ 1. *Correspondences of Matthew, Mark, and Luke.*

THE phraseology of Matthew, Mark, and Luke is in many cases very similar.[1] Two considerations will account for this. 1. As regards EVENTS recorded, any one narrating the same thing fifty or one hundred times falls inevitably into a more or less set form of words. The Apostles and their companions taught in each other's company, and the phraseology in which they taught, being used over and over again, acquired more or less of a fixed character. Matthew and Peter had doubtless taught in each other's hearing. The diction of Mark may be largely that of Peter. Luke at Antioch may have listened to more than one of the Apostles and their companions. 2. The TEACHING of Jesus, even if repeated by different listeners, would present a similarity of expression.

§ 2. *Style of John, the Evangelist.*

In the New Testament certain peculiarities of expression are found only in the language of John, and in that of others as quoted by him. This renders probable that the Evangelist, in recording when old the utterance of others, has at times done it, partly at least, in his own language, though scarcely when giving (**18**, 38) the answer of Pilate.

In the appended comparison the left-hand column gives the language of the Evangelist, the right gives that of others as reported by him. The latter is the reported language of Jesus, except where the name of another is subjoined.

---

[1] This question is somewhat fully treated by Mr. Norton in his *Genuineness*, Vol. **1**, Appendix, Note D; abridged edit. Note B.

§ 2.] TWO QUESTIONS FURTHER. 93

I. USES OF THE WORD "TRUTH."

	Evangelist John.	Jesus and Others.
	TO DO THE TRUTH (Ποιεῖν τὴν ἀλήθειαν).	
Epistle I.	1, 6. We ... do not *the truth*.	Gospel. 3, 21. Whoever *does the truth*.

TRUTH AS A DESIGNATION OF CHRISTIANITY, CHRISTIAN TEACHING, CHRISTIAN SPIRIT, RELIGIOUS DISPOSITION, ETC.

	Evangelist John.	Jesus and Others.
1, 8.	*The truth* is not in us.	**4,** 23. The true worshippers shall worship the Father in spirit and in *truth*.
2, 4.	In this man *the truth* is not.	24. They ... must worship him in spirit and in *truth*.
21.	Because you do not know *the truth*.	**8,** 32. You shall know *the truth*.
21.	No falsehood (ψεῦδος) is of *the truth*. (Compare with the foregoing the expression "Who is a deceiver (ψεύστης) save he who denies Jesus to be the Christ?")	32. *The truth* shall make you free.
		40. Who have spoken to you *the truth* which I heard from God.
3, 19.	By this we know that we are of *the truth*.	44. He doth not stand fast in *the truth* because *truth* is not in him.
4, 6.	Whoever knows God hears us, he who is not of God does not hear us. By this we know the spirit of the (?) *truth* and the spirit of error.	45. Because I speak *the truth* [teach true religion?].
		14, 6. I am the way and *the truth* and the life.
5, 6.	The spirit is *the truth*.	17. The spirit of *the truth*, which the world cannot receive.
Epistle II.		**15,** 26. When the paraclete shall come ... the spirit of the *truth* ..., he will bear witness.
1.	Whom I love in [the ?] *truth* (truly; or else as Paul would say, "in Christ").	**16,** 13. When the spirit of the (?) *truth* shall come, he will lead you into all the (?) *truth*.
1.	Who have known *the truth*.	**17,** 17. Sanctify them through *thy truth*.
2.	On account of *the truth*.	17. Thy word is *truth*.
4.	Walking in [the] *truth*.	19. That they may be sanctified by *truth*.
Epistle III.		**18,** 37. That I might bear witness to *the truth*.
1.	Whom I love in [the ?] *truth*.	
3.	Bearing testimony to *thy truth*.	
3.	That you walk in [the] *truth*.	

II. COMBINATIONS OF THE WORD "OF" (ἐκ).

	Evangelist John.	Jesus and Others.
		Gospel.
Epistle III.		18, 37. Whoever is *of the truth* hears my voice.
4.	That I may hear of my children walking in [the] *truth*.	38. What is [this] *truth*? (or, What do you mean by *truth*?) **Pilate.**
8.	That they may be fellow-laborers for *the truth*.	
12.	Demetrius has testimony from all and from *the truth* itself.	
Gospel.		
1, 14.	Full of favor and *of truth*.	
17.	Favor and the *truth* came by Jesus Christ.	

OF THE TRUTH.

		Gospel.
Epistle I.		18, 37. Whoever is *of the truth* hears my voice.
2, 21.	No lie is *of the truth*.	

OF THE DEVIL.

| **3**, 8. | He that committeth sin is *of the devil*. | 8, 44. You are *of your father the devil*. |

OF GOD.

3, 10.	Whosoever doeth not righteousness is not *of God*.	7, 17. He shall know of my teaching whether it be *of God*.
4, 1.	Try the spirits whether they are *of God*.	8, 47. Whoever is *of God* . . . you are not *of God*.
6.	We are *of God* . . . whoever is not *of God*.	

OF THE WORLD.

| **4**, 5. | They are *of the world* (τοῦ κόσμου). | 8, 23. You are *of this world* (τοῦ κόσμου τούτου), I am not *of this world* (τοῦ κόσμου τούτου). |
| 5. | Therefore speak they *of the world* (from a worldly point of view). | 3, 31. He that is *of the earth* . . speaketh *of the earth*. —John the Baptist. |

III. WALK IN DARKNESS.

Evangelist John.

Epistle I.

1, 6. If we . . . *walk in darkness.*
2, 11. He that hateth his brother . . *walketh in darkness.*

Jesus and Others.

Gospel.

8, 12. He who followeth me, will not *walk in darkness.*
12, 35. He who *walks in darkness.*

IV. ABIDE IN (μένειν ἐν) GOD OR CHRIST.[2]

ESPECIALLY WITH RECIPROCAL EXPRESSION OF GOD OR CHRIST ABIDING IN MAN.

Epistle I.

2, 6. He that saith he *abideth in* him.
2, 24. You shall *abide in* the Son and in the Father.
2, 27. You shall *abide in* him.
2, 28. *Abide in* him.
3, 6. Whoso *abideth in* him.
3, 24. He that keepeth his commandments *abideth in* him and he in him.
3, 24. Hereby we know that he *abideth in us.*

Gospel.

6, 56. Whoso eateth my flesh and drinketh my blood *abideth in* me and I in him.
14, 10. The Father who *abideth in* me, he doeth the works.
15, 4. *Abide in* me and I in you.
15, 4. Neither can you bear fruit except you *abide in* me.
15, 5. He that *abideth in* me and I in him.

---

[2] The expression "abide in," sometimes translated "remain, continue, or dwell in," is not uncommon as the designation of physical residence in a place. Thus in the New Testament the following instances occur: Luke **8**, 27, in the house; John **7**, 9, in Galilee; **8**, 35, in the house; **11**, 6, in the place; Acts **9**, 43, in Joppa; **20**, 5, in Troas; **20**, 15, in Trogyllium; **27**, 31, in the vessel; 2 Tim. **4**, 20, in Corinth. The figurative use, moreover, is not entirely peculiar to John, for there are four passages in Paul—1 Cor. **7**, 20 and 24, abide in the calling; 1 Tim. **2**, 15, if they *continue (abide) in* faith, charity and holiness; 2 Tim. **3**, 14, abide in the things which thou hast learned — which are analogous to some, though not to all of the above expressions. The frequency, however, and some forms of the figurative use, are peculiar to John. And in his Gospel alone do we find it in the reported language of the Savior. In the other three there is but one instance of its use by the Savior, and that in a physical sense: Luke **10**, 7, "in the same house remain (abide)."

Evangelist John.	Jesus and Others.

	Gospel.
Epistle I.	**15**, 6. If any man do not *abide in* me.
4, 12. If we love one another, God *abideth in* us.	7. If you *abide in* me and my sayings *abide in* you.
13. We *abide in* him and he in us.	
15. God *abides in* him and he in God.	
16. He *abides in* God and God in him.	

V. OTHER USES OF "ABIDE IN."

	Gospel.
Epistle I.	**5,** 38. Have not his *word abiding in* you.
2, 10. He . . . *abideth in* the light.	**8,** 31. If you *abide in* my *word*.
11. The *word* of God *abideth in* you.	**12,** 46. That whosoever believeth on me should not *abide in darkness*.
24. Let that *abide in* you which you have *heard* from the beginning.	**15,** 4. As the *branch* cannot bear fruit except it *abide in* the *vine*.
24. If that which you have *heard* from the beginning *abide in* you.	9. *Abide in* my *love*.
27. The *anointing* . . . *abideth in* you.	10. You shall *abide in* my *love*.
3, 9. His *seed* (God's) *abideth in* him.	10. I . . . *abide in* his *love*.
14. *Abides in* death.	11. That my joy might *abide in* you.
15. No murderer hath *eternal life abiding in* him.	
17. How *abideth* the *love* of God *in* him?	
4, 16. Whosoever *abideth in love*.	
Epistle II.	
2. The *truth* that *abides in* us.	
9. Whosoever *abideth* not *in* the *teaching* of Christ.	
9. Whosoever *abideth in* the *teaching* of Christ.	

VI. TO KNOW GOD, TO KNOW CHRIST.

Evangelist John.

Epistle I.
- **2,** 3. Hereby do we know that we *know him*.
- 4. He that saith, I *know him*.
- 13. Fathers, because you have *known him*.
- 13. Because you have *known the Father*.
- 14. Because you have *known him*.
- **4,** 6. He that *knoweth God*.
- 7. Every one that loveth . . . *knoweth God*.
- 8. He that loveth not, *knoweth* not *God*.
- **5,** 20. That we may *know him* that is true.

Jesus and Others.

Gospel.
- **8,** 55. You have not *known him*, but I *know him*, and if I should say I *know him* not, etc.
- **10,** 15. As the Father *knoweth* me, even so *know I* the *Father*.
- **4,** 7. Had you *known me*, you would have *known* my *Father*.
- 9. Hast thou not *known me*?
- **16,** 3. Because they have not *known* the *Father*.
- **17,** 3. That they may *know thee* . . . and *Jesus Christ*.
- 25. The world has not *known thee*, but I have *known thee*.

VII. TO SEE GOD, TO SEE CHRIST.

Gospel.
- **1,** 18. No one hath ever *seen God*.

Epistle I.
- **4,** 20. *God*, whom he hath not *seen*.
- **3,** 6. Whosoever sinneth hath not *seen him* (Christ)
  (i. e. hath not been conversant with his spirit).

Epistle III.
- 11. He that doeth evil hath not *seen God*.

Gospel.
- **6,** 46. Not that any one has *seen the Father* except he who is from God; he has *seen the Father*.
- **14,** 9. He who has *seen me* has *seen the Father*.

VIII. LAY DOWN LIFE (ψυχὴν τιθέναι).

Evangelist John.
Epistle I.
3, 16. He *laid down his life.*

Jesus and Others.
Gospel.
10, 11. The good shepherd *lays down his life.*
17. Because I *lay down my life.*
18. I *lay it* (my life) *down* . . . I have authority to *lay it down.*
15, 13. That any one should *lay down his life.*

IX. COMBINATIONS OF "HAVE."

TO HAVE LIFE, OR ETERNAL LIFE.

Epistle I.
3, 15. No murderer *hath eternal life* abiding in him.
5, 12. He that *hath* the *Son hath life.*
12. He that *hath* not the *Son hath* not *life.*
13. That you may know that you *have eternal life.*

Gospel.
3, 15. Should not perish, but *have eternal life.*
16. Should not perish, but *have eternal life.*
36. He that believeth on the Son *hath eternal life.*
—**John the Baptist.**
5, 24. He that heareth my word . . *hath eternal life.*
39. In them you think you *have eternal life.*
40. That you might *have life.*
6, 40. That every one who seeth the Son . . may have *eternal life.*
47. He that believeth on me *hath eternal life.*
54. Whoso eateth my flesh . . *hath eternal life.*
10, 10. I am come that they might *have life.*

TO HAVE SIN.

Evangelist John	Jesus and Others.
Epistle I.	Gospel.
1, 8. If we say that we *have no sin*.	**9,** 41. You would *have no sin*.
	5, 22. They *had not had sin*.
	5, 24. They *had not had sin*.
	19, 11. He that delivered me unto thee *hath* the greater sin.

TO HAVE THE FATHER, TO HAVE GOD, TO HAVE THE SON, ETC.

Epistle I.
5, 12. He that *hath* the *Son*, etc.
5, 12. He that *hath* not the *Son of God*.

Epistle II.
9. Whosoever transgresseth . . . *hath* not *God*.
9. He that abideth in the doctrine . . . *hath* both *the Father* and *the Son*.

X. OVERCOME (νικάω) THE WORLD, THE WICKED ONE.

	Gospel.
Epistle I.	**16,** 33. I have overcome *the world*.
5, 4. Whatsoever is born of God *overcometh the world*.	
5, 5. Who is he that *overcometh the world*?	
2, 13. You have *overcome the wicked one*.	
2, 14. You have *overcome the wicked one*.	
4, 4. You . . . have *overcome* them; because greater is he that is in you than he that is in the world.	

XI. LIGHT (φῶς).

AS A DESIGNATION OF CHRIST, CHRISTIANITY, OR OF ANY MANIFESTATION OF GOD, ETC.

Evangelist John.	Jesus and Others.
Epistle I.	Gospel.
1, 5. God is *light*, and in him is no darkness at all.	**3,** 19. *Light* is come into the world, and men loved darkness rather than *light*.
2, 8. The darkness is past; and the true *light* now shineth.	20. For every one that doeth evil hateth the *light*, neither cometh to the *light*.
9. He that saith he is in the *light*, and hateth his brother, is in darkness even until now.	21. But he that doeth truth cometh to the *light*.
10. He that loveth his brother abideth in the *light*.	**8,** 12. I am the *light* of the world : he that followeth me shall not walk in darkness, but shall have the *light* of life.
Gospel.	**9,** 5. I am the *light* of the world.
1, 4. The life was the *light* of men.	**11,** 9. If any man walk in the day . . . he seeth the *light* of this world.
5. And the *light* shineth in darkness.	10. But if a man walk in the night he stumbleth, because there is no *light* in him.
7. To bear witness of the *light*.	**12,** 35. Yet a little while is the *light* with you. Walk while you have the *light*.
8. He was not that *light*, but was sent to bear witness of that *light*.	36. While you have *light*, believe in the *light*, that you may be the children of *light*.
9. That was the true *light*, which lighteth every man that cometh into the world.	46. I am come a *light* into the world, that whosoever believeth on me should not abide in darkness.

XII. AFFIRMATION AND NEGATION.

Evangelist John.	Jesus and Others.

Epistle I.

1, 5. God is light and in him is no darkness at all.
    6. We lie and do not the truth.
    8. We deceive ourselves, and the truth is not in us.
2, 4. He . . . is a liar, and the truth is not in him.
   10. He . . . abideth in the light, and there is none occasion of stumbling in him.
   27. The same anointing . . . is truth and is no lie.
   28. We may have confidence and not be ashamed.

Gospel

1, 3. All things came into being through it, and without it not one thing came into being.
  20. He confessed and denied not.

Gospel.

3, 20. Every one that doeth evil hateth the light, neither cometh to the light.
5, 24. He . . . hath eternal life, and shall not come into condemnation.
7, 18. The same is true, and no unrighteousness is in him.
16, 29. Now speakest thou plainly and speakest no proverb. — **Disciples.**
  30. Now are we sure that thou knowest all things and needest not that any man should ask thee. — **Disciples.**

XIII. ANTITHESES: NOT, BUT (οὐκ, ἀλλά).

Epistle I.

2, 2. *Not* for ours only, *but* also, etc.
  7. I write *not* a new commandment . . . *but* an old one.
 21. I have *not* written unto you because ye know not the truth, *but* because ye know it.
3, 18. Let us *not* love in word, neither in tongue, *but* in deed and in truth.
4, 1. Believe *not* every spirit, *but* try the spirits.
 10. *Not* that we loved God, *but* that he loved us.

Gospel.

3, 17. God sent *not* his son into the world to condemn the world, *but* that, etc.
 28. That I said I am *not* the Christ, *but* that I am sent before him. — **John the Baptist.**
4, 14. Whosoever drinks of the water that I shall give him, shall *not* thirst forever, *but*, etc.
5, 22. The Father judgeth *no* man, *but* hath committed, etc.
 30. I seek *not* mine own will, *but*, etc.

Evangelist John.

Epistle I.

4, 18. There is *not* fear in love, *but* perfect love casteth out fear.

5, 6. *Not* by water only, *but* by water and blood.
18. Whosoever is born of God sinneth *not*, *but* he that is begotten of God keepeth himself.

Gospel

1, 8. He was *not* that light, *but* was sent to bear witness of that light.

Jesus and Others.

Gospel.

5, 34. I receive *not* testimony from man, *but*, etc.
6, 32. Moses gave you *not* that bread from heaven, *but*, etc.
38. *Not* to do mine own will, *but* the will of him that sent me.

APPENDIX.

APPENDIX.

NOTE A.

ACTS OF PILATE.

AMONG literary frauds by Christians in the first three centuries, the most important were two cognate documents called the "Acts of Pilate" and "Pilate's Report."[1] Differing authorships were assigned to the former of these, and it had various titles, besides the one here adopted.[2] It appears, also, to have been repeatedly remodelled, interpolated, and altered for the purpose of adapting it to various controversial wants. An elaborate translation of all these variations, though useful to a scholar, might prove distracting to an ordinary reader. To avoid such distraction and facilitate insight into the chief object of this forgery, the author has confined his translation of the document to two only of its forms,

---

[1] Justin Martyr twice mentions the former of these, and Tertullian once refers to the latter. "And that these things occurred you can learn from the ACTS prepared under Pontius Pilate." — **Justin Martyr,** *Apol.* **1,** 35. "And that he [Jesus] did these things you can learn from the 'ACTS' prepared under Pontius Pilate." — **Justin Martyr,** *Apol.* **1,** 48. "Pilate — himself already a Christian as regarded his own *conscientia*, private conviction — announced at that date to Tiberius Cæsar all those circumstances [which I have narrated] concerning Christ." — **Tertullian,** *Apol.* **1,** 21. Compare *Judaism,* p. 442.

It will be noticed that Justin uses the Latin title "Acts." This probably implies that Latin translations of the FORMER document were already in circulation. The LATTER document, even if forged in Greek, must have professed a Latin original.

According to Eusebius, *Ecc. Hist.* **1,** 9, and **9,** 5 and 7, the Heathens, a little before the year 300, invented a counter-record concerning Jesus, which bore the same name. The latter document was circulated by official authority, and was taught to children in the schools. Its object, of course, was to misrepresent and ridicule Jesus.

[2] See Ch. I. note 4.

which he has also divided into sections and supplied with headings.

The manuscripts designated by Thilo as "Paris A" and "Paris D" are the ones from which, with exceptions to be duly pointed out, the following translation is made. The heading and prologue of the former have already been given.[3] The heading of the latter is subjoined.[4]

The date when these "Acts" were likely to circulate most, and to undergo most alteration, was in the fourth and in the early part of the fifth centuries. Christians were then the dominant but not the sole party. This protected them from inconveniences to which, in earlier days, a use of this document might have subjected them. Subsequently to the fifth century the advocates of the Greek and Roman religions were scarcely so numerous as to claim any frequent appeal to Pilate's authority.

Those portions of the document which seemed most likely

---

[3] See Ch. I. note 4. Thilo (p. cxx.) gives as the literary designation of this manuscript "*Codex Paris. Catal. 770. olim Colbert. 2493. tum regius 2356.*" For the convenience of those who may wish to compare the translation with the original a table is here appended of the sections, with the pages of Thilo on which they will be found.

Preface,	pp. 494–498.	§ 8,	pp. 550–554.
§ 1,	" 500–506.	9,	" 556–564.
2,	" 506–508.	10,	" 566–574.
3,	" 508–512.	11,	" 574–588.
4,	" 512–520.	12,	" 590–594.
5,	" 520–526.	13,	" 594–604.
6,	" 526–534.	14,	" 604–616.
7,	" 534–548.	15,	" 616–626.

[4] The title or heading of *Paris D* corresponds, except the three italicized words, with that of the *Codex Venetus* given in Ch. I. note 4. It is here subjoined because of its bearing on a reading altered by Thilo in the prefatory statement. "Narrative concerning the estimable suffering of our Lord *and our Savior* Jesus Christ, and concerning his holy resurrection, written by a Jew named Enneus, which Nicodemus the Roman Toparch translated from the Hebrew language into the Romaic [that is, the common Greek] dialect." — **Thilo**, *Cod. Apoc.* p. cxxvi, compared with statement on p. cxxix, ll. 11, 12. A manuscript copy of *Paris D*, in the author's possession, has enabled him to amend Thilo's text. This copy he hopes to have printed for the convenience of any to whose studies it might be helpful.

Thilo has given copious extracts from this manuscript on pp. 500, 504, 505, 507, 510, 511, 519, 535–541, 544, 545, 548, 549, 555, 556, 558, 559, 560, 563, 564, 568, 569, 571, 572, 574, 575, 581, 589, 590, 591, 595, 597, 606, 607, 609, 610, 611, 613, 614, 616, 618, 626.

to have belonged to it as originally written are printed in larger, and the supposed additions in smaller type. This arrangement was made, however, several years ago, and if the author had eyesight thoroughly to re-examine this division he might possibly alter it in some places.

PREFATORY STATEMENT.

PARIS A.

In the FIFTEENTH year of the rule of Tiberius, — Cæsar and king of the Romans — and of Herod, king of Galilee — in the nineteenth year of his reign — on the eighth [day] before the Calends of April,[5] which is the twenty-fifth of March in the consulship of Rufus and Rubellio, in the fourth year of the two hundred and second Olympiad, under Caiaphas, high-priest of the Jews; Nicodemus prepared a narrative, and delivered it to the chief priests and other Jews, of[6] . . . and as many things

PARIS D.

Four hundred years [literally, times] having elapsed after the kingdom of the Hebrews came to an end; the Hebrews being tributary under Roman rule, the king of the Romans appointing them a king; finally while Tiberius Cæsar swayed Roman affairs, in the EIGHTEENTH year of his reign, he having appointed as king, in Judea, Herod (son of that Herod who formerly killed the children in Bethlehem) and having Pilate as governor in Jerusalem, Annas and Caiaphas having the high-priesthood in Jerusalem.

Nicodemus[8] Roman Toparch

---

[5] Thilo has here substituted the reading of *Monac. A*, instead of "April 8th," an evident corruption of text in *Paris A*. As Thilo's work is readily accessible his slighter emendations will not hereafter be mentioned. The previously mentioned fifteenth year of Tiberius was, according to Luke (**3**, 1), that in which John commenced preaching, but Tertullian (following the Acts of Pilate?) puts the crucifixion of Jesus (*adv. Judaeos*, 8) in this fifteenth year and the beginning of his ministry (*adv. Marc.* **1**, 15) in the twelfth year of Tiberius. Marcion's view (*adv. Marc.* **1**, 19) accords with Luke.

[6] There is here an obvious omission in the text. We must supply either "the things done to Jesus" or "the death and suffering" or some nearly equivalent expression.

[7] These dates must be a later addition, probably as late as the fourth or fifth century.

[8] The introduction, into the heading, of Nicodemus, a Roman Toparch, took place doubtless after the Jewish rebellion under Hadrian. It and some other peculiarities of this manuscript were caused by the wish to substitute, as far as possible, Heathen for Jewish testimony. The name of Nicodemus may already have been too closely linked with the document to admit of discarding it. For Ἰουδαίων Thilo substitutes Ἰουδαῖον. The translation would then be "Nicodemus, Roman Toparch, summoning a Jew, named Ennaeas." His conjecture would make the statement

PARIS A.
and suffering of our Lord. And as occurred after the crucifixion the composition of Nicodemus was in the Hebrew language.

PARIS D.
of the Jews, summoning [a man] named Ennæas,[9] requested him to write what had been done in Jerusalem concerning Christ in the time of Annas and Caiaphas. When the Jew had done this and delivered it to Nicodemus, he [Nicodemus] translated these things from the Hebrew manuscript into the Romaic dialect. The contents of the narrative are as follows:

§ 1. *Character of Charges against Jesus.*

PARIS A.
(The chief-priests and scribes having plotted together)[10] Annas and Caiaphas and Numes and Dothæ, [*Dathan?*] Gamaliel, Judas, Levi, Nephthalim, Jaeirus and the other Jews, came to Pilate against Jesus, accusing him of many misdeeds, saying:

PARIS D.
When our Lord was performing many great and extraordinary miracles in Judea, being envied also by the Hebrews on this account, during the governorship of Pilate over Jerusalem and the high-priesthood of Annas and Caiaphas, there came from the Jews to these same high-priests Judas, Levi, Nephthalim, Alexander, Syrus and many others accusing Christ, whom also the before-mentioned high-priests sent to tell these things likewise to Pilate the governor.

We know this man to be the son of Joseph the carpenter, born of Mary, and [yet] he claims to be Son of God and a king. And not only this, but he profanes the sabbath, and wishes to destroy the law of our fathers. For we have a law not to heal any one on the sabbath; but this man, by wrong deeds on the sabbath, heals the lame and par-

These departing said to him, A man walks about in this city whose father is called Joseph, and his mother is Mary, but he calls himself a king and Son of God; and though a Jew, he subverts the Scriptures, and destroys the sabbaths.

Pilate, the governor, questioned, therefore, to learn from them: How does he destroy the

---

in this passage accord with that in the title, and would combine Jewish with Roman testimony.

[9] The duplicate orthography of this name, Ennæus and Ennæas, is that of the manuscript.

[10] *Monac. A.*

PARIS A.

alytics and blind and the bowed [by infirmity] and the lepers and the possessed of demons, and he

is a sorcerer, and casts out demons through Beelzebub, and all things are subject to him.

Pilate says to them: This casting out of demons is not through an unclean spirit, but through [some] god. Esculapius.[11]

The Jews say to Pilate: We beseech your highness that he may stand before your tribunal and be inquired into.

Pilate addressing them says: Inform me how I, who am but a governor, can [judicially] examine a king.

They say to him: We do not call him a king, but he calls himself so.

PARIS D.

sabbaths? And they answering said that he heals the sick on the sabbath. Pilate answered: If he makes the sick well, he does nothing evil.

They say to him: If he did this properly, the evil would be small, but he does it by the use of magic and by companionship with demons.

Pilate says: Healing a sick person is not a diabolic work, but a favor from [some] god.

The Hebrews say: We beseech your highness to summon him that you may ascertain for yourself what we allege.

§ 2. Respect of Pilate and his Attendant for Jesus.

Pilate, addressing his personal messenger,[12] says: Let Jesus be brought in a becoming manner.

The personal messenger going out, and recognizing him, did him homage, and took his own *fascial*[15] and spread it upon the ground, and says to Jesus: Lord, tread on this and enter; the governor calls thee.

Thereupon Pilate the governor, taking off his *mandelium* (that is, his *fascial*),[13] gave it to one of his servants named Rachaab (that is, to his personal messenger),[14] saying to him, Go and show this to Jesus and say to him: Pilate the governor calls thee to come to him.

Therefore the servant departed and finding Jesus

---

[11] *Esculapius* may have been a marginal explanation of, or substitute for, the preceding expression.

[12] Literally, *cursor*, runner.

[13] Some copyist who had two manuscripts may have understood two different readings as being alike in meaning.

[14] The remark in the preceding note applies here also.

[15] The word here translated *fascial* and the one so translated in the second column are different. I am uncertain as to their meaning.

ACTS OF PILATE. [NOTE A.

PARIS A.	PARIS D.
	(on Palm-Sunday, sitting on an ass. And the Hebrews strewed their garments in the way, and the ass walked on the garments. And the servant, seeing such honor towards Jesus, himself also became . . .)[16] summoned him, spreading upon the ground the *mandelium* of Pilate, urging him also to walk upon it.
The Jews, perceiving this, complained to Pilate, saying: Why did you not summon him by the common crier instead of by your personal messenger? For he, as soon as he saw him, did him homage, and spread on the ground his *fascial*, and has made him to walk as a king. Pilate, calling the messenger to him, says: Why have you done this?	The Hebrews, seeing this, and being greatly chagrined, came to Pilate,[17] the governor, complaining of him. Why had he deemed Jesus worthy of such honor?

§ 3. *Regard of Common People for Jesus.*

The messenger says to him: Lord, governor, when you sent me in Jerusalem to Alexander, I saw him sitting on an ass, and the Hebrews[18] holding branches in their hands were crying, Hosanna, Blessed is he that cometh. And others strewed their garments, saying, Save [Thou] in the highest. Blessed be he that cometh in the name of the Lord.	The latter inquiring of the servant, who had been sent, why he had done this, the servant answered, saying: When you sent me to the Jew Alexander, I met Jesus entering the gate of the city, sitting on an ass, and I saw the Hebrews, that they spread their garments in the way, and the ass walked upon the garments; and others cut branches and went out to meet him, and cried, Hosanna in the highest. Blessed be he who comes in the name of the Lord. It became me therefore to do the same, and I did the same.

---

[16] An obvious interpolation, from which something has been omitted in the manuscript. Thilo (p. 507) has erroneously substituted Lord's Day of the Hebrews for *Palm Sunday.*

[17] An awkwardness in the Greek renders probable, in this and other instances on pp. 108, 109, that *Pilate* was copied from one manuscript and *governor* from another.

[18] Literally, the children of the Hebrews.

§ 3.]   REGARD OF COMMON PEOPLE FOR JESUS.   111

PARIS A.	PARIS D.

PARIS A.

The Jews say to the attendant messenger : The Hebrews were crying out in Hebrew. How then did you who are a Gentile [literally, a Greek] understand the Hebrew ?

The messenger says : I asked a certain Hebrew, What are they crying in Hebrew ? and he interpreted it for me.

Pilate says to them : What was it that they cried in Hebrew ?

They say to him : Hosanna.

Hosanna — What is the translation of it ?

(They say to him) Save.

Pilate says to them : You yourselves testify to the words uttered by the children [of the Hebrews]. What wrong has the messenger done ?

They were silent.

PARIS D.

The Jews, hearing these words, said to him : You being a Roman, how did you understand what was said by the Hebrews ?

The servant answered and said : I asked one of the Hebrews, and he told me these things.

Pilate said : What does Hosanna mean ?

The Jews said : Save us, Lord.

Pilate answered : Since you confess the utterance of these things by your own people [literally, children] unversed in evil, how can you now bring an accusation and allege what you do against Jesus ?

The Jews were silent and had nothing to reply.[19]

. . . . .

[19] Here follow several interpolations, of which the first was not improbably added soon after the Jewish war under Hadrian. It is as follows : "About that time Jesus called to him whom he wished and they went to him. He also appointed twelve, that they should be with him, and that he might send them to announce his name in the whole world. He commenced also to establish a NEW LAW for the abolition of sabbaths, the Jewish cessation [from occupation]which they had under the old covenant from God and Moses. If any Jew died on the sabbath they did not bury him before the following day. But Jesus, wishing to complete [in the sense also, of "bring to a conclusion"] that Law, gave strength to the impotent man on the sabbath. He healed on the sabbath the daughter of the chief of the Synagogue [*and* ?] her who had an issue of blood. The blind, [the] leper, and demoniac, and dead, he healed them on the sabbath. On the sabbath he awoke Lazarus [who had been dead] four days. And on this account the Jews sought to kill him, because thereafter the whole people followed him."

On the views here expressed concerning the sabbath, compare *Judaism at Rome*, Ch. XI. § 1. The word translated *to complete* is often rendered *to fulfil.*

The foregoing is followed by a copious extract from John's Gospel, having the twofold commencement, "And as recorded by (the *Evangelist*

PARIS D.

Then they bring Jesus to Pilate the governor, and it was the day of preparation, early.

And Judas seeing (that also) how they led Jesus before Pilate, was [self-] condemned in trembling and fear because of his base plotting against him, and in his despair repenting, wishing to return the thirty pieces of silver to the chief priests and to the elders of the Jews : and these evil-doers and accusers knowing (him) what Judas wished to do, uttered themselves against him in unison. At the same time also the people accused and insulted him alone, and put on him the blame ;
of the crucifixion. And they all cried out against him and said : Traitor, law-breaker, faithless one, thankless one, murderer of his teacher whose feet had been washed by that [teacher], carrier of his purse, and giving out of it as much as he wished, and hiding away as much as he wished.

at which things he being worried, and not able to bear the reproaches and what he heard, and being to such a degree condemned and insulted by all, going into the temple and finding the chief priests and scribes and Pharisees, he said, Know truly that I have done wrong, and take the silver pieces which you have given me for betraying Jesus to you that he might be murdered ; I sinned in betraying innocent blood. But they said, What is that to us, see you to that. And the Jews, not wishing to receive the silver pieces, casting these among them he fled, . . . [20] and ἐκρεμάσθη hung himself and thus ἀπήγξατο strangled himself. But the chief priests, taking the silver pieces, said, It is not lawful to cast them into the treasury because it is the price of blood, and taking counsel, they bought with them the field of the potter as a burial-place for strangers ; wherefore that field is called the field of blood TO THIS DAY. Then was fulfilled what was spoken by Jeremiah the prophet saying, And they took the thirty pieces of silver, the price of him who was valued, whom [they] of the sons of Israel valued ; and THEY gave them for the potter's field as the Lord commanded ME.[20*]

John) the *Written Books."* The *written books* might be an authority with a heathen, if he supposed them written by heathens. The *Evangelist* would not, and his name was probably added after heathenism had died out. The connection of this extract is in one or two places broken by still later interpolations. The extract itself was not likely to be added before the fourth century.

[20] The passage omitted after the word *fled* is a very late interpolation, in which a dead cock is made to flap its wings and crow. It may have been an effort to reproduce, though in a very extravagant form, the incident which (Luke **22**, 60–62) awakened repentance in Peter.

[20*] The duplicate statements and to some extent the imperfections of phraseology in the account of Judas have been retained in the translation, since they are not without bearing on the question whether the account originally belonged to, or was afterwards interpolated into, these ACTS. Other portions, however, of *Paris D* are disfigured by carelessness in copying.

The passage attributed to Jeremiah is from Zech. **11**, 12, 13.

§ 4. *Homage of the Standards to Jesus.*[21]

PARIS A.

The governor says to his personal messenger: Go out and bring him in, in such manner as you wish.

The messenger, going out, conducted himself as before, and says to him, Master, the governor calls thee.

And as Jesus entered, and the standard-bearers [stood by] holding their standards, the figure-heads of the standards bowed and did homage to Jesus.

And the Jews, seeing the behavior of the standards, that they bowed and did homage to Jesus, cried out more vociferously against the standard-bearers.

Pilate says to the Jews: Are you not filled with wonder that the figure-heads of the standards bowed and did homage to Jesus?

The Jews say to Pilate: We know that the standard-bearers bowed (the figure-heads) and did him homage.

The governor, addressing the standard-bearers, says to them: Why did you do this?

They say to Pilate: We are Greeks [i. e. Gentiles], and how could we do him homage? For as we held the figure-heads, these bowed of themselves and did homage.

Pilate says to the rulers of the synagogue, and the elders of the

PARIS D.

And as Jesus came to Pilate the governor,

Pilate's soldiers did him homage.

Others also stood in Pilate's presence holding standards, and the standards bowed and did homage to Jesus. While Pilate was wondering at the occurrence,

the Jews said to him: Lord, the standards did not do homage to Jesus, but the soldiers who were holding them carelessly.

Pilate says to the chief of the synagogue: Select twelve power-

---

[21] Christian controversialists, in their contest with heathenism, alleged with an eagerness, almost amounting to mania, the subjection to their Master's power of demons (see *Underworld Mission*, p. 78; 3d edit., pp. 74, 75) and of everything idolatrous. The figure-heads of the Roman standards were regarded by the Jews, and no doubt by many Christians, as idol emblems. This section is a fair specimen of the Master's life, as it would have been, if devised by Christians in the second century.

PARIS A.

Jewish people: Select powerful men, and let them hold the standards, and let us see whether they will bow of themselves.

The elders of the Jews, taking twelve strong and powerful men, made them six by six hold the [two] standards, and they were stationed before the tribunal of the governor.

Pilate says to his attendant messenger: Put him (Jesus) out of the Prætorium, and bring him in again in such manner as you wish.

And Jesus having gone out of the Prætorium, Pilate, addressing those who held the figure-heads, says to them: I swear by Cæsar's salvation that if the standards bow when Jesus returns I will cut off your heads. And sitting down, the governor commanded that Jesus should enter the second time. And the attendant messenger conducted himself as before, and besought Jesus earnestly to tread upon his *fascial*. And he walked upon it and entered. And as he entered, the standards again bowed and did homage to Jesus.

And Pilate, being astounded when he saw it, sought to arise from his tribunal.

PARIS D.

ful men, who can hold them firmly; and when this had been

done, Pilate commanded the servant to put Jesus out and to bring him in again. And when

he came in, again the standards bowed and did him homage.

Pilate therefore wondered greatly. But the Jews said: He is a magician, and thereby accomplishes these things.

§ 5. *Message from Pilate's Wife.*

And while he was yet intending to arise, his wife sent to him, saying: Have nothing to do with this just man, for I suffered many things on his account during the night.

Pilate, addressing the Jews, says: You know that my wife is a Monotheist, (and disposed to Judaize with you.)

§ 6.] IMPUTATION ON THE MOTHER OF JESUS. 115

PARIS A.

They say to him, Yes, we know it. Pilate says to them, Lo, my wife Procla sent, saying: Have nothing to do with this just man, for I suffered many things on his account during the night.

The Jews, answering, say to Pilate: Did we not tell thee that he is a sorcerer, and that through Beelzebub, the Prince of the demons, all things are subject to him? Lo: he sent a dream-messenger to your wife.

Pilate addressing Jesus, says to him: Such persons testify against you; (Do you not hear what these testify against you?) Do you say nothing? [Cp. § 1.]

Jesus answered: Except they had authority [for their statements?] they said nothing. Every one has authority over his own mouth to speak good and evil. They shall see.

PARIS D.

Pilate says to Jesus: You hear what these testify against you, and do you not answer? [Cp. § 1.]

Jesus answered and said: Every man has authority to speak what he wishes, whether his wish be good or evil, they also, therefore, having authority to speak their wishes.

§ 6. *Answer to Imputation on the Mother of Jesus.*[22]

The elders of the Jewish People, answering, say to Jesus: What shall we see? First, That you were born of fornication. Second, That your birth was the cause of destruction to young children in Bethlehem. Third, That your father Joseph and your mother Mary fled into Egypt, because they had no consolation (confidence?[22a]) among The People.

Certain discreet persons from

The Jews said to him: What have we to say concerning thee? First, that you were sinfully born. Secondly, that when you were born, forty-four thousand children were murdered. Third, that your father and mother fled into Egypt because they had not courage towards [meeting] "The People."

Hereupon the Jews who were present (twelve Monotheist men there)[23] answered and said: We al-

---

[22] Most of this section is doubtless an interpolation. What follows it is intimately connected, in *Paris D*, with § 4. The most probable date of the interpolation is in the latter half of the second century, when, as we can infer from the charges of Celsus, Mary's character was a subject of discussion. This discussion may have been prompted by the stress which Christians, subsequently to Hadrian's time (Justin, *Apol.* **1**, 21, 33, *Dial.* 43, 66, 75, 84, 100; *Opp.* **1**, 180 E, 206 D E A, **2**, 140 D E, 222 A, 254 A, 286 A B, 336 A) laid on the miraculous birth of Jesus as a fulfilment of prophecy.

[22a] *Monac A.* and *B.*

[23] On the substitution of (Gentile) Monotheists for Jews, see note 26.

PARIS A.

among the Jewish bystanders, say: We do not allege him born of fornication, but [on the contrary] we know that Joseph was betrothed to Mary and (Jesus) is not born of fornication.

Pilate says to the Jews, who affirmed him to be [born] of fornication: This statement of yours is not true, since the betrothing took place, as these, your fellow-countrymen, affirm.

Annas and Caiaphas say to Pilate: The multitude vociferates, and [yet] you do not believe that he is born of fornication. These are Proselytes and his disciples.

Pilate, addressing Annas and Caiaphas, says to them: And what is a Proselyte?

They say to him: They were born children of Greeks [i. e. Gentiles] and have now become Jews.

Those who maintained that he was not born of fornication — *Lazarus, Asterius, Antonius, James, Isaiah, Annas, Samuel, Isaac, Phineas, Crippius, Agrippa, Judas* — say: We have not become Proselytes, but are children of the Jews,[24] and speak the truth, for we were present at the betrothal of Joseph and Mary.

And Pilate, addressing these (*the twelve men*), who maintained that he was not born of fornication, says to them: I adjure you by Cæsar's salvation: Is it true that he is not born of fornication?

They say to Pilate: We have a law not to swear, because it is sinful. But let them swear that it is not as we have said, and we are liable to death.

Pilate says to Annas and Caiaphas: Do you answer nothing to these things?

PARIS D.

lege that his birth was not sinful, for we know that Joseph, according to betrothal, received his mother Mary, that he should have charge of her.

Pilate said: Then you speak falsely, who allege that his birth is sinful.

---

[24] This and some other portions of *Paris A* may have been specially intended to secure a circulation among Jews, or among such as had more Jewish than Gentile leanings.

PARIS A.

Annas and Caiaphas say to Pilate:
These (twelve) are believed that he was not born of fornication.

The whole multitude of us vociferate that he *was born of fornication, and* is a sorcerer and [yet] calls himself Son of God and a king; and we are not believed.

PARIS D.

They again say to Pilate: The whole people testifies that he is a magician[25]

(The Monotheists [26]) the Jews answered and said: We *were at the betrothal of his mother (and are Jews)*[27] *and* know his whole life; but that he is a magician we do not know.

Those (Monotheists) who thus affirmed, were the following: Lazarus, Astharia, Antonius, Jacob, Zaras, Samuel, Isaac, Phineas, Crispus, Dagrippus, Eumesse, and Judas.

Pilate therefore says to them: I wish you to swear by Cæsar's life whether the birth of this man is free from sin.

They answered and said: Our law ordains that we should swear to nothing, for an oath is a great sin. But by Cæsar's life we swear that his birth is free from sin. If we are falsifying, command our heads to be cut off.

When these had thus spoken, the accusing Jews answered to Pilate and said: Do you trust more to such (a dozen only) Jews than to the whole multitude, and to us who know him well [as a] magician and blasphemer who names himself Son of God?

---

[25] See § 1 and conclusion of § 4. The repetition may either be intended to support their own assertion by that of the people, or to restore the connection, which had been interrupted.

[26] *The Monotheists*, here and elsewhere, is probably a reading copied from some manuscript, wherein it had been substituted for Jews. The substitution was likely to take place during the imbitterment of heathens against Jews under Hadrian and afterwards. Compare *Judaism*, p. 463, note 4.

[27] An interpolation copied from some manuscript which was intended to circulate specially among Jews.

§ 7. *Pilate's Conviction touching Jesus.*

PARIS A.

Then Pilate commanded the whole multitude to go out except the (twelve) men who said that he was not born of fornication. and he commanded Jesus to be taken aside; Pilate then says to them: For what reason do they wish to kill him?

They say to him: They are actuated by party animosity because he heals on the sabbath.

Pilate says: Because of a good work, therefore, they wish to kill him.

They say: Yes.

Then Pilate, filled with excitement, went out of the Prætorium, and says to them:

I call the sun to witness that I find no fault in this man.

The Jews answered and said to the governor: If this man were not an evil-doer, WE [30] would not have delivered him to you.

Pilate said: Take him yourselves, and judge him according to your law.

The Jews said: It is not permitted us [by our Roman masters] to put any one to death.

PARIS D.

Then Pilate commanded all to leave the Prætorium except only the before-mentioned (twelve,[28]) and when this had taken place Pilate says to them privately: According to appearances the rulers (it appears to me that the Jews) through envy and madness wish to murder this man (him),[29] for they accuse him of but one thing, that he destroys the sabbaths. But he then does a good work, for he heals the sick. This is not a [charge which deserves] condemnation to death against the man.

They say to him (the twelve): Yes, my Lord, that is the case.

Pilate therefore went out in anger and excitement, and says to Annas and Caiaphas, and to the crowd who brought Jesus: (what accusation do you bring against this man?)[31] I call the sun to witness that I find no crime in this man.

The crowd answered and said: If he were not a (sorcerer and) magician (and blasphemer) [32] and evil-doer, WE would not have brought him and given him up to your greatness.

Pilate said: Examine him thoroughly yourselves, and, since you have a law, do as the law directs.

The Jews said: Our law does not permit us to put any man to death.

---

[28] The specific number *twelve* is in most or all cases probably an addition to the original document.

[29] The passages inside and outside of the two parentheses are evidently from different texts.

[30] An emphasis on the WE. We are no such lovers of Gentile rule as to give up our countrymen without cause.

[31] Perhaps from a different text.

[32] The previous narrative charges Jesus with being a magician and evil-doer. The terms in the parenthesis may be from some amplified text.

PARIS A.

(Pilate said to the Jews: Did God command that you should not, but that I should put to death ?)[83]

And Pilate, entering the Prætorium again, addressed Jesus privately and said to him: Are you the king of the Jews?

Jesus answered Pilate: Do you speak this of yourself, or did others say it to you concerning me?

Pilate answered Jesus, and said to him: Am I a Jew? Your nation and the chief priests gave you up to me. What have you done?

Jesus answered: My kingdom is not of [or from] this world. For if my kingdom were of [from] this world, my servants would have contended in order that I should not have been delivered to the Jews. But as it is, my kingdom [or, jurisdiction] is not thence.

And Pilate said to him: Therefore you are a king?

Jesus answered him: You say [it] that I am a king. To this end have I been born and have come, that every one who is of the truth should hear my voice.

Pilate says to him: What is the truth?

Pilate, leaving Jesus, went out of the Prætorium to the Jews, and says to them: I find no fault in him.

The Jews say to him: This man stated, I can destroy this temple, and in three days I will build it.

PARIS D.

Pilate says: If you do not wish to commit murder, by how much rather do not I.

Then Pilate returned into the palace and addressed Jesus, and said to him: Tell me, are you the king of the Jews?

Jesus answered him and said: Do you utter this, or did others (Jews) say this to you, that you ask me?

Pilate said: Am I a Hebrew? I am not a Hebrew. Your people and the chief priests delivered you into my hands; and tell me [therefore ?] whether you are king of the Jews.

Jesus answered: My kingdom is not in this world. For if my kingdom were in this world, my soldiers would not have disregarded my capture. Therefore my kingdom is not in this world.

Pilate says: Therefore you are a king?

Jesus said: You have spoken it. For this purpose I was born, to bear testimony to the truth. And if any man is of the truth, he believes my teaching and does it.

Pilate says: What is truth?

Christ[34] answered: Truth is from the heavens.

Pilate says: Is there not truth upon earth?

Christ says: I am the truth, and how is truth judged on earth by those who have earthly authority?

Therefore Pilate, leaving Christ alone, went out and says to the Jews: I find no fault in this man.

The Jews answered: May we say to your greatness what this man said? He said, I can destroy the temple of God, and in three days rebuild it.

---

[83] This is omitted in *Monac. A.* Its addition resulted doubtless from a misapprehension of the preceding statement (John **18**, 31) as referring to Jewish law instead of to Roman rule.

[34] This term *Christ* must have been a somewhat late interpolation. The original document used the name *Jesus*.

PARIS A.

Pilate says: What temple?

The Jews say: The one which Solomon built during forty-six years, but this man says he can destroy and build it in three days.

Pilate again says to them: I am innocent of the blood of this just man. You shall see to it.

The Jews say: His blood be upon us and upon our children.

Pilate calling to him the elders and chief priests and Levites, said to them privately: Do not do thus, for you accuse him of nothing which deserves death: for your accusation is of healing and of profaning the sabbath.

The elders of the people and the chief priests and Levites say to Pilate: If a man blaspheme Cæsar, does he deserve death, or not?

Pilate says: He deserves death.

The Jews say: If any one blasphemes Cæsar, he deserves death. But this man blasphemes God.

Then the governor commanded (the Jews) to go out of the Prætorium, and calling Jesus to him he says: What shall I do to you?

Jesus says to Pilate: In accordance with what has been commissioned [literally, given] you.

Pilate says: What commission has been given me?

Jesus says: Moses and the prophets foretold concerning my death and resurrection.

The Jews, paying attention and hearing, say to Pilate: What [need] have you to listen further to this blasphemy?

Pilate says to the Jews: If this remark is blasphemous (with reference to blasphemy) [36] take him and lead him away to your synagogue, and judge him according to your law.

PARIS D.

Pilate says: And what temple did he speak of destroying?

The Jews said: The temple of Solomon, which Solomon constructed in forty-six years.

Pilate says privately to the chief priests and scribes and Pharisees: I exhort you that you do no evil to this man. For if you shall do evil to this man, you will do injustice; for it is not just that such a man should die who has conferred great benefits on many men.

They spoke to Pilate: My Lord, If he who dishonors Cæsar is worthy of death, how much rather this man, who has dishonored God?

Then Pilate ordained, and all went out. Then he says to Jesus: What do you wish that I shall do to you?

Jesus says to Pilate: Do to me as is ordained.

Jesus answered,[35] Moses and the prophets wrote that I should be crucified and rise again.

The Hebrews, hearing these things, spoke to Pilate: Why do you seek to hear greater insult from him against God?

Pilate says: This is not an insolent speech against God, since it is written in the prophetical books.

---

[35] No preceding remark of Pilate appears in *Paris D*.
[36] The contents of the parenthesis are doubtless a duplicate reading copied into *Paris A*.

§ 8.] TESTIMONY OF NICODEMUS.

PARIS A.

The Jews say to Pilate : Our law contains, If a man sin against man he deserves to receive forty stripes less one ; but if against God, let him be stoned.

Pilate says : Take him yourselves and punish him in such way as you wish.

The Jews say : We wish that he may be crucified.

Pilate says : He does not deserve to be crucified.

Pilate, looking about on the surrounding crowds of Jews, sees many weeping and says : It is not the wish of the whole multitude that he should die.

The elders of the Jews say : On this account the whole multitude of us came, that he may die.

Pilate says : Why that he may die ?

The Jews say : Because he pronounced himself Son of God and king.

PARIS D.

The Hebrews spoke : Our scripture says, If a man wrong a man, or insult him, he deserves to receive forty blows with a staff, but if he insults God [he deserves] to be stoned.

(*Then came a messenger from Procle, Pilate's wife, to him. The message said : That you take care not to agree that any evil shall befall Jesus, that excellent man, since during the night I saw frightful dreams on his account.*)[37]

Pilate gave [as his] defence to the Hebrews : See : If you maintain that the speech, which you allege, that Jesus uttered, is an insult against God, take him and judge him according to your law.

The Jews said to Pilate : We wish [permission] that we may crucify him.

Pilate turning to the people saw many weeping, and said : It seems to me that it is not the wish of the whole people, that this man should die.

The priests and scribes say : We brought the whole people on this account, that you may attain certainty that all wish his death.

Pilate says : But what evil has he done ?

The Hebrews spoke : He says he is a king and son of God.

§ 8. *Nicodemus testifies to the Miracles of Jesus.*

Nicodemus, however, a certain Jew, stood before Pilate and says : I beseech your excellency, command me to speak a few words.

Pilate says : Speak.

Nicodemus says : I spoke to

Thereupon a Jew (a Monotheist) named Nicodemus, standing in the midst, spoke to Pilate : I beseech your greatness, permit me to speak a few words to you.

Pilate says : Speak.

Nicodemus says : I spoke to

---

[37] This breaks the connection, and cannot belong with what immediately precedes and follows it. Compare the beginning of § 5.

| PARIS A. | PARIS D. |

PARIS A.
the elders and chief priests and Levites, and to the whole multitude of Jews in the synagogue: What seek you with this man? This man performs many miracles and wonderful works, which no one [else ever] did or will do. Discharge him, therefore, and cherish no wishes of evil against him; for if the miracles which he performs are from God, they will stand, but if from man, they will come to nothing.

Moses also, having been sent by God into Egypt, did many miracles, which God directed him (to do) before Pharaoh, king of Egypt. And there were men there in the service of Pharaoh — Jannes and Jambres — and they also performed not a few miracles such as Moses performed, and the Egyptians held them, Jannes and Jambres, as gods. But since the miracles which they performed were not from God, they came to nothing, as did also those who believed on them. And now discharge [38] this man, for he is not deserving of death.

The Jews say to Nicodemus: You have become his disciple and argue in his behalf.

(Nicodemus says to them: Has not the governor [in your opinion] become his disciple, and does not he argue in his behalf?) [39]

Did not Cæsar appoint him [with authority] to decide this question?

But the Jews [meanwhile]

PARIS D.
the priests, and the Levites and the scribes and the people when I was present in the synagogue: What charge have you against this man? This man does many miracles, such as [any other] man never did or will do. Discharge him therefore; and if his doings are from God, they will stand, but if from men, they will end in nothing.

As happened also when God sent Moses into Egypt, and Pharaoh, king of Egypt, spoke to him that he should perform a miracle, and he performed it. Then Pharaoh had two magicians, Jannes and Jambres. And they also performed miracles by the use of magic arts, but not such as Moses performed. And the Egyptians regarded such magicians as gods. But because they themselves were not from God their performances ended in nothing.

This Jesus, indeed, raised Lazarus from the dead, and he is still alive. On this account I beseech you, my lord, that you will in no wise permit this physician and life-preserver to be murdered.

The Hebrews were incensed

---

[38] This in the Greek is plural. It may originally have been in the singular, an address to Pilate as in *Paris D*.

[39] Not in *Paris A*. Thilo copies it from three other manuscripts.

§ 9.] TESTIMONY OF THOSE WHO WERE CURED. 123

PARIS A.

were menacing, and gnashing their teeth against Nicodemus.

And Pilate says to them: Why do you gnash your teeth against Nicodemus, for he speaks truth?

The Jews say to Nicodemus: May you receive his truth and his portion.

Nicodemus says: Amen, Amen. [Be it] as you say.

PARIS D.

against Nicodemus, and said to him: May you inherit the truth of Jesus and have part with him.

Nicodemus says: Amen, Amen, Amen, be it to me as you say.

§ 9. *Those Cured testify to the Miracles of Jesus.*

PARIS A.

From among the Jews, moreover, another springing forward desired to speak a word to the governor.

The governor says: If you wish anything, speak.

(The Jew said): Thirty-eight years I lay on a couch, suffering intensely. And when Jesus came, many possessed by demons and prostrated by various diseases were healed by his presence. And some very trustful persons, having compassion on me, carried me with my couch, and brought me to him. And Jesus seeing me had compassion on me, and spoke a word, Rise, take up thy couch and walk. And immediately I was healed and took up my couch and walked.[40]

The Jews say to Pilate: Ask him on what day he was healed.

He having been asked by Pilate concerning the day says: On a sabbath.

The Jews say: Is not this in accordance with our affirmation that he cures and casts out demons on the sabbath?

PARIS D.

Nicodemus having said these things, another Hebrew getting up says to Pilate: I beseech you, lord Pilate, hear me also.

I lay helpless on a couch for thirty-eight years, and on seeing me he felt sorrow and spoke to me: Arise, take up your couch and depart to your house. And while he was speaking this speech I arose and walked about.

The Jews say: Ask him on what day of the week this (*lifting also your bed*) occurred.

He says: On a sabbath.

The Jews spoke: And therefore we say truly, that he does not keep the sabbath.

---

[40] Compare John 5, 5–16.

PARIS A.

And again another Jew springing forward said: I was born blind. I heard the voice [of others] yet saw no countenance, and, as Jesus passed by, I cried with a loud voice: Son of David, take compassion on me. And he took compassion on me, and placed his hands on my eyes, and immediately I recovered my sight.[41]

And another springing forward said: I was bowed down, and he straightened me by a word.[42]

And a certain woman named Beronice, crying out from a distance, spoke: I had had a flow of blood, and I touched the hem of his garment, and immediately the flow of blood, which had lasted twelve years, came to an end.

Then the Jews say: We have a law, not to admit a woman to testify.

And certain other men and women cried out: This man is a prophet, and the demons are subject to him.

(Pilate says: Why are not your teachers also subject to him?)[44]

They say to Pilate: We do not know.

PARIS D.

Again another standing in the midst spoke: I was born blind, and as Jesus was going along the road I cried to him, saying: Take compassion on me, Lord, son of David. And taking clay he anointed my eyes, and immediately I recovered sight.

Another spoke: I was bent down, and seeing him cried out: Take compassion on me, Lord. And taking me by the hand, immediately I arose.

Another spoke: I was a leper, and he healed me by a word alone.

A woman also named Beronice was there and spoke: That for twelve years I had a flow of blood, and I only touched the extremity of his garment, and immediately I was healed.

They say: The law does not admit a woman's testimony.

Other men[43] cried out: This man is a prophet, and the demons fear him.

Pilate says: Why do the demons have no such fear of your fathers? They say: We do not know.[45]

---

[41] Compare Mark **10**, 46–52, Luke **18**, 35–43.

[42] Compare Luke **13**, 11–13. Instead of the foregoing, *Monac. B* has the following: "I had become a leper, and he healed me by a word." Compare Matt. **8**, 2–4, Mark **1**, 40–45, Luke **5**, 12–14.

[43] "Again other Monotheists cried out: This man was a prophet. From five loaves he fed five thousand, and through four loaves four thousand, and the demons fear him." — *Codex Venet.* in **Thilo**, p. 564.

[44] *Monac. B.*

[45] "And they gave no answer." — *Codex Venet.* in **Thilo**, p. 564.

PARIS A.

Yet another spoke to Pilate: That he awoke from the sepulchre Lazarus, who had been dead since the fourth day.

And the governor, getting into a tremor, says to the whole multitude of Jews: Why do you wish to pour out innocent blood?

PARIS D.

Others again spoke: He raised, and by a word only, Lazarus, who was [already] for the fourth day in the sepulchre.

Pilate, therefore, hearing the resurrection of Lazarus, was frightened, and says to the people: Why do you wish that you may shed the just blood of a man?

§ 10. *Effort of Pilate to save Jesus.*

And summoning Nicodemus and the twelve (who had stated that he was not born of fornication) he says to them: What shall I do, for there is a tumult among the people?

They say to him: We do not know. *They shall see.*

And again Pilate, summoning the whole multitude of Jews, says: You know that it is your custom at the feast of unleavened bread [to ask me] to free you one prisoner. I have a condemned prisoner in the prison, a murderer called Barabbas, and this Jesus, on whom I find no fault (in him)." Whom do you wish that I should set free to you?

They cry: Barabbas.

And Pilate says to them: What then shall I do to Jesus, who is called the Christ?

They say: Let him be crucified.

Another Jew said: You are plainly no friend of Cæsar, because he proclaimed himself son of God and king. You, there-

Then he summoned Nicodemus and the twelve Monotheists (Jews) and spoke to them: What do you say that I should do, for the people is in commotion?

They say: We do not know. *Do what you wish. What the people do [is done] that they may find out this, [namely, your will.]*

Pilate again went out and says to the people: You know that, during the feasts of unleavened bread, it is customary that I should set free on my [your?] account one of the arrested liable to confinement. I have in prison an evil-doer, a robber named Barabbas. I have also Jesus, who never did evil. Which of the two do you wish that I should set free for you?

The people say: Free Barabbas for us.

Pilate says: What then shall I do with Jesus?

They say: Let him be crucified.

Again others cried out: If you free Jesus you are no friend of Cæsar, for he calls himself son of God and king, and if you

---

⁴⁶ Doubtless from two texts.

PARIS A.

fore, wish him for king and not Cæsar.

Pilate, being angry, says [48] to the Jews: Your nation is always turbulent and you oppose your benefactors.

The Jews say: What benefactors?

Pilate says: As I hear, your God led you out from oppressive slavery, out of the land of Egypt, and saved you through the sea as if it had been dry land, and nourished you with manna in the desert and gave you a measure of quails, and from a rock supplied you with water to drink, and gave you a law. And after all these things you provoked your God, and sought out a molten calf, and incensed your God and he sought to kill you. And Moses interceded for you and you were not destroyed. And now you charge me that I hate the king.

And Pilate rising from the tribunal sought to go out.

And the Jews cried to Pilate, saying: We recognize Cæsar as king, but not Jesus. For the magi offered him gifts as to a king, and Herod, hearing from the magi that a king was born, sought to kill him. But his father Joseph, knowing thereof, took him and his mother and fled to Egypt. And Herod hearing of it destroyed the children in Bethlehem.

(*And Pilate hearing these words from the Jews was frightened.*

And Pilate silencing the multi-

PARIS D.

should free him he (becomes king)[47] will take the kingdom of Cæsar.

Pilate thereupon got angry, and spoke: [48] Your race was always devilish and faithless, and you were always adversaries of your benefactors.

The Hebrews spoke: And who were our benefactors?

Pilate says: God, who freed [you] from the hand of Pharaoh, and passed you through the Red Sea as if on dry land, and fed you [49] ... with water from the rock and who gave you a law, which you disregarded, denying God; and, unless Moses had stood beseeching God, you would all have perished by a bitter death. You, indeed, forget all those things, and after the same manner, say now that I do not love Cæsar, but hate him, and wish to plot against his authority.

And having said these things Pilate rose in anger from his seat, wishing to fly from them.

The Jews thereupon cried out: We wish Cæsar to reign over us and not Jesus, because Jesus received gifts from the magi. And Herod also heard this, that he would become a king and [Herod] wished to put him to death and, to this end, sent and killed all the children in Bethlehem. And on this account Joseph, his father, and his mother fled, from fear of these things, into Egypt.

Pilate therefore, hearing such statements, and being frightened, silenced the people [and said]:

---

[47] Either two texts are copied or *and* must be supplied, which Thilo has done.

[48] The remarks of Pilate were doubtless interpolated, not long after the Jewish rebellion against Hadrian, at a time when some Christians addressed the Jews in a similar strain.

[49] The MS. must have omitted something.

PARIS A.

tudes because of their crying out, says :)[60] So, this is he whom Herod sought?
The Jews say: Yes, this is he.

Then Pilate, taking water, washed his hands publicly,[62] saying: I am innocent of the blood of this just man. You shall see [to it, or, the result of it].

And again the Jews cry out, that his blood [be] on us and on our children.

PARIS D.

Then this is the Jesus whom Herod at that time sought to kill?
They say to him: Yes.
Pilate, therefore, becoming aware that he [Jesus] belonged to Herod's jurisdiction, *because descended from the race of Jews,*[61] sent Jesus to him.
And Herod having seen him rejoiced greatly, for he had been desiring to see him, hearing of the miracles which he was accustomed to perform. Therefore he clothed him with white garments, and began to ask him: Whence are you, and of what race?
But Jesus gave him no answer.
But Herod wishing to see some miracle, such as [had been] formerly performed by Christ, and not seeing [any], but [perceiving] that he did not even give him a civil answer, sent him again to Pilate.
But the people cried out: Let him be crucified.
Pilate, noting this, spoke to his servants to bring water, and these brought it. Washing his hands, therefore, with the water, he said to the people: I am innocent of the blood of this excellent man. You shall see that you are murdering this man unjustly, since neither did I find fault in him, nor yet Herod. For on this account [Herod] sent this man back to me.
The Jews spoke: His blood [be] upon us and upon our children.
But the chief priests raised an uproar among the people, that they should destroy him promptly.

---

[60] *Monac. B.*

[61] This is a sample of mistakes which would have found place in the Gospels, had they been of late origin.

[62] Literally, *in presence of the sun,* or, to use a modern expression, *in sight of heaven.*

PARIS A.	PARIS D.
	And the people again to Pilate [. . . ?]
	Then says Pilate to Jesus: You are the king of the Jews?
	But Jesus gave him no answer.
	Pilate says: Do you not speak to me? Do you not know that I have authority to crucify you and authority to free you?
	Jesus spoke to him: You have not a particle of authority against me, except what was given you from above.

§ 11. *Crucifixion of Jesus.*

Then Pilate commanded the accused[53] to be brought before the tribunal where he was sitting,	Then Pilate seated himself on his official seat, that he might give judgment against Jesus. He decreed, therefore, and Jesus came before him.
	And they brought a crown of thorns and placed it upon his head and a reed upon [in his] right hand.
and gave judgment as follows against Jesus.	Then he gave judgment, and says to him:
SENTENCE BY PILATE. Your own nation has convicted you as [claiming to be] a king, and on this account I have decreed that he [you]	Your race says and testifies [concerning] you that you wish to reign. On this account I decree that
be first scourged, because of the ordinance of the pious kings, and then	they shall first strike you with a staff forty blows, as the laws of the kings decree, and that they shall make sport of you, and finally that
be hung on a cross,	they shall crucify you.
in the garden where he was seized and two malefactors with him.[54]	
	Such judgment, therefore, from Pilate having taken place, the Jews began to strike Jesus, some with staves, others with their hands, others with their feet, and others spit in his face.

---

[53] Τὸ Βῆλον. The translation is conjectural.

[54] "Let Dysmas and Stegas, the two malefactors, be crucified with you."— *Monac. A.*

PARIS A.

And immediately they led Jesus from the Prætorium with the two malefactors.

PARIS D.

Immediately, therefore, having prepared a cross, they took [him] away to crucify him. And having given this [the cross] to him, they hurried to be on their way.

And as he was thus going, carrying also his cross, he came to the gate of the city of Jerusalem. But as he was not able to walk, because of the many blows, and because of the weight of the cross, these [people] because of the desire which the Jews had to crucify him, meeting[55] a certain man, — a Cyrenian named Simon, who was coming from the country, who had two sons, Alexander and Rufus, (*and he was from the city of Cyrene*) — gave him, therefore, the cross. Not out of compassion towards Jesus, and to lighten him of the burden, but desiring, as has been said, to murder him sooner, they impressed Simon that he should carry his cross. And they bring him to the place Golgotha, which translated is, Place of a Skull.[56]

And, when they arrived at the spot,

Then they reached safely the place called Skull, which was strown [*or*, paved] with stones; and there the Jews placed the cross.

the soldiers divested Jesus of his garments, and girded him with a linen cloth,

And the soldiers took off his garments and divided these things among themselves.

and encircled his head with a crown of thorns,

And they offered him to drink wine mingled with myrrh, which he did not take.

And they put on him a purple

---

[55] The Greek is ungrammatical and confused, owing apparently to the mingling of two, or more, narratives.

[56] Here follows in *Paris D* an interpolation which must be later by several centuries than the original document, for it styles Mary *Mother of God*.

PARIS A.	PARIS D.
	cloak, that is a purple Rosos [Rasos?], and weaving a crown of thorns they put it on his head, and bending their knees before him they mocked him, saying: Hail, king of the Jews! And spitting on him, they took a reed and struck him on his head. And after they had mocked him they took off the cloak, that is the Rasos [Rosos?], which is called purple. And they put on him his own garments and led him away that he might be crucified. And crucifying him they divided his garments, casting lots upon them [to determine] what each one should take.[57]
and crucified him, and at the	And it was the sixth [58] hour of the day. They lifted him on the cross, and crucifying him destroyed [59] him.
	And the inscription of his alleged crime was written over him in Greek and Romaic and Hebrew letters, saying, This is the king of the Jews.
same time suspended the (?) two malefactors with him.	And they crucified with him two robbers, one on the right and one on the left.
	And the passers-by uttered abusive language towards him, shaking their heads and saying: Oh, you, who destroy the temple and build it again in three days, save yourself and descend from the cross. In like manner the chief priests with the scribes said mockingly to each other: The Christ, the son of Israel, saved others. He cannot save himself. Let him descend from the cross, that we may see and believe him.[60]

---

[57] The reference by Justin Martyr (*Apol.* 1, 35) to this passage implies that in the middle of the second century it was to be found, in the *Acts of Pilate*, corresponding apparently with the text here given.

[58] The manuscript here uses a numeral.

[59] The translation of this word is conjectural.

[60] Here follows in *Paris D* an interpolation of monkish times, a long lamentation by the "Mother of God."

§ 11.] CRUCIFIXION OF JESUS.

PARIS A.

But Jesus said: Father, forgive them, for they know not what they do.

And the soldiers divided his garments.

And the people stood looking on. And the chief priests and elders of the people sneered at him saying: He saved others and cannot save himself. If he is the Son of God, let him descend from the cross and we will believe on him. And the soldiers made game of him, coming and offering him vinegar and gall and saying: If you are the Christ, the king of the Jews, save yourself.

And Pilate, after the sentence, commanded an inscription to be written, the charge against him, in Greek letters.[61]

And a certain one of the suspended malefactors, Gestas by name, said to Jesus: If you are the Christ save yourself and us.

But Demas, the other, answering, rebuked him, saying: Have you no fear of God, because of being under the same condemnation? And we [are condemned] justly, for we receive the proper [consequences] of what we have done. But this man has committed no crime. And he said to Jesus, Remember me, Lord, when you shall come in your kingdom. Jesus spoke to him: Verily I

PARIS D.

Then Jesus cried with a loud voice: Do not charge this sin to them, for the wretched [ones] do not know what they are doing.

Then he says: I am thirsty. And immediately one of the soldiers ran, and taking a sponge and filling it, and placing it on a reed, gave him to drink. And having tasted he did not wish to drink.

But the Jews standing and looking on ridiculed him and said: If you said truly that you are the Son of God, descend from the cross, and immediately, that we may believe on you. Others ridiculing him, said: He saved others, he cured and healed others, infirm, palsied, lepers, demoniacs, blind, lame, dead, and he cannot likewise save himself.

And the robber, crucified on his left hand, said to him: If you are the Son of God, descend from the cross and save yourself and us. His name was Gestas. But the robber crucified on the right, named Dysmas, reproached that same robber, saying: O miserable and wretched [man], do you not fear God? We indeed have done things which deserve what we suffer. But he has done and committed no crime whatever. And this robber on the right turning, addressed and says to Jesus: Lord, remember me when you shall come in your kingdom. But Jesus spoke to him: So be it: I say to you,

---

[61] "In Romaic *and Hebrew* letters, that, in accordance with what the Jews stated he is king of the Jews."—*Monac. B.* The same with omission of "*and Hebrew*" is found in *Monac. A.*

PARIS A.	PARIS D.
say to you, Demas : To-day you shall be with me in Paradise.[62]	this day you shall be with me in Paradise.[63] Then Jesus crying with a loud voice, spoke : Father, into thy hands will I commit my spirit. And with this utterance he expired. [Cp. § 12 of Paris A.]

§ 12. *Accompaniments of the Crucifixion.*

And it was about the sixth hour.	And it was about the sixth hour. And immediately a very great earthquake occurred over the whole earth, so that the whole world shuddered. And because of the excessive earthquake the rocks were rent and the sepulchres were opened, and many bodies of the Just were awakened,[64] and the sun was darkened, and the veil of the temple was rent in the middle, and the darkness occurred over the whole earth until the ninth hour.
And darkness took place upon the earth until the ninth hour, the sun being darkened. And the veil of the temple was rent in two from top to bottom.	
And Jesus crying with a loud voice, spoke : Father, into thy hands I commit my spirit. And having said this he gave up the spirit.[65] [Cp. § 11 of Paris D.]	
The centurion, seeing what took place, glorified God, saying that : This man is just. And all the crowds who were passing to see this spectacle, when they saw the occurrences, returned, beating their breasts.	And these things having taken place, the Jews being frightened, some of them said that "in reality this man was just." Longinus, the centurion, standing up boldly, spoke : Truly, this man was Son of God. Others coming and seeing him, [commenced] beating their breasts, and immediately turned back again from fear.

---

[62] This can scarcely have been added before the fourth century. See *Underworld Mission*, pp. 144, 145 ; 3d edit. pp. 138, 139.

[63] Another monkish interpolation of *Paris D* occurs here. It narrates that when Joseph and the "Mother of God" fled to Egypt thirty-three years previously, the leprous child of the right-hand robber was cured by being washed in the same water which had been used for the infant Jesus.

[64] The genuineness of the similar passage in Matthew **27**, 52, 53, has been questioned. See Norton, *Genuineness of the Gospels*, Vol. **1**, Appendix, Note A, Section v.

[65] In some of the MSS. the Hebrew of Psalm **31**, 5 (*Septuagint*, **30**, 6) is here copied with the Greek appended as a translation.

§ 12.] ACCOMPANIMENTS OF THE CRUCIFIXION.

PARIS A.

But the centurion reported to the governor all the occurrences. And the governor and his wife hearing of it were grieved [depressed?] and neither ate nor drank on that day. And Pilate summoning the Jews spoke to them: You have beheld the occurrences.

But they spoke to him: An eclipse of the sun has taken place, a usual thing.⁶⁶

PARIS D.

But the centurion, having noticed all such wonders, going to Pilate, narrated these things. But he hearing [the narration] wondered and was astounded, and because of his fear and grief, would not eat nor drink on that day. He gave notice, moreover, and the whole Sanhedrim came so soon as the darkness had passed. And Pilate spoke *to the people:* You see how a great earthquake took place; You see how the veil of the temple was rent in the midst; You see how darkness took place over the inhabited earth from the sixth to the ninth hour. In reality I did well in exhorting you not to murder the excellent man.

But all the miscreants were utterly unbelieving. On the contrary they said to Pilate, that: Such darkness is an eclipse of the sun, similar to what has occurred in other times.

Pilate says to them: If this darkness be an eclipse of the sun as you say, what do you pronounce the other marvels and shuddering prodigies?

And they had nothing to answer.

And while he was saying these things, the Jews coming *and* (?) spoke to Pilate: My Lord, they did not write properly the inscription above the head of Jesus, for it testifies that he is our king. Therefore we beseech you, that you decree and write there, that he said that he was king of the Jews.

---

⁶⁶ This oversight was subsequently remedied in some copies by an interpolation. According to *Monac. A*, " Pilate said to them: Foulest of men, this is your truthfulness in all things. I know that this never occurs except at new moon [literally, at the moon's birth]. You ate your passover yesterday on the fourteenth of the month, and [yet] you say an eclipse of the sun occurred." — **Thilo**, p. 594, n.

PARIS A.

PARIS D.

Pilate said to them: What I have written, I have written.

Then they say to him: We have the feast of unleavened bread all of to-morrow, and we beseech you, since the crucified yet breathe, that their bones may be broken, and that they may be taken down.

Pilate spoke: Let this take place. He sent soldiers, therefore, and they found the robbers breathing, and broke their limbs. But finding Jesus dead, they did not touch him. Then one soldier leaving [his companions] pierced Jesus also with a spear in the right side, and immediately there came out blood and water.

§ 13. *Joseph esteems and buries Jesus.*

And, behold, a man named Joseph, a councillor, a good and just man, this man had not assented to their design nor action — from Arimathea, a city of the Jews — himself also awaiting the kingdom of God, this man

And towards evening of the *Preparation*, that was closing, Joseph, a certain well-born and wealthy man, a *Monotheist*, a Jew, finding the Nicodemus whom the previous treatise has made known, says to him: I know that you loved Jesus while he was alive, and I saw you combating the Jews on his account. If it seems good to you, therefore, let us go to Pilate and ask the body of Jesus for burial, since it is a great sin that it should be unburied.

I am afraid, says Nicodemus, lest [owing to] Pilate being angry I should suffer some injury. But if you, going alone and asking, should receive the dead, then I will accompany you and will co-operate in per-

§ 13.] JOSEPH ESTEEMS AND BURIES JESUS.

PARIS A.	PARIS D.
coming to Pilate, requested the body of Jesus. And Pilate permitted [or, directed] that the body be given him. And taking it he wrapped it in pure linen and placed it in a rock-hewn sepulchre, in which no one had ever yet been.	forming thoroughly all things appropriate to burial.[67]
And the Jews, hearing that Joseph had asked for the body of Jesus, were seeking for him also,	The Jews having learned that these things had been done by Joseph and Nicodemus, were very indignant at them, and the high-priests, Annas and Caiaphas, manifesting [it] to Joseph, spoke to him: Why did you perform this sepulture for the dead Jesus?

and for the twelve who had said that Jesus was not born of fornication, and for Nicodemus and many others, who, springing forward before Pilate, had made manifest his good works.

And all [others of them] having concealed themselves, Nicodemus only made his appearance to them, because he was a ruling man of the Jews. And Nicodemus says to them: How can you [dare] enter the synagogue?

The Jews say: How do you [dare] enter the synagogue? For you are his accomplice and his portion [be] yours in the future life.

Nicodemus says: Amen, Amen.

In like manner Joseph, coming forward from [his concealment?][68] said to them: Why are you vexed at me because I asked the body of Jesus? Behold, I put it in my sepulchre, wrapped it in pure linen, and I rolled a stone against the

---

[67] Here follows a passage in which Mary is called Mother of God. It is of course later by centuries than the original document.

[68] Παρεκβάς.

PARIS A.

door of the sepulchre. And you have not done well towards the just man, that having crucified him you did not repent, but raised a spear against him.

PARIS D.

Joseph says: I knew Jesus [to be] a just man, true and good in all things, and I knew you, that from envy you accomplished his murder, and therefore I took charge of his burial.

The Jews, having heard these things from Joseph, immediately seizing him, commanded that he be made safe until the first day of the week, saying: The hour does not permit doing anything against you, because the sabbath is about dawning, and you will not be deemed worthy of sepulture, but we will give your flesh to the birds of heaven.

Joseph says to them: This is the speech of the arrogant Goliath, who uttered contumely towards the living God and the holy David. But God spoke through the prophets: To me [belongs] thorough vengeance; I will repay, says the Lord. And now the uncircumcised in flesh, but circumcised in heart, taking water, washed his hands in presence of the sun, saying: I am innocent of the blood of this just man, you shall see. And answering Pilate you said: His blood [be] upon us and upon our children. And now I fear lest the anger of the Lord be close upon you and upon your children, in accordance with your speech.

But the Jews having heard these words were embittered in spirit, and laying hold of Joseph, seized him and shut him into a house where there was no win-

Then the high-priests getting angry and seizing Joseph, threw him into prison and said to him: If we do not to-morrow murder you as we did him! For the present remain under guard, but

§ 13.] JOSEPH ESTEEMS AND BURIES JESUS.

PARIS A.

dow. And guards remained at the door.

PARIS D.

on the LORD'S DAY[60] early you will be delivered to death. They spoke these things, and marked with a seal the prison, which was secured by all manner of keys.

The Preparation having come therefore thus to an end, the Jews, early on the sabbath, went off to Pilate and spoke to him: That deceiver, while yet alive, spoke [to the effect] that after three days he should be raised. Lest his disciples, stealing him by night, should mislead the people by such a falsehood, command, we pray you, that his sepulchre be guarded.

Pilate, therefore, gave them five hundred soldiers, who seated themselves on the sepulchre to guard it. Placing also seals [upon] the stone of the sepulchre, they guarded it during the sabbath until the first dawn of the LORD'S DAY.

After that a great earthquake again took place first, then a lightning-bearing angel of the Lord came from heaven and rolled the stone from the sepulchre and sat upon it. And from [fear] of the angel the soldiers became as dead. Then the Lord arose, wakened Adam and all the prophets, whom the devil had in his power. He there wakened also all believers on him.[70]

---

[60] Anachronisms like this would have crept into the Gospels had they been written after the first century.

[70] The original document seems to have ended here. The following *doxology* is subjoined in *Paris D* and *Cod. Venet.*:
"The name of the Lord be praised
With his Father and the all holy spirit
Now and always and to ages of ages."
as also the following subscription in *Paris D*:
"End of the Holy Sufferings and beginning of HIS resurrection; of our Lord Jesus Christ."

§ 14. *Heathens testify to the Resurrection.*

And on the sabbath the chiefs of the synagogue and priests and Levites decreed that all should assemble [literally, be found] in the synagogue on the first day of the week. And rising early, all plotted in the synagogue, by what death they should kill Joseph.

And while the council [or Sanhedrim] was sitting, they commanded him to be brought with much ignominy. And having opened the door they did not find him. And the whole people was astounded, and they became amazed, because they found the seals and doors sealed, and that Caiaphas had the key. And for the rest, they no longer dared to lay their hands on those who had spoken before Pilate concerning Jesus.

And while they were yet sitting in the synagogue, and wondering on account of Joseph, some of the guard came, whom the Jews had requested from Pilate to watch the sepulchre of Jesus, lest the disciples coming should steal him. And they announced to the chiefs of the synagogue and priests and Levites, stating the events which had taken place, how "a great earthquake occurred while we were watching the sepulchre, and we saw how an angel descended from heaven and rolled away the stone from the door of the sepulchre and he sat upon it.

And his appearance was like lightning, and his garment white as snow, and from fear of him we became as dead.[71]

When, therefore, the Lord's Day dawned, the chief [or high] priests held a council with the Jews, and sent to put Joseph out of prison, for the purpose of killing him. And having opened [it] they did not find him. And they were surprised at this, as to how, the doors being shut and the keys safe, and the seals having been found [unbroken] *but* Joseph was become invisible.

And hereupon a soldier, one of those who had guarded the sepulchre, coming up, spoke in the synagogue: Learn that Jesus has risen.

The Jews say: How?

But he said: "First a great earthquake took place, then a lightning-bearing angel of the Lord descended from heaven, rolled the stone [from] the sepulchre and sat upon it, and from fear of him all we soldiers became as dead, and were unable either to fly or speak. And we

---

[71] In *Monac. A* this reads, "and we lay in great fright."

PARIS A.

And we heard the angel saying to the women who stayed by the tomb of Jesus, and he said: Be not afraid, for I know that you seek Jesus the crucified. He is not here, for he has risen in accordance with what he spoke. Approach; see the place where the Lord was lying; and going quickly speak to his disciples, that he has risen from the dead, and behold, he precedes you into Galilee. There ye shall see him in accordance with what he spoke to you."

The Jews say: To what women was he talking?

The guards say: We do not know who they were.

The Jews say: Why did you not seize the women?

The guards say: We were become as if dead from fright, not hoping to see the light of day; and how could we seize them?

The Jews say: As the Lord lives we do not believe you.

The guards say: You see so many miracles in relation to that man and you believe not, and how can you believe us? For you swore well that as the Lord lives, we do not believe you. For the Lord does live.

And again the guards say: We have heard that you shut up him who asked for the body of Jesus, sealing also the door, and having opened it, you did not find him. Give us Joseph, and we will give you Jesus.

The Jews say: We will give you Joseph; Give us Jesus also.

The guards say: First give us Joseph, and then we will give you Jesus likewise.

PARIS D.

heard the angel saying to the women, who had come thither to see the sepulchre,
that: Be not afraid, for I know that you seek Jesus. He is not here, but has risen as he told you beforehand. Bend down and see the sepulchre where the body of Jesus lay.
Go, however, and state to his disciples that he has risen from the dead, and that they shall go in [into] Galilee, for there they shall find him."

On this account I [the soldier] tell you this previously.

The Jews say to the soldiers: What women were they that came to the sepulchre?

and why did you not seize them?

The soldiers say: From fear, and from the sight alone of the angel, we were unable to speak or to move.

The Jews spoke: As the Lord of Israel lives *that* we believe nothing of what you say.

The soldiers say: Jesus performed such miracles and you did not believe him, and [how] are you to believe us now? You say truly, that God lives, and in reality that he truly lives whom you crucified.

But did we not hear that you had Joseph shut up in prison, then opening the doors you did not find him. Give us Joseph, and we will also, on this condition, give you Jesus.

PARIS A.

The Jews say: Joseph has departed to his own city.

The guards say to the Jews: And Jesus is in Galilee, as we heard from the angel who rolled away the stone, that: He precedes you into Galilee.

And the Jews, having heard these words, were greatly excited, saying: This account must by no means be heard [lest] all be inclined towards Jesus. And holding a council among themselves, they laid down a sufficient quantity of silver and gave it to the soldiers, saying: State, that His disciples, coming by night, stole him while we were asleep. And, if this should be heard by the governor, we will persuade him and will save you any anxiety.

But they taking the silver did as they had been taught. And this report has circulated among the Jews UNTIL THE PRESENT TIME.[72]

PARIS D.

The Jews say: Joseph, a fugitive from prison, you will find him in Arimathea, his country.

The soldiers also say: Go you also to Galilee and you will find Jesus, as the angel stated to the women.

Hereupon, being frightened, the Jews stated to the soldiers: See that you state to no one this account, and [lest?] all shall believe on Jesus. To which end also they gave them much silver, that they might state: While we slept his disciples came and stole him.

The soldiers spoke: We fear lest Pilate should hear that we took silver and should put us to death.

The Jews spoke: Take it and we pledge ourselves to render an apology to Pilate in your behalf. Only state that you slept.

And the soldiers took the silver, and stated as they had been ordered, and UNTIL THE PRESENT DAY such a false account is circulated by the Jews.

§ 15. *Jews testify to the Resurrection.*

But a certain Phineas, a priest, and Addas, a teacher, and Angæus, a Levite, coming down from Galilee into Jerusalem, narrated to the chiefs of the synagogue and to the priests and Levites, that

And, after a few days, three men came from Galilee to Jerusalem. One was a priest named Phineas: another a Levite named Angæus, but the remaining one a soldier named Adas. These came to the chief-priests and stated to them and to the

---

[72] The language coincides closely with that of Matthew, **28**, 11–15. See p. 89.

PARIS A.

they saw Jesus and his disciples sitting on mount Admonition. And he said to his disciples:

Going into the whole world, proclaim to the creation that whoever believes and is baptized will be saved, but the unbeliever will be condemned.

And these miracles shall follow believers. In my name they shall cast out demons, they shall speak in [to them] new languages, and shall take serpents into their hands, and if they shall drink anything deadly, it shall not injure them. They shall lay their hands on the sick and these shall get well.

While Jesus was yet speaking to his disciples, we saw him taken up into heaven.

The elders and priests and Levites say: Give glory to the God of Israel and make acknowledgment to him if ye have heard and seen what ye narrate.

The narrators say, that: As the Lord God of our fathers lives, the God of Abraham and the God of Isaac and the God of Jacob, we have heard these things and we saw him taken up into heaven.

The Jews say: Did you come for this, to make a glad announcement, or did you come that you might offer prayer to God?

They say: That we may offer prayer to God.

The Jews say to them: To what purpose then is this silly talk which you have been nonsensically talking before all the people?

Phineas says, as also Addas, the teacher, and Angæus the Levite, to the chiefs of the synagogue and to the priests and Levites: If these words which we have spoken are sinful, lo, we are before you. Do

PARIS D.

people: We saw in Galilee that Jesus, whom you crucified, with his eleven disciples on the mount of Olives, teaching them and saying: Go into the whole world and proclaim the gospel, and who believes and is baptized will be saved, but the unbeliever will be condemned. And having said these things he ascended to heaven.

And not only we, but many others of the five hundred there, saw him.

And the chief priests and Jews, having heard these things, spoke to those three men: Give glory to the God of Israel, and repent of these, your falsehoods.

These three answered: As lives the Lord God of our fathers, of Abraham, Isaac, and Jacob, we do not falsify but tell you the truth.

PARIS A.

to us what seems good in your eyes.

But they, taking [a book of] the Law, adjured them to narrate these accounts no further to any one. And they gave them to eat and drink and put them out of the city, having given them also *silver and* three men [who were] to place them again in Galilee. And they departed.[73]

PARIS D.

Then the high-priest adjured them, and giving them money sent them away to another place, that they should not proclaim the resurrection of the Lord in Jerusalem.

The foregoing not only comprises everything in *Paris A* and *Paris D*, which can reasonably be regarded as part of the original *Acts of Pilate*, but includes many of the additions. The remainder of these documents, as printed by Thilo,[74] cannot have formed part of the original composition.

NOTE B.

PILATE'S REPORT.

ASIDE from the Acts of Pilate which have been given in the preceding Note, a letter from Pontius Pilate to Tiberius was fabricated, either as a support to the preceding document or as an independent fraud. Tertullian (see Note A, footnote 1)

---

[73] "And they gave them to eat and drink, and putting them out of the city, let them go, having given them also three men so as to take them safely [without any talking?] as far as Galilee." — *Monac. A*, **Thilo**, p. 626.

[74] A portion of the remainder is weak and objectless. A search through the country, prompted by Nicodemus, finds nothing of Jesus, but does find Joseph, who gives a lecture to the murderers of Jesus.

Another portion is a narrative by two sons of that Simeon, who blessed Jesus when a child. They had died and been buried some time previously. They were among those raised at the resurrection of Jesus. They narrate to the Jewish rulers the deeds of Jesus in the Underworld, of which the reader will find a brief abstract in *Underworld Mission*, pp. 161, 162; 3d. edit. pp. 155, 156. These omitted portions constitute about half of the whole document as printed by Thilo.

refers to it. At present this letter appears in several forms, occasioned perhaps by the different wants of controversialists. The longer Latin form of the letter is herewith translated. I understand Thilo to mean that he takes it as given in his text from the Einsiedlen MS.,[1] and as given in his notes from the Orthodoxographa.[2]

§ 1 *Longer Latin Form.*

Codex Einsidlensis.

PONTIUS PILATE TO HIS SOVEREIGN CLAUDIUS,[3] GREETING.

Lately it happened with my sanction that the Jews through envy punished themselves and their posterity by cruelly sentencing [a person] concerning whom, when their fathers had a promise that their God would send to them from his holy Heaven [one] who should deservedly be called their king, and had promised that he would send this king to the earth through a virgin.[4] When the God of the Hebrews during my procuratorship had sent that king into Judea, and when the Hebrews had seen him give light to the blind, purify the lepers, cure paralytics, drive demons out of men, call to life even the dead, control the winds, walk with dry feet over waves of the sea, and do many other miraculous wonders, and when many of the Jewish people believed him to be

Monumenta Orthodoxographa.

Lately it happened, of which thing I can bear testimony, that the Jews through envy destroyed themselves and all their posterity by cruelly sentencing [a person]. For when by the promise of oracles received by the authority of their ancestors they expected as follows, namely, that their God would through a young virgin send [one] who should justly be called their king, he sent this [person] into Judea during my presence there. He, as is known to all, restored sight to the blind, cleansed lepers, cured paralytics. They saw him also drive out demons and liberate those possessed by impure spirits. He also resuscitated from their sepulchres the dead. The storms of wind obeyed him; he walked on the sea with dry feet. He did also very many other miracles so that he was commonly called among Jews and the common people the Son of God.

---

[1] Thilo, p. 796 n. The letter, subjoined in this MS. to the Acts of Pilate, is given in **Thilo**, *Cod. Apoc.* pp. 796–800.

[2] Thilo states, p. cxxxiv, that he knows not the MS. origin of the Latin which he has given in notes on pp. 798–800, and which is here translated. It is perhaps nearer than the Einsiedlen MS. to the original letter.

[3] This was a portion of the fuller name Tiberius Claudius Cæsar.

[4] The sentence is imperfect in the Latin. In the corresponding passage of the Orthodoxographa the expression is *virginem juvenculam.* Possibly this may be intended to mean an immature virgin.

Codex Einsidlensis.

the Son of God, the chief priests and scribes, and Pharisees of the Jews experienced envy towards him, and seizing, delivered him to me as procurator, and stated to me falsely a variety of things concerning him, asserting that he was a magician and acted[5] contrary to their law. I, however, believed their charges, and delivered him after a scourging to their decision. They, however, crucified him *on a wooden cross*[6] and burying him when dead placed guards, the soldiers of my Prætorium guarding his sepulchre and sealing it. On the third day he arose from the sepulchre. The wickedness of the Jews, however, flamed out to such a degree that they gave money to my soldiers, saying: State that[7] his disciples stole his body by night. But my soldiers, after they had received the money, could not be silent as to the truth of what had occurred, but testified that he had risen from the sepulchre, and said that they had received money from the Jews.

Therefore I suggest to the sovereign that no one *spread a contrary falsehood and* decide[8] to credit untruths of the Jews.

Monumenta Orthodoxographa.

The chief priests, however, moved by rivalry and envy, were opposed to him, and delivered him, captured, to me, charging him as a criminal with fictitious crimes: they called him a magician, a renegade from, and transgressor of, their law, by which persuasions I, misled, credited their complaints and delivered him, scourged, to them that they should proceed against him as they deemed proper. But they thereupon crucified him and placed guards over the sepulchre in which he was deposited, among which guards also were some of my soldiers, who saw him on the third day rising from the dead. The wickedness of the Jews, however, flamed out the more hereupon, and they paid a large sum of money to the soldiers as an inducement to affirm that his disciples had stolen the body by night. The soldiers accepted the money, but nevertheless affirmed and testified publicly everywhere that they had seen visions of angels, and that that Jesus had truly risen from the dead.

I, however, have written these things to the end that no one may credit the triflings and false-

---

[5] For *magnum* read *magum*.

[6] The words in Italics, omitted in one MS., were probably added during the rage for using arguments from the Old Testament. Compare in *Judaism*, p. 345, a remark of Middleton.

[7] *Quia* is used here in the sense of the Greek word ὅτι. If not a translation it would indicate, that Latins who resided in Greek countries, or Greeks who wrote Latin, had affixed this meaning to the word.

[8] For *æstimans* read *æstimet*. The preceding words in Italics may be an interpolation. Otherwise we might treat *et* as interpolated and translate "that no one spread a contrary falsehood [*and*] deciding to credit untruths of the Jews."

Codex Einsidlensis.	Monumenta Orthodoxographa.
I have directed to your mightiness [a record of] all things done touching Jesus in my Prætorium.[9]	hoods of the Jews if they give a different account of what has occurred. Farewell.

§ 2. *Shorter Latin Form.*[10]

PONTIUS PILATE, PROCURATOR OF JUDEA, TO TIBERIUS CÆSAR, EMPEROR, S. P.

Concerning Jesus Christ, — on whom in my last communications I made a plain declaration to you, that severe punishment was inflicted by desire of the people, I being unwilling and reluctant, — no previous age had or will have a man, by Hercules, so pious, so [morally] austere. But there arose a wonderful effort of the people itself, and a concurrence of the scribes and chiefs and elders, (although their prophets, who according to us would be called Sibyls, warned against it) to crucify this ambassador of truth, supernatural signs making their appearance while he was suspended [on the cross], such as threatened, in the opinion of philosophers, ruin to the whole world. His disciples flourish, not proving untrue in work and continence of life to their master; nay, being most beneficent in his name. Unless I had been in the utmost fear lest a sedition should arise of the people who were almost boiling over, perchance that man would still live for us. Although fidelity to your dignity, rather than my own will, prevented my opposing with all my strength the sale and suffering of just blood, void of any accusation, merely through the malignity of men [and] yet [to eventuate], as the Scriptures make plain, in their own destruction. Farewell. — *V. Cal. April.*

---

[9] The paragraph in Italics is probably a later addition.

[10] The letter in this form cannot be the one to which Tertullian (see Note A, footnote 1) refers. Thilo prints it in his Codex Apocryphus, pp. 801, 802. He mentions that it is nowhere found appended in manuscripts to the Acts of Pilate, or, to use his words, *a nemine, quod sciam, cum Nicodemi evangelio conjuncta est.* The letters S. P. appended to the inscription are an abbreviation probably of *Salutem Plurimam,* "utmost prosperity."

§ 3. *Greek Form.*

REPORT OF PONTIUS PILATE, PROCURATOR OF JUDEA, SENT TO
TIBERIUS CÆSAR, AT ROME.

Pontius Pilate, administering the Eastern government, to Tiberius Cæsar, most powerful and sacred.[11]

I have thought proper, filled [as I am] with much fear and trembling, most powerful king, to indicate by this, my own writing, to your Practical-piety, the ῥοπὴν contingency [to nature][12] of this date as the event made it known.

While I, O master, according to the command of thy Serenity, was administering this eparchy, (*which is one of the eastern cities called Jerusalem, in which is situated the temple of the Jewish race*)[13] the whole multitude of the Jews being assembled, delivered to me a man named Jesus, bringing many and unusual accusations against him, but they were not able by any statement to convict him. There was one party of them [who charged][14] against him that he said the sabbath was not their true rest.

That man performed many cures in addition to good works. He made the blind to see, purified lepers, raised the dead, healed paralytics who were totally unable to move, except that they retained speech and the articulation of their bones, and he gave them power to walk about and run, imparting it by a mere word. He did another more powerful work, which was strange even for our gods [to perform] : he raised from the dead a certain Lazarus, dead since the fourth day, commanding by a word only the dead man (whose body was already destroyed by worms and vermin) to awake, and he commanded that foul-smelling body which was lying in the sepulchre to run, and this [dead man], like a bridegroom from

---

[11] The translation of the title follows *Codex C*, which is less bombastic than that adopted by Thilo. His text for the remainder will be found in his *Codex Apoc.*, pp. 804 - 812. It is there followed (pp. 813 - 816) by a much later document entitled Παράδοσις Πιλάτου, "Surrender of Pilate," which represents Tiberius and the senate as sitting in judgment on Pilate and having him put to death.

[12] See Tertullian's remarks on this "accident to the world" quoted in *Judaism*, p. 442.

[13] The passage in parenthesis is probably a later addition.

[14] This insertion seems necessary to the sense.

his chamber, came out of the sepulchre filled with the most fragrant perfume.

Also certain hopelessly insane who had their dwelling in the deserts eating flesh of their own limbs, fellow-livers with the reptiles and wild beasts, [these] he placed as inhabitants of cities in their own houses, and by a mere word, exhibited them in their sound mind and intelligent; and others, in whom were a crowd of unclean spirits, he made to be men of repute, and driving out the demons who were in them into the sea, in a herd of swine, he choked them.

Also by a mere word he rendered sound another man who had a withered hand, who with pain acquired his living, not even having the half of his body sound.

Also a woman who had a flow of blood for a great length of time, so that because of it the joints of her bones were visible, and the body which she carried round had hardly a human appearance, but looked like alabaster, and as if it were a dead body because of her loss of blood, for all physicians proclaiming her hopeless, paid no attention to her, for there was no hope of preservation in her. Then as Jesus was passing, she receiving strength from his shadow, touched the hem of his garments, and in the same hour the strength of her body was restored, and she became sound as one who had had no disease, and began to run at full speed to her own city Paneas.

And these things were as narrated, but the Jews charged that Jesus did these things on the sabbath. But I know wonderful things done by him beyond what the gods, whom we recognize, perform.

Herod therefore, and Archelaus, and Philip, and Annas, and Caiaphas, with the whole people, delivered this man to me for examination, stirring up much tumult against me as regarded their accusations against him.

At first scourging him, I found no fault in the matters which they charged against him. Afterwards I gave him again to them, when THEY [15] had crucified whom, a darkness occurred over the whole world, the full-orbed sun being hidden and the firmament of darkness appearing in daytime [so that the stars were *not* visible],[16] but nevertheless having its

---

[15] Crucifixion was a Roman, not a Jewish form of punishment. The statement that the Jews crucified Jesus is one of those mistakes which would have crept into the Gospels had they been of later origin.

[16] The bracketed passage may be an interpolation. *Codex C* omits *not*. If it be genuine the translation should be, "so that [even] the stars were not visible."

far-shining brilliancy darkened as is not unknown to your Practical-piety, since in the whole world they lighted lamps from the sixth hour until early. And the moon being as blood did not disappear during the whole night, although she was full. And the whole world was shaken by unheard-of portents, and the whole creation was about to be swallowed up by the underworld; likewise the veil of their temple was rent from above downwards as thunder and a great noise from heaven occurred so that the earth shook and trembled.[17]

[Subsequent Addition.]

In the midst of the fright dead persons appeared rising up. As the Jews themselves, who had seen, stated: That we have seen Abraham, and Isaac, and Jacob, and the twelve Patriarchs, those (who had previously died) after Moses[18] (twenty-five hundred years ago) and many others. (And we saw Noah visibly in the body.) But the stars and Orion made lamentation on account of the Jews, because of their lawlessness.

And after the sabbath, about the third hour of the night, the sun became visible as it never before shone, and the whole heaven was bright. And as winter lightnings make their appearance, thus certain men on high, of brilliant clothing and of inexpressible glory, appeared in the air, and an unnumbered multitude of angels, calling out: The crucified Christ has arisen, [*being a god*].[19] And a voice was heard, powerful as thunder, saying: Glory in the highest to God and upon earth peace, among men good-will. Ascend from the underworld, you who have been enslaved in its subterranean regions. And at their cry all the mountains and hills were shaken, and the rocks were rent, and mighty chasms took place in the earth, so that the contents of the abyss were visible. And many bodies of the dead who had fallen asleep arose, to the number of

---

[17] The subsequent portion of this report must be of later date, since it implies a well-developed existing belief in Christ's mission to the underworld, and bears plain traces of the discussions connected with that subject. Probably the original termination of the letter has been displaced by this new subject.

[18] The reader will find in the *Underworld Mission*, § II., that a Gnostic teacher maintained the unwillingness of Jews in the underworld to follow Christ. In § III. of the same work will be found that some restricted the benefits of his underworld mission to Jews and their monotheistic predecessors. The contradiction in the text has perhaps been caused by efforts to include or omit followers of Moses. Its origin from two texts may be elucidated by printing as follows: εἴδομεν ... τοὺς δώδεκα Πατριάρχας, τοὺς [προτετελευτηκότας] μετὰ Μωσέα [πρὸ δισχιλίων πεντακοσίων ἐτῶν] καὶ ἑτέρους πολλούς.

[19] *Cod. A* omits the words in brackets.

five hundred, and the whole multitude walked around and hymned God with a loud voice, saying: He who rose from the dead, the Lord *our God*, restored to life all of us dead, and plundering the underworld, destroyed it.

The whole of that night, therefore, O Royal Master, the light did not cease, but many of the Jews died and were engulfed and swallowed up in the chasms on that night, so that their bodies were not visible. Those of the Jews I mean, O Master, had disappeared who spoke against Jesus [*so that I seemed to see some vision, the multitudes of ancient dead whom we have never seen*]. One synagogue was left in Jerusalem, where all those synagogues which opposed Jesus, were swallowed up.

Being therefore beside myself with fear and seized with much trembling, determining that very hour to write the things which were done among them all, I sent them to your mightiness.[20]

NOTE C.

CORRESPONDENCE.

OPENED BY KING ABGARUS WITH JESUS.

The following spurious correspondence is found in **Eusebius** (*Ecc. Hist.* 1, 13), who alleges that his Greek is translated from the original Syriac in the public archives at Edessa. It must belong to the close of the third or beginning of the fourth century. The translation here adopted is that of Lardner altered.

Copy of a Letter written by Abgarus the Toparch to Jesus, and sent to him at Jerusalem by the Courier Ananias.

Abgarus, Toparch of Edessa, to Jesus the good Saviour, who has appeared at Jerusalem, sendeth greeting.

---

[20] Subjoined to the letter is the following : " When these documents arrived in Rome and were read, all were astounded that because of Pilate's wickedness the darkness and earthquake took place over the whole world. And Cæsar being filled with anger, sending soldiers, commanded to bring Pilate as a prisoner."
Appended to this is the "Surrender of Pilate," mentioned in note 11.

I have heard of thee and of thy cures, performed without herbs, or other medicines. For it is reported that thou makest the blind to see, and the lame to walk: that thou cleansest lepers, and castest out unclean spirits and demons, and healest those who are tormented with diseases of a long standing, and raisest the dead.

Having heard of all these things concerning thee, I concluded in my mind one of these two things, — either that thou art God come down from heaven who doest these things, or else thou art the Son of God who performest them. Wherefore I now write unto thee, entreating thee to come to me, and to heal my distemper. Moreover, I hear that the Jews murmur against thee, and plot to do thee mischief. I have a city, small indeed, but neat, which may suffice for us both.

ANSWER OF JESUS TO ABGARUS THE TOPARCH.

(Through Ananias the Courier.)

Abgarus, thou art happy, forasmuch as thou hast believed in me, though thou hast not seen me. For it is written concerning me, that they who have seen me should not believe in me, that they who have not seen me might believe and live.[1] As for what thou hast written to me desiring me to come to thee, it is necessary that all those things, for which I am sent, should be fulfilled by me here: and that after fulfilling them, I should be received up to him that sent me. When therefore I shall be received up, I will send to thee some one of my disciples, that he may heal thy distemper, and give life to thee, and to those who are with thee.

Subjoined to the foregoing correspondence in Eusebius is a narrative, taken also professedly from the public archives at Edessa, concerning cures performed by Thaddeus in that city. It will be found hereafter in Note F, being separated from the foregoing in order that the reader may, by the aid of such classification, distinguish more readily the fabrications of testimony concerning the Master from those which concerned chiefly his followers.

---

[1] The reference must be to John's Gospel, **20**, 29, which at the assumed date of this letter had not yet been written.

NOTE D.

LETTER OF LENTULUS.

THE following letter is not quoted by any early Christian writer. The fact that it is attributed to a heathen implies that it is not of later date than the fourth century. Possibly it belongs to the third. Its origin and object may be seen by recurring to Ch. III. § 14. The text of its Latin copies or translations differ from each other. One of these, a translation from the Persian, will be found in Fabricius, *Cod. Apoc. Nov. Test.* pp. 301, 301*, 302. He mentions another, substantially the same, but different in phraseology, as existing in the *Orthodoxographa*. It will be found in the Biblical Repository, Vol. 2, pp. 373–375, in an article by Professor E. Robinson, who has also given in footnotes the readings of different manuscripts. The letter must have had but little currency or it would have been quoted by some early writer.

Of the two versions here subjoined, one is from **Calmet's Dictionary,** made from De Dieu's Latin version of a Persian copy,[1] which was perhaps a modern translation from the Latin. Another, in the second column, is my own from the text of the *Orthodoxographa* as given by **Robinson.**

[A LETTER ... WHICH WAS SENT TO THE SENATE BY A *certain* LENTULUS.[2]]	LENTULUS, PREFECT OF JERUSALEM, TO THE SENATE AND ROMAN PEOPLE, GREETING.
There has a man appeared here, who is still living, named Jesus Christ, whose power is extraordinary. He has the title	In the present age a highly endowed man has appeared who is yet with us, named Jesus Christ, who by Gentiles is styled

---

[1] In the sixteenth century Francis Xavier, during his missionary work in Asia, published a church history in Persian, in which the above-mentioned Persian copy of the letter from Lentulus is found. The supposition is reasonably certain that he supervised a translation of it from the Latin. "Xavier, at command of the Persian Emperor Acabar, composed, as it seems, this history in the Portuguese language, *lingua Lusitanica*, in Agra, the principal city of the whole kingdom; and his teacher Abdel Lenarin Kasen, originally from Lahore, translated it into Persian." — **Walch,** *Bibliotheca Theolog.* Vol. 3, p. 405.

[2] The heading is taken from the Jena MS. No. 2.

given to him of the Great Prophet; his disciples call him the Son of God. He RAISES THE DEAD, and HEALS all sorts of DISEASES.

He is a tall, well-proportioned man; there is an air of serenity in his countenance, which attracts at once the love and reverence of those who see him. His hair is of the color of new wine from the roots to his ears, and from thence to the shoulders it is curled, and falls down to the lowest part of them. Upon the forehead it parts in two, after the manner of the Nazarenes. His forehead is flat and fair, his face without any defect, and adorned with a very graceful vermilion; his air is majestic and agreeable. His nose and his mouth are very well proportioned, and his beard is thick and forked, of the color of his hair; his eyes are gray and extremely lively; in his reproofs he is terrible, but in his exhortations and instructions amiable and courteous; there is something wonderfully charming in his face, with a mixture of gravity. He is never seen to laugh, but he has been observed to weep. He is very straight in stature; his hands are large and spreading, and his arms very beautiful. He talks little, but with great gravity, and is the handsomest man in the world.

the Prophet of Truth,[3] whom his disciples call the Son of God; [one] who AWAKENS THE DEAD and HEALS INFIRMITIES.

He is a man of prominent stature, arresting attention, having a countenance which inspires reverence, whom those that regard him can both love and fear; having curly and wavy hair, somewhat dark and glossy, floating on his shoulders, parted in the middle, according to Nazarene custom; having a smooth, serene forehead, a face without wrinkle or speck — which a moderate degree of color renders attractive — a faultless nose and mouth, a copious and auburn beard, like his hair in color, not long but forked; with clear and animated eyes. [He is] terrible in reproof, placid and lovable in his admonitions, genial without loss of gravity, who was never seen to smile but often to weep. He is distinguished[4] in stature, having hands and limbs which it is a delight to look upon, sedate in speech, peculiarly modest, beautiful among the sons of men.[5] Farewell.

---

[3] Prophet of Truth, *or* of the Truth. This term occurs in the Clementine Homilies **2**, 5, 6, 9; **3**, 11, as also the term True Prophet, **1**, 19, 21; **3**, 11.

[4] All copies save this read "erect." See Biblical Repository, **2**, p. 375, note 13.

[5] Ps. **45**, 2.

NOTE E.

INTERPOLATIONS OF JOSEPHUS.

§ 1. *Concerning Christ.*

THERE are three passages in Josephus which have been regarded as interpolated, namely, *Antiq.* **18**, 3, 3; **18**, 5, 2, **20**, 9, 1. One of these, a passage concerning Jesus, is probably a fraud by some Christian. Whether the same can be said of the other two is doubtful. The passage concerning Jesus stands between narratives of two events which Josephus classes together as calamities.

"But Pilate undertook to bring a current of water to Jerusalem, and did it with the sacred money. . . . Myriads of the people got together, and made a clamor against him. . . . He bid the Jews himself go away; but they, boldly casting reproaches upon him, he gave the soldiers that signal which had been beforehand agreed on; who laid upon them much greater blows than Pilate had commanded them. . . . And thus an end was put to this sedition.

"[Now there was about this time Jesus, a wise man, if it be lawful to call him a man; for he was a doer of wonderful works, a teacher of such men as receive the truth with pleasure. He drew over to him both many of the Jews, and many of the Gentiles. He was [the] Christ. And when Pilate, at the suggestion of the principal men among us, had condemned him to the cross, those that loved him at the first did not forsake him; for he appeared to them alive again the third day; as the divine prophets had foretold these and ten thousand other wonderful things concerning him. And the tribe of Christians, so named from him, are not extinct at this day.]

"About the same time also another sad calamity put the Jews into disorder, and certain shameful practices happened about the temple of Isis that was at Rome." [1]

---

[1] *Antiq.* **18**, 3, 2–4; *Whiston's trans.* This other calamity of which Josephus treats occurred in A. D. 19 at Rome (see *Judaism,* p. 188) about eleven years before Jesus entered on his ministry.

§ 2. *Concerning John the Baptist.*

The passage in the works of Josephus concerning John the Baptist is probably due to some disciple of John, or to some adherent of the popular party, rather than to any Christian. Even if correct, it does not, at first sight, accord with the Gospel narrative,[2] nor does it refer in any way to Christ or Christianity. Whether it be an intentional interpolation or a marginal comment innocently copied into the text may admit question.

"Aretas, the king of Arabia Petræa, and Herod had a quarrel. . . . Herod the tetrarch had married the daughter of Aretas. . . . However, he fell in love with Herodias. . . . Aretas made this the first occasion of his enmity between him and Herod, who had also some quarrel with him about their limits at the country of Gemalitis. So they raised armies on both sides. . . . All Herod's army was destroyed. . . . Herod wrote about these affairs to Tiberius, who being very angry at the attempt made by Aretas, wrote to Vitellius to make war upon him, and either to take him alive, and bring him to him in bonds, or to kill him, and send him his head [?]. This was the charge [?] that Tiberius gave to the president of Syria.[3]

---

[2] According to Matthew (**14**, 3) and Mark (**6**, 17) the cause of John's imprisonment was his statement that Herod ought not to marry his brother's wife. According to Luke (**3**, 19, 20) it was for this and other causes. That John, who spoke with equal boldness of prince and people, should be arrested by Herod is comprehensible enough. If, however, Herod, as **Mark** tells us (**6**, 20) "feared John . . . and did many things as he told him and listened to him readily," Herod must for a time have striven to gain John over to his side, that he might use his influence with the people. Failing in this, the request by a daughter of Herodias, for the head of John, as also the king's previous oath, may have been preconcerted by himself to lessen the odium of what he intended doing, or by his wife and the aristocracy as a means of pushing him to a decision at which he hesitated.

The date of John's death must have been in A. D. 31, while the aristocracy at Rome (see *Judaism*, pp. 522–531) were preparing for the rebellion, which broke out in October. In the spring of A. D. 32, when this rebellion had been suppressed, Pilate and Herod (Luke **23**, 12) were reconciled, which not improbably means that Herod had previously sympathized with the aristocracy and Pilate with Tiberius, from whom he held his office.

[3] Josephus repeatedly falsifies history with the object of favoring the Roman and Jewish aristocracy. The above is doubtless one of his fictions. See remarks near the close of the section.

"[Now, some of the Jews thought that the destruction of Herod's army came from God, and that very justly, as a punishment of what he did against John, that was called the *Baptist*, for Herod slew him, who was a good man, and commanded the Jews to exercise virtue, both as regarded justice towards one another, and practical recognition towards God, and so to come to baptism ; for that the washing [with water] would be acceptable to him, if they made use of it, not in order to the putting away, [or the remission] of some sins [only,] but for the purification of the body ; supposing still that the soul was thoroughly purified beforehand by righteousness. Now when [many] others came in crowds about him, for they were greatly moved [or pleased] by hearing his words, Herod, who feared lest the great influence John had over the people might put it into his power and inclination to raise rebellion, (for they seemed ready to do anything he should advise,) thought it best, by putting him to death, to prevent any mischief he might cause, and not bring himself into difficulties by sparing a man who might make him repent of it when it should be too late. Accordingly, he was sent a prisoner, out of Herod's suspicious temper, to Macherus, the castle I before mentioned, and was there put to death. Now the Jews had an opinion, that the destruction of this army was sent as a punishment on Herod, and a mark of God's displeasure to him.]

"So Vitellius prepared to make war with Aretas, having with him two legions of armed men. . . . Leading his army through Judea, the principal men met him, and desired that he would not thus march through their land : for that the laws of their country would not permit them to overlook those images which were brought into it. . . . Whereupon he ordered the army to march along the great plain, while he himself, with Herod the tetrarch, and his friends, went up to Jerusalem to offer sacrifice to God, an ancient festival of the Jews being then just approaching ; and when he had been there, and been honorably entertained by the multitude of the Jews, he made a stay there for three days, within which time he deprived Jonathan of the high-priesthood, and gave it to his brother Theophilus. But when, on the fourth day, letters came to him, which informed him of the death of Tiberius, he obliged the multitude to take an oath of fidelity to Caius ; he also recalled his army, and made them every one go home, and take their winter-quarters there, since, upon the devolution of the empire upon Caius, he had not the like authority of making the war which he had before." [4]

---

[4] **Josephus,** *Antiq.* **18,** 5, 1-3 ; *Whiston's trans. altered.* The chronology of the passage is somewhat as follows : Herod's substitution of

In the foregoing an omission of the passage concerning John would cause no break in the connection between what precedes and follows it. Some may think that the connection would thus become even closer.

It is plain, moreover, that Josephus wishes us to regard Tiberius as having espoused Herod's cause, and to understand Vitellius as being very deferential to the aristocracy. We can feel reasonably certain that if Josephus for any cause had wished to commend John, he would not have selected this connection for so doing. John's designation for the aristocracy, "brood of vipers" (**Matt. 3, 7**), and the whole tone of his teaching, were not calculated to inspire reverence for those in high places.

The habitual untruthfulness of Josephus (concerning which see *Judaism*, pp. 553–560) renders it a fair question whether the expedition of Vitellius[5] had the slightest connection with Aretas. Vitellius may before moving have received orders from Tiberius, who felt the approach of death, that he should guard against any rebellion by the Jewish aristocracy on the accession of Caligula. His troops may have been intended to intercept communication between the aristocracy at Jerusalem and senatorial sympathizers on the sea-coast. The need of this will appear from a study of events two years afterwards.[6]

§ 3. *Concerning James.*

The extant interpolation concerning James may, or may not, have originated in an honest marginal comment copied subsequently through ignorance into the text.

"The king [Agrippa] deprived Joseph of the high-priesthood, and bestowed the succession to that dignity on the son

---

Herodias for his former wife cannot have been later than A. D. 31, if so late. The advent of Vitellius into Syria cannot have been earlier than A. D. 35, seeing that he was consul in A. D. 34. The death of Tiberius occurred March 16, A. D. 37.

[5] Vitellius was a member of the popular party, and, equally with other of its prominent men, has been grossly abused and misrepresented by Tacitus. The following, forced probably from that writer by public opinion in provinces more intelligent than Rome, should be well weighed. "In governing the provinces he acted with pristine [a patrician term for *commendable*] uprightness." — **Tacitus**, *An.* **6**, 32.

[6] See *Judaism*, pp. 96 - 107.

of Ananus, who was himself called *Ananus*. . . . But this younger Ananus, who, as we have told you already, took the high-priesthood, was a bold man in his temper, and very insolent : he was also of the sect of the Sadducees, who are very rigid in judging offenders above all the rest of the Jews, as we have already observed. When, therefore, Ananus was of this disposition, he thought he had now a proper opportunity [to exercise his authority]. Festus was now dead, and Albinus was but upon the road ; so he ASSEMBLED THE SANHEDRIM of Judges.

"[And brought before them the brother of Jesus, who was called CHRIST, whose names was JAMES, and some others. And when he had formed an accusation against them as breakers of the law, he delivered them to be stoned.]

"But as for those who seemed the most equitable of the citizens, and such as were most uneasy at the breach of the laws, they disliked what was done ; they also sent to the king, [Agrippa,] desiring him to send to Ananus that he should act so no more, for that what he had already done was not to be justified : nay, some of them went also to meet Albinus, as he was upon his journey from Alexandria, and informed him, that it was not lawful for Ananus to ASSEMBLE A SANHEDRIM without his consent." [7]

The foregoing interpolation may be a correct piece of history which some one has noted in the margin of Josephus. It can have had no theological bearing, and presented therefore no motive for FRAUDULENT insertion.

Besides the above there would seem in Origen's time to have been in some copy, or copies, of Josephus a somewhat different statement concerning James, which, instead of pertaining merely to fact, included opinions.[8]

---

[7] **Josephus,** *Antiq.* **20,** 9, 1 ; *Whiston's trans.*

[8] "Josephus . . . says : 'These things befell the Jews in vindication of James called the Just, who was the brother of Jesus called the Christ : forasmuch as they killed him who was a most righteous man.' . . . With how much more reason might he have said that this had happened for the sake of Jesus who was the Christ." — **Origen,** *cont. Cels.* **1,** 47 ; *Opp.* ed. Lommatzsch, **18,** p. 87 ; ed. de la Rue, **1,** p. 363 A ; *Lardner's trans.*

"Titus destroyed Jerusalem, according, indeed, to Josephus, 'because of James the Just, the brother of Jesus, who is called Christ,' but in

NOTE F.

EDESSENE ARCHIVES OR PSEUDO-THADDEUS.

In Eusebius is our earliest mention of the above document, which he gives in a Greek translation, with the following prefatory remark:—

"To these epistles [1] . . . are subjoined the following things, in the Syriac language.

"'After Jesus had been taken up, Judas, called also Thomas, sent the APOSTLE Thaddeus,[2] one of the seventy; who, when he came to Edessa, took up his abode with Tobias, son of Tobias. When his arrival was rumored about, and he had begun to be known by the miracles which he had wrought, it was told to Abgarus, that an APOSTLE was sent to him by Jesus, according to his promise. Thaddeus therefore by the

---

truth because of Jesus Christ the Son of God." — **Origen**, *cont. Cels.* **2**, 13; *Opp.* ed. Lommatzsch, **18**, p. 161; ed. de la Rue, p. 399 D.

"'Flavius Josephus, who wrote the Jewish Antiquities in twenty books, being desirous to assign the cause why that people suffered such things, so that even their temple was demolished to the foundation, says that those things had happened because of the anger of God against them, for what they had done to James the brother of Jesus called the Christ.'" — **Origen**, *Comment. in Matt.* Tom. **10**, 17 (*Opp.* ed. Lommatzsch, **3**, p. 46; ed. de la Rue, **3**, p. 463 C); *Lardner's trans.*

[1] Epistles of Abgarus and Jesus, already given in Note C.

[2] In the enumeration of the Apostles by Matthew, Mark, and Luke, we find that after mention of James, the son of Alpheus, **Luke** (6, 15, 16) mentions "Judas, the brother of James"; **Mark** (3, 18) mentions "Thaddeus"; and **Matthew** (**10**, 3) mentions "Lebbeus, whose surname was Thaddeus." Probably the author of the present document meant that Judas, otherwise called Thaddeus, the apostle, had gone to Edessa. Some one who noticed that in Matthew and Mark there is no mention of any other Judas than the traitor, or some one who used Luke's gospel and found no such name as Thaddeus appended to the brother of James, undertook to remedy the difficulty by making Thaddeus one of the seventy, and a different person from Judas. This may have caused him to be sometimes called an apostle and sometimes one of the seventy.

Eusebius in his introductory remarks, prior to the correspondence of Abgarus with Jesus, calls Thomas "one of the twelve Apostles," and Thaddeus, "in the number of the seventy." He had probably noticed the confusion, and intended his remarks as the suggestion of an explanation.

power of God healed all sorts of maladies, so that all wondered.

"'But when Abgarus heard of the great and wonderful works which he did, and how he healed men in the name and by the power of Jesus Christ, he was induced to suspect [ἐν ὑπονοίᾳ γέγονεν] that he was the person about whom Jesus had written to him, saying, "When I am taken up, I will send to thee some one of my disciples, who shall heal thy distemper." Sending therefore for Tobias, at whose house he was, he said to him: "I hear that a man, endowed with great power, and come from Jerusalem, is at thy house, and that he works many cures in the name of Jesus." To which Tobias answered, "Yes, sir; there is a stranger with me, who performs many miracles." Abgarus then said: "Bring him hither to me." Tobias, coming to Thaddeus, said to him: "The toparch Abgarus has bid me bring thee to him that thou mayest heal his distemper." Whereupon Thaddeus said: "I go; for I am sent to him by [an impelling] power."

"'The next day, early in the morning, Tobias taking Thaddeus came to Abgarus. As he came in, the nobles being present, there appeared to Abgarus somewhat very extraordinary in the countenance of the APOSTLE Thaddeus, which when Abgarus saw, he did reverence to Thaddeus; which appeared strange to all present, for they did not see that sight which appeared to Abgarus only. He then asked Thaddeus: "Are you indeed the disciple of Jesus the SON OF GOD, who once said to me: I will send to thee some one of my disciples who shall heal thy distemper, and give life to all with thee?" Thaddeus answered: "Forasmuch as thou hast great faith in the Lord Jesus, therefore am I sent unto thee: and if thou shalt increase in faith in him, all the desires of thy heart will be fulfilled according to thy faith."

"'Then Abgarus said to him: "I have so believed in him, that I would go with an army to extirpate the Jews who crucified him, if I were not apprehensive of the Roman power." Then Thaddeus said: "Our Lord [*and God*][3] Jesus Christ has fulfilled the will of his Father: and, having fulfilled it, he has been taken up to his Father." Abgarus then said: "I have

---

[3] The words *and God* are omitted by the three manuscripts mentioned in the next note, and are deemed spurious by the editors Valesius and Heinichen, though in following the copy which they had adopted they have kept them in their text.

believed in him and in his Father." And thereupon said Thaddeus: "Therefore I put my hand upon thee in the name of the Lord Jesus." And, upon his so doing, Abgarus was healed of his distemper. And Abgarus wondered, that as it had been reported concerning Jesus, so it had been done by his disciple [*and apostle*]⁴ Thaddeus; insomuch as he had healed him without herbs, or other medicines. Nor did he heal him alone, but also Abdus, son of Abdus, who had the gout. For he came to him, and fell down upon his knees before him, and by the laying on of his hands with prayer he was healed. The same [*apostle*]⁵ healed many other citizens of the same place, and wrought many and great miracles as he preached the word.

"'After which Abgarus spoke to this purpose: "Thou Thaddeus doest things by the power of God, and we admire thee. But I beseech thee to inform me about the coming of Jesus, how it was, and of his power, and by what power he did all those things which we have heard of." To which Thaddeus answered: "Now I forbear, though I am sent to preach the word; but to-morrow gather together all the citizens, and then in their hearing I will preach the word, and sow in them the word of life, and will inform them of the coming of Christ, how it was, and concerning his mission, and for what cause he was sent by the Father, and concerning the power of his works, and the mysteries which he spoke in the world, and by what power he did these things, and concerning his new doctrine, and about the meanness and despicableness of his outward appearance,⁶ and how he humbled himself, (and died, and lessened his deity; how many things also he suffered from the Jews, and how he was crucified,)⁷ and descended into the underworld, and rent asunder the inclosure never before rent, and arose, and raised up the dead who had been buried many ages; and how he descended alone, but ascended to his Father with a great multitude; and how he is set down on the right hand of the Father with glory in the heavens; and how he will come again with glory and power to judge the living and the dead."

"'Abgarus therefore issued out orders that all the citizens

---

⁴ The Mazarine, Medicæan, and Fuketian MSS. omit the words in brackets.

⁵ Omitted by the three MSS. mentioned in the preceding note.

⁶ See Ch. III. § 14.

⁷ The parenthesis must include two or more varying texts.

should come together early the next morning, to hear the preaching of Thaddeus. And after that he commanded that gold and silver should be given to him, but he did not receive it, saying: "When we have left what is our own, how should we receive those things which belong to others?"

"'This was done in the four hundred and thirtieth year.'"[8]

NOTE G.

CORRESPONDENCE OPENED BY SENECA WITH PAUL.

FOURTEEN letters, professedly of Seneca and Paul, have come down to us, — eight by the former and six by the latter, — which will be found in editions of **Seneca** and of the **Apocrypha**.[1] They were extant before the close of the fourth century, for Jerome alludes to them.[2] They are part of the

---

[8] **Eusebius**, *Ecc. Hist.* **1**, 13; *Lardner's trans. altered*. His translation is in his *Works*, **6**, 598 – 600. Eusebius says that the above narrative which he gives in Greek is translated from the Syriac. Heinichen's edition gives other *various-readings* than those heretofore cited.

The four hundred and thirtieth Syrian year corresponds with the fifteenth of Tiberius; see note of Valesius on this passage in his edition of Eusebius, *Ecc. Hist.*, Appendix, pp. 22, 23, copied in Heinichen's edition, Vol. **1**, pp. 88, 89.

[1] See Seneca, *Opp. Philos.* **4**, pp. 474 – 479, ed. Le Maire; Fabricius, *Cod. Apoc. Nov. Test.* **1**, pp. 892 – 904 (where the last letter is misnumbered 13). Jones in his work on the Canon, Vol. **2**, pp. 45 – 53, gives the text of Fabricius, which differs from that in Seneca. He accompanies it with an English translation by himself, which has been copied with a few verbal oversights into Hone's Apocryphal New Testament, pp. 84 – 88. This translation of Jones is, with some alterations, the one adopted above.

[2] "Lucius Annæus Seneca, . . . whom I would not place in the catalogue of holy men unless prompted by those Epistles, read by most persons, of Paul to Seneca, and Seneca to Paul, in which . . . he says that he wishes he occupied the same place among his countrymen as Paul among Christians."— **Jerome**, *de Vir. Illust.* 12; *Opp.* **2**, col. 849 – 851; edit. Vallars.

Augustine also remarks: "Seneca, who lived in apostolic times, some of whose letters to the apostle Paul are in circulation, truly says: *He who hates the wicked hates all men.*" — *Epist.* 54 (edit. Benedictin. **1**, 53) *ad Macedonium.*

conflict between Christians and heathens, and were intended as evidence of Seneca's respect for Paul. When heathenism had lost political power, Paul's authority outweighed that of Seneca. A consequence of this has been that in the title of the correspondence, as now extant, Paul's name precedes that of Seneca.

1 ANNÆUS SENECA *to* PAUL *Greeting.* I suppose, Paul, that you have been informed of that conversation, which passed yesterday between me and my Lucilius, concerning hypocrisy and other subjects; for there were some of your disciples in company with us; for when we were retired into the Sallustian gardens, through which they were also passing, and would have gone another way, by our persuasion they joined company with us. I desire you to believe, that we much wish for your conversation. We were much delighted with your book of many Epistles, — which you addressed to some states and chief towns of provinces, — containing wonderful instructions for moral conduct: such sentiments, as I suppose you were not the author of, but only the instrument of conveying, though sometimes both the author and the instrument. For such is the sublimity of those doctrines, and their grandeur, that I suppose the age of a man is scarce sufficient to be instructed and perfected in the knowledge of them. I wish your welfare, my brother. Farewell.

2. PAUL *to* SENECA *Greeting.* I received your letter yesterday with pleasure; to which I could immediately have written an answer, had the young man been at home, whom I intended to have sent to you; for you know when, and by whom, at what seasons, and to whom, I must deliver everything which I send. I desire, therefore, you would not charge me with negligence, if I wait for a proper person. I reckon myself very happy in having the judgment of so valuable a person, that you are delighted with my Epistles: for you would not be esteemed a censor, a philosopher, or be the tutor of so great a prince, and a master of everything, if you were not sincere. I wish you a lasting prosperity.

3. ANNÆUS SENECA *to* PAUL *Greeting.* I have completed some volumes, and divided them into their proper parts. I am determined to read them to Cæsar, and if any favorable opportunity happens, you also shall be present, when they are read. But if that cannot be, I will appoint and give you notice of a day, when we will together read over the performance. I had determined, if I could with safety, first to have your opinion of it, before I published it to Cæsar, that you might be convinced of my affection to you. Farewell, dearest Paul.

4. PAUL *to* SENECA *Greeting*. As often as I read your letters I imagine you present with me; nor indeed do I think any other than that you are always with us. As soon therefore as you come we shall mutually see each other nearer. I wish you all prosperity.

5. ANNÆUS SENECA *to* PAUL *Greeting*. We are very much concerned at your too long absence from us. What is it, or what affairs are they which obstruct your coming? If you fear the anger of Cæsar, because you have abandoned your former religion, and made proselytes also of others, you have this to plead, that your acting thus proceeded not from inconstancy, but judgment. Farewell.

6. PAUL *to* SENECA *and* LUCILIUS *Greeting*. Concerning those things, about which ye wrote to me, it is not proper for me to mention anything in writing with pen and ink: the one of which leaves marks, and the other evidently declares things. Especially since I know that there are near you, as well as me, those who will understand my meaning. Deference is to be paid to all men, and so much the more, as they are more likely to take occasions of quarrelling. And if we show a submissive temper we shall overcome effectually in all points, if they be such as can repent of their doings. Farewell.

7. ANNÆUS SENECA *to* PAUL *Greeting*. I profess myself extremely pleased with the reading your letter to the Galatians, Corinthians, and people of Achaia. For the Holy Spirit has in them by you delivered those sentiments which are very lofty, sublime, deserving of all respect, and beyond your own invention. I could wish, therefore, that when you are writing things so extraordinary, there might not be wanting an elegancy of speech agreeable to their majesty. And I must own, my brother, — that I may not at once dishonestly conceal anything from you, and be unfaithful to my own conscience, — that the emperor is extremely pleased with the sentiments of your Epistles. For when he heard the beginning of them read, he declared, That he was surprised to find such notions in a person who had not had a regular education. To which I replied, That the gods sometimes speak by the 'mouth of babes' [Ps. **8**, 2; Matt. **11**, 25], and gave him an instance of this in a rustic, named Vatienus, who, when he was in the country of Reate, had two men appear to him, called Castor and Pollux, and received a revelation from the gods. Farewell.

8. PAUL *to* SENECA *Greeting*. Although I know the emperor is both an admirer and favorer of our matters, yet give me leave to advise you against your suffering any injury [by showing any favor to us]. I think indeed you ventured upon a very dangerous attempt, when you would

declare [to the emperor] that which is so very contrary to his religion, and way of worship; seeing he is a worshipper of the heathen gods. I know not what you had particularly in view, when you told him of this; but I suppose you did it out of a too great respect for me. But I desire that for the future you would not do so; for you had need be careful, lest by showing your affection to me, you should offend your master: His anger indeed will do us no harm, if he continue a heathen; nor will his not being angry be of any service to us: And if the empress act worthy of her character, she will not be angry; but if she act as a woman, she will be affronted. Farewell.

9. ANNÆUS SENECA *to* PAUL *Greeting*. I know that you are less disturbed on your account by my letter, acquainting you that I had given the emperor your Epistles, than by the condition of things which so powerfully diverts men's minds from good manners and practices, [as to occasion] that I at present should not be esteemed because among many documents I deem this [of yours] the most noteworthy. Let us, therefore, begin afresh; and if anything heretofore has been imprudently acted, do you forgive. I have sent you a book *de copia verborum*. Farewell, dearest Paul.

10. PAUL *to* SENECA *Greeting*. As often as I write to you, and place my name before yours, I do a thing both disagreeable to myself and contrary to our religion; for I ought, as I have often declared, to become all things to all men, and to have that regard to your quality, which the Roman law has honored all senators with; namely, to put my name last in the [inscription of the] Epistle, that I may not at length with uneasiness and shame be obliged to do that which it was always my inclination to do. Farewell, most respected master. Dated the fifth of the calends of July, in the fourth consulship of Nero and Messala [A. D. 58].

11.[3] ANNÆUS SENECA *to* PAUL *Greeting*. All happiness to you, my dearest Paul. If a person so great, so every way agreeable as you are, become not only a common, but most intimate friend to me, how happy will be the case of Seneca! You, therefore, who are so eminent, and so far exalted above all, even the greatest, do not think yourself unfit to be first named in the inscription of an Epistle; lest I should suspect you intend not so much to try me as to banter me; for you know yourself to be a Roman citizen. For I could wish to hold among my people the position which you hold among yours. Farewell, dearest Paul. Dated the tenth of the calends of April, in the consulship of Aprianus [Apronianus] and Capito [A. D. 59].

---

[3] No. 12 in Le Maire.

12.[4] ANNÆUS SENECA *to* PAUL *Greeting*. All happiness to you, my dearest Paul. Do you think that I am not saddened and grieved at the punishments inflicted on your innocent [sect?] and that all the people should suppose you [Christians] so criminal, and imagine all the misfortunes befalling the city, to be caused by you? But let us bear the charge with a patient temper, appealing [for our innocence] to the court [above], which is the only one our hard fortune will allow us to address, till at length our misfortunes shall end in unalterable happiness. Former ages have produced [tyrants] Alexander the son of Philip, and Dionysius; ours also has produced Caius Cæsar; whose inclinations were their only laws. As to the frequent burnings of the city of Rome, the cause is manifest; and if a person in my mean circumstances might be allowed to speak, and one might declare these dark things without danger, every one should see the whole of the matter. The Christians and Jews are indeed commonly punished for the crime of burning the city; but that impious miscreant, who delights in murders and butcheries, and disguises his villanies with lies, is appointed to, or reserved till, his proper time; and as the life of every excellent person is now sacrificed instead of that one person [who is the author of the mischief], so this one shall be sacrificed for many, and he shall be devoted to be burnt with fire instead of all. One hundred and thirty-two houses and four whole squares [or islands] were burnt down in six days: the seventh put an end to the burning. I wish you all happiness. Dated fifth of the calends of April, in the consulship of Frigius [Frugi] and Bassus [A. D. 64].[5]

13. ANNÆUS SENECA *to* PAUL *Greeting*. All happiness to you, my dearest Paul. You have written many volumes in an allegorical and mystical style, and, therefore, such mighty matters and business, being committed to you, require not to be set off with any rhetorical flourishes of speech, but only with some proper elegance. I remember you often say, that many by affecting such a style do injury to their subjects, and lose the force of the matters they treat of. But in this I desire you to regard me, namely, to have respect to true Latin, and to choose just words, that so you may the better

---

[4] No. 11 in Le Maire.
[5] In Le Maire the Consuls mentioned at the end of Letter 11, and also of Letter 12, are Apronius and Capito.

manage the noble trust, which is reposed in you. Farewell. Dated fifth of the nones of July, Leo and Savinus consuls.

14. PAUL *to* SENECA *Greeting*. Your serious consideration is requited with those discoveries, which the Divine Being has granted but to few. I am thereby assured that I sow the most strong seed in a fertile soil, not anything material, which is subject to corruption, but the durable word of God, which shall increase and bring forth fruit to eternity. That which by your wisdom you have attained to, shall abide without decay forever. Believe that you ought to avoid the superstitions of Jews and Gentiles. The things which you have in some measure arrived to, prudently make known to the emperor, his family, and to faithful friends; and though your sentiments will seem disagreeable, and not be comprehended by them, seeing most of them will not regard your discourses, yet the Word of God, once infused into them, will at length make them become new men, aspiring towards God. Farewell, Seneca, who art most dear to us. Dated on the calends of August, in the consulship of Leo and Savinus.[6]

At a date when some writers maintained the genuineness of these letters, extracts were made from Paul's writings and the Epistle to the Hebrews, which he was supposed to have written, and were placed parallel with similar extracts from Seneca. They will be found in Le Maire's Seneca, *Opp. Philos.* **4**, pp. 465 – 467. The similarity is due to the fact that not only Paul and the Writer to the Hebrews, but Seneca, like his brother Stoics, copied more or less from Judaism.

The two extra letters of Seneca, over and above the number written by Paul, are due probably to the substitution by later writers than the original forger, of one letter for a different one. The later substitutes and the original have been preserved and copied.

---

[6] The consuls for A. D. 65 were A. Licinius Nerva Silianus and M. Vestinus Atticus. Those for A. D. 66 were C. Lucius Telesinus and C. Suetonius Paullinus. The forger of the Epistles must have intended to name the consuls for one or the other of these years, since the execution of Paul could not have been placed at any later date. Either some corruption of the text has taken place, or the forger made some blunder.

NOTE II.

LETTER OF MARCUS ANTONINUS.

During a war waged by Marcus Antoninus in Germany (A. D. 174) he and his army were almost famished with thirst, being cut off doubtless from water by their enemies. An opportune shower relieved them. The Antonine-column attributes this to Jupiter Pluvius. Christians attributed it to the prayers of a Christian legion; some Heathens to an Egyptian Astrologer named Arnuphis, others to a Chaldæan named Julian.[1]

Christians invented a letter, professedly by the emperor, indorsing their account. This letter must have existed by the beginning of the third century, for Tertullian alludes to it.[2] A copy of it has come down to us, appended by some scribe to Justin's first *Apology*. In *Maran's edition* of Justin, it will be found on pp. 85 – 87, and in *Otto's edition*, Vol. **1**, pp. 276 – 280. Lardner's translation, the one here given, will be found in his *Works*, Vol. **7**, pp. 184, 185. He accompanies it with various citations and arguments from different writers. His heading of the letter includes the titles "Augustus" and "high-priest," omitted by Maran's text and Otto's.

The Emperor Cæsar, Marcus Aurelius Antoninus [Augustus], Germanicus, Parthicus, Sarmaticus [high-priest], to the People of Rome, and to the Sacred Senate, *Greeting*.

I gave you an account of the greatness of the enterprise which I had undertaken, and what great difficulties came upon me in Germany; how I was surrounded and besieged in the midst of it, and afflicted with heat and weariness: at which time I was overtaken at Carnutum by seventy-four regiments, who were not more than nine miles off from us. Now when the enemy was come very near us, our spies gave us notice of it: and Pompeianus, my general, informed me also

---

[1] Dio Cass. **71**, 8; Suidas, *Lex.*, articles *Arnuphis* and *Julian*.
[2] In his *Apology* (c. 5) Tertullian refers to the letter of Marcus Antoninus as attesting that the shower was, *perhaps*, obtained by the prayers of Christian soldiers.

of what I knew before. In our army we had only the first, the tenth, the double, and the Fretensian legions, to contend with an innumerable company of barbarians. When I had computed my own numbers with those of the enemy, I addressed our gods in prayer; but not being regarded by them, and considering the distress we were in, I called for those whom we call Christians; and upon examination I found that they were a great multitude, at which I was much displeased, though I should not have been so; for afterwards I understood how powerful they are. For which reason they began, not by preparing their darts, or other weapons, or their trumpets, inasmuch as such things are disagreeable to them on account of God, whom they bear in their consciences: for it is reasonable to believe that they, whom we call atheists, have God within them for a bulwark. As soon, therefore, as they had cast themselves down upon the ground, they prayed, not for me only, but also for the whole army, for relief under our great thirst and hunger. For it was the fifth day we had no water, because there was none in that place. For we were in the midst of Germany, surrounded by their mountains. But as soon as they had cast themselves upon the ground and prayed to a God, who was unknown to me, water came down from heaven immediately. Upon us it was very cool, but upon our enemies it was fierce hail. And immediately after their prayers we found God to be present with us, as one that is impregnable and invincible.

Beginning here, therefore, let us permit these men to be Christians, lest they should pray for the like weapons against us and obtain them. And I declare that no man who is a Christian is to be called in question as such. And if any man accuse a Christian, because he is a Christian, I declare that the Christian may appear openly; and that if he confesseth himself to be so, but showeth that he is accused of no other crime but that he is a Christian, let his accuser be burnt alive. And as to him that confesseth himself to be a Christian, and gives full evidence of the same, let not the governor of the province oblige him to renounce his religion, nor deprive him of his liberty. I will that this be confirmed by the decree of the senate. And I command that this my edict be set up in Trajan's forum, that it may be read by all. Vitrusius Pollio, præfect of the city, will take care that it be sent into the provinces; nor is any one who desires to have it and make use of it, to be hindered from taking a copy of this our edict which is publicly set up by me. Farewell.

NOTE I.

ASCENSION OF ISAIAH.

A WORK, or collection of works, entitled ASCENSION OF ISAIAH, originally written in Greek,—probably in Egypt,—and known perhaps to Origen,[1] has come down to us in an Æthiopic version. Laurence first translated it into English. Dillmann's edition, forwarded by the kindness of a friend, has reached me too late to make due use of it. In the "Ascension" some views must be peculiarities of an individual, or at most of a small class. The work or compilation is too long for transcription here, but the subjoined outline will give a general idea of its contents.

Ch. 1, 1 – 3, 11. Introductory statement.   ⎫ *These consti-*
3, 12 – 4, 22. Causes of Isaiah's seizure.[2] ⎬ *tuted perhaps*
5, 1 – 16. Isaiah's death.   ⎭ *one work.*

---

[1] "And Isaiah is recorded to have been sawed by The People. But if any one pays no attention to this record on account of its being contained in the secret [or apocryphal] Isaiah, let him believe what is written, as follows, in the Epistle to the Hebrews."— **Origen**, *Comment. in Matt.* **10**, 18, *Opp.* **3**, p. 465.

[2] "Then Manasseh sent and seized Isaiah. For Berial was highly indignant with Isaiah, on account of the vision and the manifestation, which manifested Samael, and because by him was revealed the coming of the Beloved from the seventh heaven, his change, descent, and form, when he shall be changed into the form of man, his rejection, and the torments with which the children of Israel shall torment him, as also the coming and doctrine of his twelve Disciples, his suspension on a tree the day before the sabbath, his suspension in company with men the workers of iniquity, and his burial. 'Moreover,' said Isaiah, 'the twelve,' who shall be with him, shall be scandalized at what shall happen to him ; and watchmen shall be appointed to guard his sepulchre. There shall likewise be a descent of the Angel of the Christian Church, which in the latter days will exist in heaven ; and of the angel of the Holy Spirit, and of Michael the Archangel, to open his sepulchre on the third day, when the Beloved shall go forth sitting on the shoulders of the Seraphim, and shall send his twelve disciples, to teach all the [?] people and all nations his resurrection from the dead, so that those who believe in his crucifixion shall be saved ; and finally his assumption shall be into the seventh heaven from whence he came. Many also, who shall believe in him, shall speak by the Holy Spirit. And frequent signs and wonders shall take place in those days. But afterwards upon the subject of his second advent his disciples shall forsake the doctrine of the twelve Apos-

THE VISION WHICH ISAIAH SAW.

6, 1 – 17. Circumstances under which it took place.
7, 1 – 10, 6. He narrates his ascent to the seventh heaven.
10, 7 – 11, 40. Also what he heard and saw concerning Christ's mission.[3]

In the last two headings are items which illustrate common Christian opinions, while others illustrate only eccentricities of the author, or of a small class to which he belonged.

Christians generally regarded the heathen deities, or demons, as the powers of the air, who had control of mankind, and whose spirit was that of contention.[4]

The author personifies without plainly deifying the spirit, whom with the pre-existent Jesus he depicts as joint worshippers of God.[5] He terms Jesus "the Beloved," "the Lord." Once we find "thy lord [*God*] the lord Christ,"[6] but the bracketed word is suspicious because absent from parallel expressions (**9**, 37, 39, 40 ; **10**, 7) and nowhere else applied to Jesus.

---

tles, their beloved and pure faith; while much contention shall take place respecting his coming and the proximity of his approach. In those days there shall be many attached to office, destitute of wisdom; multitudes of iniquitous elders and pastors injurious to their flocks, and addicted to rapine; nor shall the holy pastors themselves diligently discharge their duty. Many likewise shall barter the honorable clothing of the saints for the garment of him, who delights in gold. Abundant shall be the respecters of persons in those days, and lovers of this world's honor.' " — **Ascension of Isaiah, 3**, 12 – 25.

[3] "On account of these visions and prophecies, Samael Satan sawed asunder, by Manasseh, Isaiah the son of Amos, the prophet. And such were the things which Hezekiah delivered to Manasseh in the twenty-sixth year of his reign; Who nevertheless forgot them, . . . abandoning himself to the service of Satan." — **11**, 41 – 43.

[4] "We then ascended into the firmament, I and he, where I beheld Samael and his powers. Great slaughter was perpetrated by him, and diabolical deeds, while each contended one against another. . . . I said to the angel, 'What is this contention?' He answered : 'Thus has it been from the foundation of the world, and this slaughter will continue, until he, whom thou shalt behold, shall come and put an end to it.' " — **7**, 9 – 12.

[5] "I saw that my Lord worshipped and the angel of the Holy Spirit, and that both of them together glorified God." — **9**, 40.

[6] **9**, 5. Dillmann, for a reason entirely different from the above, deems "thy lord" the only genuine part of the quotation. Here and in cc. **2**, 2 ; **9**, 39, 40 ; **11**, 1, 10, the word God is in his translation followed by O. M. If this imply that the Æthiopic word so translated designates the Supreme Deity, that word must here be spurious. Isaiah was unable (**9**, 37 ; **11**, 32) to behold the Supreme Being.

He represents Jesus, in accordance with directions from his Father,[7] as descending from the seventh through the six lower heavens, recognized by the inhabitants of the sixth, but altering his form in each of the five lower ones, so as not to be recognized by their inhabitants. He represents him as born without the knowledge of his mother,[8] and subsequently gives in a condensed shape some of his history.[9]

---

[7] " For the Lord shall descend into the world in the latter days, and after his descent shall be called Christ. He shall take your form, be reputed flesh, and shall be man. Then shall the God of the world be revealed by his Son. Yet will they lay their hands upon him, and suspend him on a tree, not knowing who he is. In like manner, also, shall his descent, as thou wilt perceive, be concealed from the heavens, through which he shall pass altogether unknown. But after he has escaped from the angel of death, on the third day he shall rise again, and continue in the world five hundred and forty-five days. And many also of the saints shall ascend with him, whose spirits shall not receive their clothing, until the Lord Christ shall ascend himself, and with him shall they ascend. Then, therefore, shall they assume their clothing, and thrones, and crowns, when he shall have ascended into the seventh heaven." — **9**, 13 – 18. Compare directions, **10**, 7 – 15, and the compliance with them, **10**, 19 – 31 ; **11**, 19 – 32.

Irenæus (*Cont. Hæres.* **1**, 3, 2 and **1**, 30, 14) mentions some Gnostics who held that Jesus remained on earth after his resurrection eighteen months, which, counting the year at three hundred sixty-five days, and the six months at thirty days each, would make five hundred forty-five. The author of the Ascension, though not a Gnostic, held some Gnostic views. In this case, however, I suspect that the teaching of Gnostic leaders may have been misunderstood by their less attentive followers, or by their Catholic opponents. The Valentinians held (**Irenæus 5**, 31, 2) " that the Lower Regions, *Inferos*, are this world of ours." If they held with some moderns, that the ministry of Jesus lasted eighteen months, they may have said that after his descent to this, our underworld, he taught during a year and a half.

[8] " I beheld . . . a woman by name Mary, . . . betrothed to a man by name Joseph. . . . I saw that . . . after she was betrothed, she was found pregnant. . . . After, however, two full months . . . while Mary was attentively gazing on the ground, she suddenly perceived with astonishment a small infant lying before her. . . . The Lord was come to his inheritance. . . . Many affirmed that she did not bring forth at all, . . . all knew that he was, but knew not whence he was. Then they took him and came to Nazareth of Galilee." — **11**, 2 – 15. Compare in Norton's *Genuineness* (**3**, 167) the Valentinian view that the Æon Savior " passed through Mary . . . without receiving anything from her substance."

[9] " When, however, he was grown up, I saw that he performed great signs and wonders in the land of Israel and Jerusalem ; that foreigners hated him and raised up the children of Israel against him, not knowing who he was ; that they delivered him to the king, and crucified him ; and that he descended to the angel of death. In Jerusalem I beheld him hanging on a tree ; and after the third day rising again, and remaining

If cc. **6–11** be a distinct document its object was to develop what preceded. Dillmann has translated the work into Latin.[10] He thinks (*Proleg.* § 4) that he finds in it three documents, namely; a Jewish one, cc. **2,** 1–**3,** 12; **5,** 2–14; a Christian one, cc. **6,** 1–**11,** 1, 23–40, to which, he thinks, another Christian prefixed ch. **1** (except verse 3) and added **11,** 42, 43.

NOTE J.

SIBYLLINE ORACLES.

Mention has been made in a former work[1] of two acrostics by Christian writers, one complete and the other imperfect, which remain to us in the Sibylline Oracles. Whether they were written with controversial intent may be a question. The finished one treats of the future Judgment. The unfinished one has more to do, though not very plainly, with Christ's life on earth, and was the better calculated of the two for controversy with heathens.

Three pieces which deal more plainly with Christ's life on earth are here subjoined, as also a fourth which does so in a slight degree. Any argument from them implies that to no one save Jesus were they applicable. Their applicability to him, when not conceded, must have been based on Pseudo-Heathen records.

No. 1.

Then to men shall a son of the Great God come
In the flesh, being likened to mortals on earth,   325
[His name] has four vowels; but its consonants
I announce as two; and will tell the whole number;
Eight units, and as many tens,

---

on earth for a certain period. Then the angel, who was conducting me, said: 'Understand, Isaiah.' When immediately I saw him send forth his twelve Disciples, and ascend from the world." — **11,** 18–22.

[10] Ascensio Isaiæ, Æthiop. et Lat. cum Proleg. Adnotat. [etc.], edita ab A. Dillmann, Lips. 1877. Its author had access to two manuscripts besides the one which Laurence used. There is also a late English translation of this work by G. H. Schodde which I have not seen.

[1] See *Judaism*, p. 444.

And eight hundreds to the incredulous
His name will exhibit ;[2] but apprehend thou mentally   330
The Christ of the Immortal God, Son of the Highest.

He will fulfil the law of God, not destroy it ;
Furnishing an antitype[3] copy, and will teach all things [needful].
 To him priests shall bear an offering of gold,
Myrrh and frankincense ; for all these things will he [?] perform. 335
 But when a certain voice in the desert
Shall come proclaiming to mortals, and shall cry out to all : —
"Let us make straight paths, and throw away
Wickedness from the heart, and let every mortal body
Be enlightened with water, that being born from above,   340
They may no longer transgress what is just,"
(But a barbarous mind,[4] persuaded by dancing,
Cutting off [his head] shall give it as a reward.) Then a sign to
        mortals
Shall suddenly take place, when guarded there shall come
From the land of Egypt a beautiful stone, but against this   345
The Hebrew people shall stumble ; but the Gentiles shall assemble

```
² — I   10
    H    8          8 Units =    8
    Σ  200          8 Tens      80
    O   70          8 Hundreds 800
    Υ  400                     —
    Σ  200                     888
       ———
       888
```

Perhaps repetition of the number "eight" was connected in the writer's mind with an idea of some secret signification belonging to it. Justin (*Dial.* 24, 41) and Barnabas (*Epist.* 15) term Sunday the eighth day. The former says : "I can show you, gentlemen, . . . that the Eighth Day had a mystery, proclaimed through these [before-mentioned circumstances] by God, superior to [that of] the Seventh." — **Justin Martyr,** *Dial.* 24. Compare 41.

In Egypt, where Greeks, by attention to astronomy, had detected, as was supposed, an eighth sphere or heaven — that of the fixed stars — far above and beyond the one in which the planet Saturn was supposed to move, the Valentinian Gnostics selected this eighth sphere as the dwelling-place of the Supreme Being who had sent Christ. Compare *Judaism,* p. 334.

[3] On the meaning of antitype compare (*Judaism,* p. 349) the antitheses of Irenæus. After an imbittered war between Jews and Romans an idea was advanced by some Christians that the events of the Old Testament were antithetically repeated in the New. Perhaps the idea may be intended above.

[4] Compare Note E, footnote 4.

Under his lead ; for the God who rules from on high,
Through him they shall know, and the straight path of universal
    light.

For he will show eternal life to mortals,
To the chosen, but inflict fire eternally on the lawless.   350
And then he will heal the sick, also the blameworthy,
[Of their sins?] all who put trust in him.
The blind shall see, the lame shall walk,
The deaf shall listen, the dumb shall talk ;
He shall eject demons ; the dead shall rise ;   355
He shall walk the waves and in a desert place
From five loaves and a marine fish
Shall satiate five thousand, and the remnants of these
Shall fill twelve baskets for [the *Sacred Virgin*].[5]
    And then Israel being drunk shall not perceive   360
Nor hear, being burdened with dull ears.

But when anger of the Highest shall visit the Hebrews
In its rage, and shall take away their faith,[6]
Because they destroyed the Heavenly Son of God.

And then blows and vile spittle   365
Shall Israel with polluted lips inflict on him.
For food gall, and for drink undiluted vinegar
They shall godlessly give him, impelled by wicked frenzy
In their breast and heart, but not seeing with their eyes —
Blinder than moles, more frightful than reptiles   370
Poisonous serpents — fettered by heavy sleep.
    But when he shall spread out his hands and embrace all
        things,
And shall bear a crown of thorns, and his side shall
They pierce with spears (wherefore during three hours,
Dark monstrous night shall come in mid-day),   375
Then indeed the temple of Solomon to mortals
Shall give a great sign, when He shall enter
The underworld, announcing resurrection to the dead.

---

    [5] The corresponding line, Book **8**, 278, instead of "Sacred Virgin," reads "Hope of the Peoples." Lactantius quotes it, "Hope of the Multitude."

    [6] This may mean, destroy their worship by destruction of their temple. The passage breaks the connection. Were line 364 amended thus, "So that they SHALL destroy the Heavenly Son of God," part of the difficulty would be removed.

But when he shall come in three days to light again,
And shall show mortals his sleep,[7] and teach all things,   380
Ascending in the clouds he shall journey to heaven,
Leaving to the world the gospel dispensation.
In his name a new shoot shall sprout
From the Gentiles, guided by God's law.
    After these things there shall be Apostle [8] guides,   385
And then shall be a cessation of prophets.
    Thenceforward Hebrews shall reap an evil harvest.
And much gold and silver shall the Roman king
Plunder.   And afterwards other kings
Shall continually arise, as former ones perish,   390
And shall afflict mortals.   But to those men shall be great
Destruction, when they shall rule with haughty injustice.
But when the temple of Solomon on the mighty earth
Shall fall, cast down by men of barbarous speech,
Brazen-breastplated, and Hebrews be expelled the land   395
Wanderers [and] slaughtered, and shall mix much darnel
With their wheat, noxious sedition shall be among all
Mankind ; cities, mutually insulted,
Shall bewail (since they performed an evil act),
Receiving the great God's anger in their bosom.   400

Sibylline Oracles, 1, 324 – 400.

No. 2.

I heartily sing the Immortal's great and famous Son
To whom the Highest Parent granted assumption of the
    throne

When not yet born, since a second time in flesh
Was he born, being washed by the pouring of the river
Jordan, which is borne along in a blue course ;   5
Who, escaping the fire,[9] shall first see the sweet
Spirit[10] coming on [him] with the white wings of a dove.
There shall sprout a pure shoot ; the fountains shall bubble up ;

---

[7] The meaning probably is, "shall narrate to mortals the events of his three days below." There is, however, a different reading : "shall show mortals a type."

[8] The Greek word στόλοι is perhaps an abbreviation for 'Απόστολοι. Otherwise the meaning must be "multitudinous guides," though the expression would be an unusual one.

[9] An allusion possibly to the idea (Justin, *Dial.* 88) that the Jordan took fire at the baptism of Jesus. Another reading gives a different sense.

[10] For πνεύματι γινόμενον read πνεῦμ' ἐπιγινόμενον.

He shall show men the ways, shall show the paths
To heaven; shall teach all in wise parables; 10
Shall lead to rectitude and persuade a contrary people,
Boasting a praiseworthy descent from his Heavenly Father.
He shall walk the waves, free men from diseases,
Raise the dead, drive off multitudinous ailments,
From one ῥίζης roll of bread men shall be satiated. 15

      Sibylline Oracles, 6, 1–15.

The remaining thirteen lines of Book **6** are by a later writer. Some of them speak in the past, not in the future tense.[11]

No. 3.

Not in glory, but as mortal [about] to be judged[12] he will come,
Pitiable, dishonored, formless,[13] that he may give hope to the pitiable.
Also [fair] form to perishable flesh and heavenly faith
To unbelievers he will give; and [anew] form man,
(Originally moulded by God's hands) 260
Whom the serpent misled, that he should stray

---

[11] When the house of David shall produce a plant in whose hand
The whole world, earth, heaven and sea shall be.
Lightnings on earth shall be [such] as formerly they saw
The two who were born from each other's side;
It shall be [thus] when the earth shall rejoice in hope of the Son.
On you alone, Land of Sodom, misery shall lie,
For senseless, you did not recognize your God,
Trifling with mortal perceptions, but from the thorn
Crowning him with a crown, mixed frightful gall
For insult and ὦμα drink, which shall cause you grievous suffering.
O wood most blessed on which God was suspended;
Earth shall not have you, but you shall see heaven,
When the fiery eye of God shall dart lightning on the temple.
      Sibylline Oracles, 6, 16–28.

[12] It was customary in ancient times for one awaiting his trial to indicate by his apparel and by his unshaved or unwashed countenance that he was in a pitiable condition. This was intended as an appeal to sympathy and compassion. "Cicero . . . changed his attire, and assuming the garb of one accused, went round the forum soliciting the compassion of all whom he met."—**Smith**, *Dict. of Biog.* **1**, p. 713, col. 2, *art.* Cicero.

[13] See Ch. III. § 14.

To a deadly fate, and take knowledge of good and evil,
So that leaving God he should serve mortal customs :
To him the All-ruler, taking [him] specially as adviser,
Said in the beginning : " Child, LET US BOTH [14] make 265
(Forming from our own image) mortal tribes.
I now with my hands, then you by teaching shall heal
Our form, that we may establish a mutual work."
Mindful therefore, of this purpose, he will come to be judged,
[*Furnishing an antitype* [15] *representation of the undefiled virgin* [16]]
Enlightening with water by the hands of the elders. 271
Doing all things by a word, healing every disease,
He shall lay the winds with a word, and calm the sea
When raging, with his feet, treading it in peace and trust.
From five loaves and a marine fish 275
He shall satiate five thousand men in a desert,
And taking all the surplus fragments,
Shall fill twelve baskets as a hope for the people.
He will invite souls of the blessed and love the wretched
Who, scoffed at, shall do good for evil, 280
[While] beaten, scourged, desiring poverty.
[He] perceiving and seeing and hearing all things,
Shall look into the interior, and lay it bare for conviction,
For he is the hearing, understanding and sight of all,
The Logos creating forms, whom all things obey, 285
Savior of the dead, healer of all disease.
He will fall at last into LAW-less and FAITH-less [17] hands.
They will give God blows with unholy hands,
And with polluted lips vile spittle.
He will give to the blows an utterly undefiled back ; 290
[For he will give himself to the world undefiled in virginity,[18]]
And buffeted, will be silent, that no one may recognize
Who, of whom, he is, whence he came, that he may talk to
  the dead.[19]

---

[14] See Note M, text prefixed to footnote 17.
[15] See note 3.
[16] That is Eve, who was deemed by many a virgin until her expulsion from Paradise. Compare line 201 and see *Underworld Mission*, Appendix, Note H.
[17] LAW-less means heathen. FAITH-less may mean Jews or heathens.
[18] Literally, "an undefiled virgin."
[19] The meaning seems to be that, if recognized, he would not have been put to death, and could not have fulfilled his mission in the underworld. Compare *Underworld Mission*, 3d edit. p. 79.

He [20] will bear a crown of thorns: for of thorns [21]
The eternal crown of chosen saints shall come.   295
They shall pierce his side with a spear on account of their law,
Since from reeds,[22] moved by another spirit,
The soul's inclinations, anger and revenge, are nourished.
He will spread his hands and measure all the world.
Giving gall for food and vinegar to drink,   300
They shall spread this table of inhospitality.
  But when all these things mentioned shall be finished,
Then in him the whole Law is abolished which at first
Was given to mortal opinions because [23] of a disobedient people.
Rent is the veil of the temple, and in mid-day   305
Shall be dark monstrous night for three hours.
For, cessation of service to temple and concealed Law,
Veiled by worldly fantasies, was again manifested
On the Ruler's descent into the enduring earth.
He will come to the underworld announcing to all   310
The consecrated, hope, end of ages and the last day,
And will abolish death by sleeping till the third day;
And then, freed from the departed, will come to light,
The first to show the chosen a beginning of the resurrection.

[Washed in the waters of an immortal fountain   315
From their former wickedness, that born again from above
They may no longer be slaves to immoralities of the world.]

  First the Lord is seen by his own [disciples]
In the flesh as formerly. On hands and feet he will show
To his own, four marks impressed on his members.   320
The East, the West, the South, the North,
For so many kingdoms of the world shall fulfil
The lawless reprehensible deed on our image.

Sibylline Oracles, 8, 256–323.

---

[20] The next half-dozen lines, 299–304, are given in the order of Alexandre.

[21] The word ἄκανθος has a double meaning, indicating thorn and also (according to Liddell and Scott) "a plant much used in works of art, especially Corinthian capitals."

[22] The word for spear and reed κάλαμος is the same in the original.

[23] Compare Justin Martyr, *Dial.* 43, quoted in *Judaism* on p. 343.

No. 4.

Hail, Zion, much suffering daughter,
Thy king enters riding on a colt,   325
Appearing gentle to all, that our yoke,
Slavish, grievous, on the neck he may carry off,
And end godless laws and galling fetters.
Know him thy God, the Son of God,
Praising him and having him in thy heart;   330
Love him with thy soul and bear his name,
Reject those who preceded,[24] and wash from his blood.
For observances and petitions do not propitiate him;
Nor, Immortal, does he heed perishable sacrifices,
But, uttering with thy mind the cure of his holy teaching,   335
Know this one, and you shall see his Parent.
                    Sibylline Oracles, 8, 324 – 336.

NOTE K.

HERMES TRISMEGISTUS, MERCURY THRICE GREATEST.

In the early part of the second century astrological and other works — doubtless of heathen origin — were circulating in the name of Mercury.[1] This probably suggested to some Christian of the less scrupulous sort, that Mercury might be made to teach better things than astrology. In order that his production might seem even more authoritative than prior ones in the name of that god, he ascribed it to **Hermes Trismegistus,** or Mercury, Thrice Greatest, and designates the production as λόγος τέλειος, the "*Perfect Discourse,*" or the "*Final*[2] *Discourse,*" intending probably to give it position above all other productions of the same personage.

---

[21] The meaning seems to be, reject the Jews and by so doing wash your hands from the crime of putting Jesus to death.

[1] Clement mentions (*Strom.* **6,** 35; *Opp.* edit. Potter, p. 757) four books on astrology and two others, one of which contained hymns to the gods, while the second contained a computation of, or rules for, a regal life.

[2] A passage attributed to **Orpheus** (cited in *Judaism,* pp. 337–338) represents him as saying to his son, "I speak truth lest [my?] former views should rob you of longed-for eternity." Perhaps in the present case the heading of the Discourse meant that the views here given were the latest teachings of Mercury.

In the first half of the fourth century Lactantius prefixes to his quotations from this work an account of Mercury,[3] which can hardly have originated earlier than the latter half of the third century. In it Mercury is made to proclaim a Supreme Being devoid of name, also one subordinate and created God, and some other views common among Christians.

"This [Mercury] wrote books, and indeed many of them, pertaining to the knowledge of divine things, in which he asserts the majesty of the Supreme and Sole God, and calls him by the same names as ourselves, 'GOD and FATHER,' and lest any one should ask his name, says that he is ἀνώνυμον, 'WITHOUT NAME.' . . . His words are these: 'GOD IS ONE, BUT THE ONE DOES NOT NEED A NAME, FOR THE SELF-EXISTENT IS WITHOUT NAME.'" — *Div. Inst.* **1**, 6.

"Hermes [Mercury] . . . who not only said that man had been made in the image of God, but also tried to explain it." — *Div. Inst.* **2**, 11.

"**Hermes** [Mercury] affirms that those who have known God are not only safe from attacks of demons, but are not even subject to fate. He says: 'THE SOLE PROTECTION IS PRACTICAL MONOTHEISM, FOR NEITHER AN EVIL DEMON NOR FATE HAS CONTROL OF THE PRACTICALLY MONOTHEISTIC MAN, FOR GOD FREES THE PRACTICAL MONOTHEIST FROM EVERY EVIL, FOR PRACTICAL MONOTHEISM IS THE ONE AND SOLE GOOD IN MEN.'" — *Div. Inst.* **2**, 16.

"Trismegistus, who, I hardly know how, investigated almost all truth, often described the excellence and majesty of the Word." — *Div. Inst.* **4**, 9.

"The Father God, . . . since he lacks parents, is justly named by Trismegistus, 'FATHERLESS and MOTHERLESS.'" — *Div. Inst.* **4**, 13.

---

[8] **Lactantius**, after devoting five chapters to other matter, says: "Let us now pass to divine testimonies, but first I will bring forward one which is akin to divine, both because of its exceeding age, and because he whom I shall name was transferred from mortals into the category of gods.

"In the writings of Cicero, **C. Cotta**, high-priest, disputing against the Stoics, . . . states that there were five Mercuries, and after enumerating four of them in order, [says] the fifth was that one by whom Argus was killed, and who 'fled on that account into Egypt, and delivered laws and literature (*litteras*) to the Egyptians.' . . .

"He also founded a town which even now is in Greek called Hermopolis; . . . who, although a man, was most ancient and most instructed in every kind of learning, so that [his] knowledge of many things and arts fixed on him the name of Trismegistus." — *Div. Inst.* **1**, 6.

"**Hermes Trismegistus**, . . . who agrees in words as well as substance with us, that is, with the prophets whom we follow, and speaks thus concerning justice : ' O Son, adore and worship this *verbum* Teaching,' but the sole worship of God is not to be evil. . . . 'These [frankincense and spices], and things similar to these, are not appropriate to Him, for he is full of all things which exist and has not the slightest need of any thing, but we adore him by giving thanks, for his sacrifice is simply benediction.'" — *Div. Inst.* **6,** 25.

"Hermes [Mercury] did not ignore that man was formed by God and in the image of God." — *Div. Inst.* **7, 4.**

"I have made clear, as I think, that the soul is not dissoluble. It remains to cite the witnesses by whose authority my arguments may be corroborated. Neither will I call the prophets to testify . . . but those [witnesses] rather to whom it is necessary that the rejecters of true religion *veritatem* should yield credence. **Hermes,** describing the nature of man, . . . introduces these [remarks]. God ' made the same from both natures, the mortal and the immortal, [into] the one nature of man, making him partly immortal, partly mortal, and placed him half-way between a divine immortal nature and a mortal mutable one, that, seeing all things [mortal and immortal], he might admire all things.'" — *Div. Inst.* **7,** 13.

"In that book which is called the *Perfect* (or *Final*) *Discourse*, after enumeration of the evils concerning which we have spoken, he adds these things: ' But when these things shall thus take place, O Esculapius, then the Lord, and Father, and God, and Creator, of the first and one [subordinate] God, looking at the things which take place — even such [as occur] by His will — opposing to disorder what is good and recalling what wanders, and purifying what is wicked, sometimes dissolving by much water, and sometimes burning out by the fiercest fire, and sometimes crushing out by wars and famines, leads [back again] to the ancient condition and replaces His world.'" — *Div. Inst.* **7,** 18.

NOTE L.

ALLEGED UNCANONICAL GOSPELS.

Luke in the beginning of his Gospel (1, 1, 2) mentions that "many have undertaken to arrange a narrative of the events accomplished among us, conformably to the accounts given us by those who were eye-witnesses from the beginning, and [who] have become ministers of the religion." No trace remains of the narratives to which he refers unless Matthew's Gospel, then extant only in Hebrew, was among those which he had in mind. His form of expression renders probable that some individuals after listening to detached portions of the Master's history had endeavored in writing to connect and arrange them. Probably these imperfect attempts were laid aside by their authors or readers so soon as fuller and more connected narratives appeared.

Some modern writers suppose that various Gospels existed in the second century, from which the four now in use were selected, or out of which they were formed or in opposition to which they were fabricated. This view, in a crude shape, is expressed by Hone and Tischendorf.[1] It is also held

---

[1] "After the writings contained in the New Testament were selected from the numerous Gospels and Epistles then in existence, what became of the books that were rejected by the compilers?" — *Apoc. N. Test.* p. v. **Hone,** in answer to the foregoing, presents his reader a collection of documents classified by him as Gospels and Epistles, not one of which professes to record the MINISTRY of Jesus.

"The definition of Apocryphal Gospels is [Gospels] opposed to Canonical ones; unless you prefer to contend that in the earliest times Canonical Gospels were [created?] in opposition to apocryphal ones. . . . When first the Canonical Gospels by consent of the Church began to be separated from the great number of writings in circulation, it is obvious that yet other and new [writings] which were issued could not aspire to evangelical authority unless they feigned the same valued peculiarity (*virtutem*) with those [canonical ones]. . . .

"Whence it is to be concluded that no Gospels were reckoned apocryphal before the Canon of Sacred Books existed in the ancient church." — C. **Tischendorf,** *De Evang. Apoc. Origine et Usu,* pp. 1, 2.

Tischendorf, after arguing (pp. 3, 4) from Irenæus, Tatian, and Theophilus, writers after the middle of the second century, that "in the opinion of the most numerous and of the principal [Christian] teachers the Gospel Canon *pœne jam constitisset* had now been almost established,"

in several shapes by other writers, especially in Germany, an extract from one of the more thoughtful of whom is subjoined.[2] Attention to four meanings of the word Gospel and to some historical facts should precede examination of these uncanonical works.

One meaning of this term is A RECORD OF THE LIFE OF JESUS. A second meaning, common among early Christians, was THE FOUR RECORDS or Gospels in contradistinction from the Epistles. A third meaning is THE INTERPRETATION PUT UPON CHRIST'S TEACHING, or that of his Apostles, by an individual or a sect. Thus the Gospel according to Calvin, or according to Wesley, would be readily understood as meaning the interpretation by those individuals of New Testament teaching. A fourth meaning is, A GOSPEL, or THE FOUR GOSPELS, AS TRANSLATED OR ANNOTATED BY SOME INDIVIDUAL. Thus "Campbell's Four Gospels" would be readily understood to mean his translation of, and annotations on, the four Gospels. Among early Christians such a work would have been termed Campbell's Gospel, the latter word distinguishing the four collectively from the Epistles.

In the days of Irenæus and of Tatian, probably about A. D. 170, it is obvious that four Gospels only were in common use.

---

adds (p. 4), "therefore from the time which immediately preceded the middle of the second century until almost the close of the fourth, was the era of Apocryphal Gospels."

It would — with the exception of our four Gospels — be difficult or impossible to point out in the era mentioned a single document professedly of Christian origin, which assumed to narrate the life or ministry of Jesus.

An earlier and common error in Europe paved the way for such views as the foregoing. It appears in the following extract from **Mosheim**: "Not long after the Savior's ascension, various histories of his life and doctrines, full of impositions and fables, were composed by persons, . . . superstitious, simple, and piously fraudulent ; and afterwards, various other spurious writings were palmed upon the world, falsely inscribed with the names of the holy Apostles." — *Ecc. Hist.* Century I. Part **2**, Ch. 2, § 17, Murdock's trans. **1**, p. 73. Mosheim, however, did not suppose that the Gospels and other writings of the New Testament had merely been selected out of this mess by the good or bad judgment of men.

[2] "In addition to our canonical Gospels, Christian antiquity was acquainted with several others ; and it is in the last degree needful to obtain as accurate a knowledge of these as possible, for the opinion is pretty wide-spread that some of them are older and more original than our canonical Gospels." — **De Wette**, *Introduct. to N. Test.*, p. 87 ; *Frothingham's trans.*

The effort of Irenæus to explain WHY this precise number existed implies that its existence was well recognized.[3] Tatian also made a *Diatessaron*,[4] a harmony or synopsis of the four.

Somewhat earlier we find two classes of men, intensely unlike each other, called Gnostics. Both classes originated after an imbittered war between Jews and Gentiles, and both held that the God of the Jews was not the God of the Christians, but a different being.[5] Marcion, the leader of one class, adopted, or made special use of, the Gospel of Luke, who was a Gentile and a companion of Paul.[6] From this he expurgated what he could not, even by forced explanation, fit into his system, but

---

[3] **Irenæus**, after specifying (*cont. Hæres.* 3, 1, 1) Matthew, Mark, Luke, and John as having each written one of the Gospels, adds as follows : "Nor can there be more or fewer Gospels than these. For as there are four regions of the world in which we live, and four cardinal winds, and the Church is spread over all the earth, and the Gospel is the pillar and support of the Church, and the breath of life ; in like manner is it fit that it should have four pillars." — *Cont. Hæres.* 3, 11, 8 ; *Opp.* **1**, pp. 467, 468, edit. Stieren, *Norton's trans.* On. p. 467 Stieren has erroneously c. 12 for c. 11.

Eusebius (*Ecc. Hist.* 3, 37) mentions Quadratus as engaged in teaching at the same time with the daughters of Philip, and states that the disciples of that age were accustomed "to distribute the writing of the divine Gospels." As Philip was executed in A. D. 52 (see *Judaism*, p. 238) the ministry of his daughters can scarcely be placed later than the close of the first century. Quadratus lived into the first quarter of the second century, for he presented an Apology to Hadrian. Eusebius would not have termed any Gospels DIVINE except the four recognized in his day, and unless his information were inaccurate, these four must in the time of Quadratus have had an established authority.

[4] "**Tatian** putting together, I know not on what plan, a synopsis and harmony of the evangelists, called this τὸ διὰ τεσσάρων, 'The four collated,' which even yet is in circulation among some." — **Eusebius**, *Ecc. Hist.* 4, 29. In the fifth century Theodoret (*Hæret. Fab.* **1**, 20) took away two hundred copies of this Diatessaron which he found used and esteemed by churches that he regarded as sound in the faith. His only charge against it is its omission of the genealogies (which perhaps Tatian could not harmonize) and of the descent from David.

[5] See touching these men *Judaism*, pp. 331 – 336.

[6] **Irenæus** speaks (**3**, 11, 7) of Marcion "as mutilating the Gospel according to Luke." Compare Irenæus **1**, 27, 2. **Tertullian** says : "Marcion seems to have selected Luke as the [one] whom he would cut up." *Adv. Marc.* 5. Compare in Norton's *Genuineness*, Vol. **3**, Appendix, Note C, his remarks on this Gospel.

Apelles, the disciple of Marcion, seems to have used the same expurgated copy of Luke. The term Gospel of Marcion, or Gospel of Apelles, meant sometimes this expurgated copy, and sometimes, perhaps, the system which they based upon it. Neither of these two individuals doubted the authorship of the four Gospels, but they supposed the evangelists, be-

used from the other Gospels what he thought could be pressed into its support.

The chief division of the other class was the Valentinians, or followers of Valentinus. These used especially, but not exclusively, John's Gospel.[7] Heracleon, one of them, wrote a commentary on it, the remnants of which will be found collected by Massuet in his edition of Irenæus, pp. 362 – 376, in which work also an extract from his commentary on Luke will be found on p. 362. Another portion of this class used Mark's Gospel.[8] Basilides will be subsequently mentioned.

It seems impossible that other records concerning the ministry of Jesus should have been afloat in Gentile communities, and that the Gnostics, instead of drawing from them, should have needed forced interpretation and, in the case of Marcion, mutilation of the records yet in use.

We have the direct testimony of Irenæus that the Heretics, under which title he specifies the Ebionites, Marcionites, Valentinians, and others, used our Gospels.[9] This testimony comes from one who would have been prompt to point out any tendency of the Heretics to use records other than what he deemed sanctioned. We have, moreover, the statement of **Tertullian** that the Heretics should not be allowed to use the Christian Scriptures,[10] — a superfluous statement, if the records which they used were from other hands than those recognized by Christians generally.

---

cause of their Jewish education, to have misunderstood the Master's teaching.

A letter of Origen preserved only in a Latin translation, implies that Marcion and Apelles, even if they made most use of Luke, must have used the remaining three Gospels. "You see . . . with what expurgation Marcion expurgated the Gospels or the Epistles *Apostolum*, or with what his successor, Apelles, after him [did the same]." — Origen, *Epist. Opp.* **1**, p. 6 B, edit. de la Rue.

[7] "The Valentinians making copious use of that [Gospel] which is according to John." — Irenæus, **3**, 11, 7.

[8] "Those who distinguish Jesus from the Christ, and say that Christ remained without suffering, but that Jesus suffered, preferring the Gospel according to Mark, if they read it with the love of truth, can be corrected." — *Ibid.* This perhaps means that Mark's Gospel admitted less easily than John's of vague and fanciful interpretations.

[9] "Such is the established authority of the Gospels that the Heretics themselves render testimony to them, and each one of them who goes out [from Christianity] endeavors to confirm his teaching out of them." — Irenæus, *cont. Hæres.* **3**, 11, 7. The passage is found only in the Latin translation.

[10] "They (the Heretics) offer the Scriptures, and by this their auda-

We will now endeavor to classify these supposed uncanonical Gospels. Lack of leisure and sight prevent that fuller treatment which I could wish. The general reader will find all that he needs in Norton's *Genuineness*, **3**, pp. 214 – 286; abridged edit. pp. 340 – 391.

1. RECORDS. Matthew and Luke under other names. Matthew's Gospel, in what was then called Hebrew,[11] was used by Hebrew Christians, also called Nazarenes or Ebionites, and hence received the name of "Gospel to the Hebrews," "to the Nazarenes," "to the Ebionites," and also according to Jerome "Gospel of the Apostles," otherwise called, perhaps, "of the Twelve Apostles."[12] Some copies of it had interpolations not extant in Matthew.[13]

Bartholomew is said to have carried this Hebrew Gospel

---

city at once influence some. . . . We interpose that they are not to be admitted to a dispute from the Scriptures." — *De Præscript. Hæret.* 15; *Opp.* p. 236 C. "The reason for what we propose is obvious; that the Heretics are not to be admitted to enter upon an argument from the Scriptures. . . . Not being Christians, *nullum jus capiunt Christianarum literarum*, they have no legal right to the Christian records." — *De Præscript. Hæret.* 37; *Opp.* 242 D.

[11] The Nazarenes "have the Gospel according to Matthew in its fullest shape, in the Hebrew language." — **Epiphanius**, *Hæres.* **29**, 9. The Ebionites "also receive the Gospel according to Matthew, for they, as also the followers of Cerinthus, use this Gospel; they call it [the Gospel] according to the Hebrews." — *Hæres.* **30**, 3. "Matthew . . . composed the Gospel of Christ in Hebrew letters and words. . . . Further: the Hebrew itself is preserved until this day in the library at Cæsarea." — **Jerome**, *de Vir. Illust.* 3; *Opp.* **2**, 833, *edit. Vallars.* "The Gospel also which is called according to the Hebrews, and which was lately translated by me into the Greek and Latin, and which Origen often used." — *De Vir. Illust.* 2; *Opp.* **2**, 831. Cp. Euseb. *Ecc. Hist.* **3**, 255 "The Gospel which the Nazarenes and Ebionites use . . . and which is called by many [*or* most], *a plerisque*, the authentic [Gospel] of Matthew." — **Jerome**, *Comment. in Matt.* **12**, 13; *Opp.* **7**, 77.

[12] "The Gospel *according to the Hebrews* . . . which the Nazarenes yet use — [that, namely] *according to the Apostles*, or as many think, *according to Matthew* [in its genuine form?] — which is in the library of Cæsarea." — **Jerome**, *cont. Pelag.* 3; *Opp.* **2**, col. 782, edit. Vallars. Compare Hom. 1 on Luke, Origenis *Opp.* **3**, 933 B (**5**, 87). Jerome omits, and the Homilies use, the word "Twelve" before Apostles. If the Apostles while working collectively in Judea used any written Gospel it must have been this, the others being in Greek.

[13] See ancient quotations from the Gospels in Grabe, *Spicileg.*, **1**, pp. 25 – 31. Those by Clement and Origen (pp. 26 – 27) must have existed in the second or third century. Those quoted by other writers may in several instances have found their way into it at a later date. The

to India.[14] Cerinthus is said to have made special use of it.[15] Hence the terms (Jerome Præfat. in Matt.) "Gospel of Bartholomew," (Epiphan. Hæres. 51, 7) "Gospel of Cerinthus." These terms, however, can never have had much currency, and may have been unknown to the first three centuries.

The Gospel of Marcion or of Apelles (see note 6) was an altered copy of Luke.

2. COMMENTARIES AND EXPOSITIONS. Basilides wrote an exposition of the Gospels in twenty-four books,[16] which at a later date seems to have been called his Gospel.[17] The Gospel of Thomas, judged by our only extract from it,[18] may have been some exposition of passages in the Gospels. A Gospel of Truth, attributed to the Valentinians by Irenæus (3, 11, 9, cp. Tertullian, *de Præscript. Hæret.* 49), must have been expository or doctrinal. Nothing historical from it is quoted or controverted by any one.

3. DOCTRINAL WORKS. Serapion early in the third century mentions the Gospel of Peter.[19] The work, obviously not historical, may have been some portion of the Clementines,[20] or

---

Jewish Christians who used Matthew in the original, soon became an unimportant sect. It is hardly possible that they had among them trained copyists equal to those in the Greek book-markets. Some passages from Luke and John (not always closely translated into Hebrew), or marginal paraphrases and comments on the same, seem, with a little other matter, to have been copied into the text.

[14] "Pantænus . . . is said to have gone to the Indians; where, it is commonly said, he found the Gospel of Matthew, which before his arrival had been delivered to some in that country, who had the knowledge of Christ: to whom Bartholomew, one of the Apostles, is said to have preached, and to have left with them that writing of Matthew in Hebrew letters, and that it was preserved among them to that time." — **Eusebius,** *Ecc. Hist.* **5**, 9, 10; *Lardner's trans.*

[15] **Epiphanius,** *Hæres.* **30**, 14.

[16] Agrippa Castor, cited by Eusebius, *Ecc. Hist.* **4**, 7.

[17] Hom. **1** on Luke, Origenis *Opp.* **3**, 933 C (5, 87).

[18] In the **Philosophumena** (**5**, 7, p. 101, edit. Miller) is an extract at second hand from the Gospel of Thomas. "He who seeks me will find me in children after their seventh year, for there — to become concealed in their fourteenth year — I am manifested." — Cp. Matt. **18**, 5. The work is also mentioned in Hom. **1** on Luke, Origenis *Opp.* **3**, 933 C, (5, 87).

[19] Eusebius, *Ecc. Hist.* **6**, 12.

[20] In early writers a subject is sometimes presented (see *Judaism*, p. 177) by selecting disputants on either side into whose mouths the arguments of respective schools are put. The author of the Clementine Homilies and Recognitions selects Peter as the person who shall present true views, and Simon Magus as the opponent who is to present

of a similar work. A Gospel of Matthias (cp. Acts **1**, 26) is mentioned by Eusebius (*Ecc. Hist.* **3**, 25) and by the Homilies on Luke (**1**, Origen. *Opp.* **3**, 933 C). Absence of any appeal to it implies that it was not a history of Jesus. It must have been something doctrinal.

4. GOSPEL ACCORDING TO THE EGYPTIANS.[21] Uncertainty as to whether this belongs under the first or third of the preceding heads, leads me to treat it separately. The citations from it suggest that it was a doctrinal homily (on Matthew **22**, 30?) exceptional in that it selects Jesus as speaker. The citations refer to the absence of sex in the next life, and the fact that while marrying and bearing of children continue death also will continue. There may have been some casual reason for the title "Gospel according to the Egyptians." As no such reason, however, is apparent, I think the fol-

---

false views of the subjects discussed. In another document called the Preaching of Peter it is also obvious that Peter is merely selected as spokesman. Their authors had no thought of passing off these productions as written or uttered by that Apostle. They merely meant, by selecting him as spokesman, to indicate their adherence to a belief in both dispensations — the Jewish and Christian — as having proceeded from the same God. They were prompted to this, perhaps, by the fact that, of the two bodies opposed to this view one, the Marcionites, made great use of Paul's writings, while the other, the Valentinians, used chiefly those of John.

In the latter of these documents Peter is made to argue from the Scriptures of the New Testament (Clem. Alex. *Strom.* **6**, 11) an appeal which would have been deemed needless, or even derogatory to him by one who was trying to palm off the work as his genuine production.

In one portion of the work where the author appeals to Sibylla and Hystaspes — books regarded as prophecies addressed to heathen communities — Paul is introduced (Clem. Alex., *Strom.* **6**, 42, 43 ; *Opp.* p. 761, edit. Potter) as the personage to make THIS appeal. Probably it would have been deemed out of place in the mouth of Peter.

[21] In the third century it is mentioned by Clem. Alex. *Strom.* **3**, 63, 92, 93 (cp. 45, 64) and by the author of the Philosophumena, **5**, 7, p. 98, edit. Miller. Later mentions are found in the Homilies on Luke (see note 19) and Epiphan. *Hæres.* **62**, 2, *Opp.* **1**, 514, who probably confused a view which the Philosophumena ascribes to this Gospel with others which it ascribes to the Mystics. Cp. pseudo Clem. Rom. *Epist.* **2**, 12 ; *al.* 5. The quotation from it by Clement (*Strom.* **3**, 92) speaks of a time "When . . . the male with the female shall be neither male nor female" (cp. Matt. **22**, 30). This may have been the passage on which the Ophites are said (Philosophumena, p. 98) to have based their view of transmutation in the soul or its affections. That the Philosophumena should treat this work as the source of but one error accords with its being an almost unknown doctrinal treatise, or a translation either of Matthew or the four Gospels, in some manuscript or manuscripts of which one or two notes or interpolations had attracted attention.

lowing explanation probable. A translation of Matthew,[22] if not of the four Gospels, may already have been made into some Egyptian dialect. In one or more manuscripts of this some scribe may have appended as a note, or perhaps interpolated, an extract or extracts from this Homily. On this supposition the term Gospel according to the Egyptians would be natural, and would accord with the fact that Clement of Alexandria who quotes, does not appear to have seen the work.

The foregoing includes, I believe, every uncanonical Gospel mentioned in the first three centuries. So far as concerns Eusebius, Jerome, Epiphanius, or the Homilies on Luke,[23] it includes mentions of later date.

When Christianity gained the upper hand, there was a motive which did not previously exist for fabricating documents in the name of venerated Christians. Yet even then any fabricated histories of Jesus concerned themselves with his earlier years, not with his ministry. The authority of the four Gospels seems to have been so firm as to preclude other accounts concerning this portion of his life.

---

[22] The number of Jews in Egypt gives plausibility to the supposition that Matthew's Gospel may have been translated earlier than the others for some of the non-Greek-speaking communities of Jewish Christians.

[23] In de la Rue's edition of Origen's Works, Vol. **3**, p. 932, and in the edition of Lommatzsch, **5**, XXVII, XXVIII, and in the edition of Jerome by Vallarsius, **3**, col. 245 – 248, is a letter of Jerome, which in the last-mentioned work is addressed to Paula and Eustochium. In all these it is entitled Prologue to Homilies on Luke, there attributed to Origen. In this letter **Jerome** says that a lady named Blæsilla had, at a former date, asked him to issue in the Latin, Origen's "thirty-six [*Vallars.* twenty-five] books on Matthew and five others on Luke and thirty-nine [*Vallars.* thirty-two] on John," — a request, as he said, beyond his strength and leisure, but, as the friends who now addressed him had asked only for the translation of the Homilies on Luke, he had complied. *Quam tamen idcirco nunc faciam, quia sublimiora non poscitis.*

In a preceding portion of the letter he says that the persons whom he addressed had asked him to translate the [thirty-nine??] Homilies on Luke of "our Adamantius," that is, of Origen. De la Rue and Lommatzsch omit the bracketed number thirty-nine. It is doubtless an interpolation. It contradicts the statement in the same letter (a statement in which all texts agree) attributing to Origen but five Homilies on Luke. If this be so the thirty-nine Homilies must, even if translated by Jerome, have been from some other writer than Origen. Jerome mentions in his *de Viris Illustribus* (109, *al.* 118, *Opp.* **2**, col. 939, edit. Vallarsius; **1**, p. 193, Frankfort edit.) a Didymus of Alexandria, then living, as having written commentaries on Matthew and John which he (Jerome) had translated into Latin. Possibly the thirty-nine Homilies on Luke were from the same source. They are evidently from an Alexandrine writer.

NOTE M.

DATE WHEN JESUS WAS DEIFIED.

In the early part of the third century the deification of Jesus had, at least in some localities, considerable foothold among Gentile Christians, though it was rejected by all Jewish ones, and was treated by many Gentiles as a dangerous innovation.[1]

In the third quarter of the second century Justin Martyr, the earliest extant defender of this view, advocated it in his discussion with a Jew, but manifests a feeling of uncertainty touching it,[2] which he does not on other points. At a yet earlier date — probably about the middle of the century [3] — he wrote an *Apology* addressed to a heathen emperor, in which he designates Jesus as the ANGEL and APOSTLE [4] of the Supreme Being, basing in one case his argument on a use of the former term in the Old Testament.[5] Throughout this somewhat

---

[1] See *Judaism*, Ch. XI. notes 56, 57, 58, 60.

[2] "'But, O Trypho,' I said, 'his being the Christ of God is not annulled even if I am unable to show that he pre-existed as a God, son of the Maker of all things and was born a man.'" — **Justin Martyr**, *Dial.* 48; *Opp.* **2**, 154 C.

[3] In the *Apology* (**1**, 46; *Opp.* **1**, 228-230) Justin places the birth of Christ 150 years previously. In his *Dialogue* (120; *Opp.* **2**, 400 C) he alludes to the *Apology* as already written. The date of either work has however been much discussed and differently decided by different writers. The war mentioned by the Jew may have been the Jewish one under Hadrian, or that under Antoninus Pius, or may have been a non-Jewish war under the latter, or even under Marcus Antoninus. If the first-mentioned be the one referred to, then we must suppose that Justin wrote out the discussion long after its occurrence. Cicero's work *de Nat. Deorum* was written thirty years after the discussion which it professes to narrate.

[4] "Our teacher — who is both son of the FATHER OF ALL THINGS and MASTER GOD and also his apostle — foretold us that these things would happen." — **Justin Martyr**, *Apol.* **1**, 13; *Opp.* **1**, 162 A. "These [Old Testament] teachings are given as proof that Jesus Christ is the Son and Apostle of God, having previously been his Logos, and appeared sometimes in the guise of fire [at the burning bush] and sometimes in the likeness of incorporeal things." — *Apol.* **1**, 63; *Opp.* **1**, 262 A. "We do homage to . . . the son . . . and to the host of OTHER good angels who are his followers and like to him. . . ." — *Apol.* **1**, 6; *Opp.* **1**, 148, 150 C. Compare fuller quotation in *Judaism*, p. 470.

[5] The Jews — "having it expressly stated in the compositions of

elaborate *Apology* there is not a paragraph nor even a sentence devoted to argument for, nor yet to a statement of, the deity of Jesus. With a possible exception soon to be considered, that doctrine is not even mentioned.[6] The omission cannot have been occasioned by Gentile repugnance, since after the doctrine was in existence it met less opposition from Gentile converts than from Jewish ones,[7] and the only natural explanation of it is that the view, if held, had not yet taken such possession of Justin's mind as it afterwards did.

The only mention of the doctrine in the *Apology* is appended,[8] a mention so parenthetical and brief that its omission would not impair connection of the sentence.

Justin in his larger *Apology* would, by any reader ignorant of his *Dialogue*, be understood as meaning and affirming that

---

Moses (**Exod. 3**, 2, 6, 14, 15), 'The ANGEL of God spoke to Moses in a fiery flame, in the bush, and said: I am THE BEING, the God of Abraham and the God of Isaac and the God of Jacob' — affirm that it was the Father and Artificer of all things who spoke these words." — *Apol.* **1**, 63; *Opp.* **1**, 262 A, 264 B.

[6] The above remark holds true of the second or shorter *Apology* without any exception; but that work is quite brief and was written with special reference to an occurrence at Rome, so that nothing can be confidently inferred from its omission of the view.

[7] See *Judaism*, Ch. XI. notes 57, 58, 60.

[8] "The Jews therefore who constantly maintain that the FATHER OF ALL THINGS spoke to Moses, when the speaker was in reality the Son of God, who is called his ANGEL and APOSTLE, are justly convicted by the prophetic spirit and by Christ himself, of knowing neither the Father nor the son. For those who say that the son is the Father are convicted of not understanding the Father and of not knowing that the FATHER OF ALL THINGS has a son, who being the first-born Logos of God, (*also is God*) also formerly appeared in the semblance of fire and in the image of what was incorporeal, to Moses and to the other prophets." — *Apol.* **1**, 63; *Opp.* **1**, 264 C D. If the words in a parenthesis be from Justin the word "and" should be substituted for "also" immediately afterwards. The Greek will bear either translation. In this latter case Justin, who had more than once quoted the words spoken to Moses, "I am the God of Abraham and of Isaac and of Jacob" (**Exod. 3**, 6), may have deemed it necessary to admit parenthetically that the term God, equally as the term angel, was applied to the speaker in the Old Testament. The parenthesis, however, may be a later insertion. Our means of determining the text of Justin are very scanty, and therefore have less weight in deciding the question. Only two manuscripts of the *Apology* (Smith, *Dict. of Biog.* art. *Justin*) are in existence. If the parenthesis stood in a different connection its genuineness might be less suspicious, but here it seems to contravene the point of Justin's argument, which consists in keeping out of view the term God while laying stress on the term angel.

Jesus was merely a pre-existent angel.[9] This certainly is the view to which he gives prominence. Probably in his first efforts to meet objections raised against the Old Testament, this was his means of defence. It is equally plain that at a later date, when he wrote his *Dialogue*, he substitutes the view that Jesus, though called an angel, was a subordinate god.[10]

---

[9] In one place **Justin** affirms: "We are followers of the ONLY God, the Unborn, through the Son." — *Apol.* **1**, 14; *Opp.* **1**, 164 B. By the "Unborn God" Justin always means the Father. He never applies this term to Jesus. The passage implies that Justin at this date recognized NO god save the Father.

[10] "As to your saying that this Christ pre-existed before the ages as a God, . . . it appears to me not only PARADOXICAL but foolish." — **Trypho** in *Dial.* 48; *Opp.* **2**, 154 B. It is noteworthy in the foregoing that Justin takes this method of introducing what he had not previously affirmed. Again, his opponent is made to say: "Answer me first how you can show that there is another God besides the Maker of all things." — **Trypho** in *Dial.* 50; *Opp.* **2**, 162 E. "I will endeavor to persuade you who understand the Scriptures, that there is and is said to be another god and lord BENEATH the MAKER OF ALL THINGS, one who is also called an angel." — *Dial.* 56; *Opp.* **2**, 178 C. "If I could not show you from the Scriptures that one of those three [**Gen. 18**, 2] is a god and is called an angel, . . . it might be reasonable for you to think him, as your whole nation thinks, the God who existed BEFORE CREATION OF THE WORLD." — *Dial.* 56; *Opp.* **2**, 180 D E. "I will endeavor to persuade you that this being who is said to have appeared to Abraham, to Jacob, and to Moses, and is termed god, is a different one from the GOD WHO MADE ALL THINGS." — *Dial.* 56; *Opp.* **2**, 182 E.

"Begin and explain to us how this god, who appeared to Abraham, and who is a SERVANT to God the MAKER OF ALL THINGS, being born of a virgin, became, as you have alleged, a human being, similar in suffering to others." — **Trypho** in *Dial.* 57; *Opp.* **2**, 190 E A. "This [being] called a god, who appeared to the patriarchs, is called also angel and lord, so that from these [appellations] you may recognize him as SERVANT to the FATHER OF ALL THINGS." — *Dial.* 58; *Opp.* **2**, 192 C D. "It is necessary that I explain to you the words which announce how there appeared to him flying from his brother Esau this being who was angel and god and lord, and who appeared in the form of a man to Abraham, and in the form of a mortal wrestling with Jacob." — *Dial.* 58; *Opp.* **2**, 194 E. "Bear with me, I said, while I show you from the book of Exodus how this same [being] angel and god and lord and man and mortal, who appeared to Abraham and Jacob, appeared in a flame of fire from a bush to, or associated with, Moses." — *Dial.* 59; *Opp.* **2**, 196 C D. "If, O friends, it was an angel and god at the same time who appeared to Moses, as has been shown you by the previously written words, the god who spoke to Moses, will not be the MAKER OF ALL THINGS . . . but [will be] he who was shown you to have appeared to Abraham and to Jacob: a SERVANT to the will of the MAKER OF ALL THINGS." — *Dial.* 60; *Opp.* **2**, 198 A B. The Scripture, "by saying that an angel of the Lord appeared to Moses, and afterwards indicating that it was the Lord him-

This is the view to which he there gives prominence. It seems to have been adopted by him after his *Apology* was written, though at what date we can only conjecture, and this conjecture will doubtless vary according to the date assigned to the *Dialogue*.

The *Dialogue*, though professedly a discussion with a Jew, must have been written with expectation of finding its readers chiefly or wholly among Gentiles.

An examination of writers coeval with, or slightly later than Justin may, by showing us the greater or less foothold which this view had attained, give us more grounds for determining its date. There are probably eight or nine such writers who have left us one, or more than one, work each.

We will first consider three of these who shared more or less nearly Justin's view of a subordinate deity. Each (cp. p. 75) addressed a work to heathens, or to a heathen, and in these works neither the word Jesus nor the word Christ can be found.[11] The only cause for this omission which would not be equally applicable to preceding and subsequent writers[12] is as follows. The reign of Marcus Antoninus was very reactionary. Judaism, since the war under Hadrian, had almost lost its influence in Europe, and heathens who felt that they were now dealing chiefly with Christianity laid great stress on the argu-

---

self who was also a god, points out the same [being] whom it indicates by many other statements as a SERVANT to the (GOD OVER THE WORLD." — *Dial.* 60; *Opp.* **2**, 200 A. "I will give you another testimony ... from the Scriptures that originally, prior to all his creations, God produced from himself a certain reasoning power which is called by the holy spirit the glory of the Lord, but sometimes son, sometimes wisdom, sometimes god, sometimes lord and logos, and sometimes he calls himself chief commander, when appearing in form of a mortal to Joshua, son of Nun. For he has all these appellations because of serving his Father's will and being born by the will of the Father." — *Dial.* 61; *Opp.* **2**, 200 A – 202 B. See also cc. 68, 73, 86, 87, 113, 115, 126, [bis], 127, 128 [bis], 129; *Opp.* **2**, pp. 332 C, 246 D, 294 A B, 298 C, 376 D, 384 B, 420 D, 422 C, 424 C D, 426 A B C, 428 E. It is possible that Justin had found difficulty in maintaining the position taken in his *Apology*, that the Being mentioned in the Old Testament was simply an angel. He needed to account for the application to that being of the term God, and took this method of doing it. Compare note 32.

[11] Athenagoras, besides his *Apology* addressed to the heathen emperors, wrote a work on the resurrection. The above remark is not applicable to this latter work.

[12] Inability to quote the Gospels against heathens as a trustworthy record of their Master's life, would not at this date have been more of an impediment than it was previously and subsequently.

ment from antiquity. The emperor lent his aid to foster the veneration for what was ancient. It was through observance of Ancient Customs, he said, that Rome would be perpetuated;[13] atrocious barbarity, misnamed Ancient Discipline for the legions, received his commendation.[14]

Christians in meeting this tendency were tempted to ignore the Master who had lived, taught, and died in the days of Tiberius. Such a teacher would have been less ancient than most heathen ones. Some preferred to concentrate attention on the idea developed in controversy with the Gnostics, that their leader was an angel or subordinate god. In their statements of this it is noteworthy that although one of their number, Theophilus, quotes from the Old Testament passages in which the term God is plainly applied to the being whom they ALLEGE as subordinate, yet they in their own persons almost never apply that term to him.[15]

Another yet more noteworthy circumstance is that while treating creation as almost exclusively the work of this subordinate being they never apply to him the term Creator, but restrict it exclusively to the Supreme Being under whom he acted.

We will now attend to the views of these writers on the subject in question. **Theophilus** addressed a work to his heathen friend Autolycus. He instructs him that the Supreme Being dwelt from eternity, having inside of him his reason or creative power; that before creating the world he, without divest-

---

[13] See *Judaism*, p. 36 n.
[14] See *Judaism*, p. 361 n.
[15] **Theophilus** once speaks (2, 22; *Opp.* p. 120 C) of the Logos as "being God." **Athenagoras** applies to the Son (*Supplicat.* 10; *Opp.* p. 48 A) the term God. The word "God," if dropped out, would cause no break in the connection, and therefore its interpolation after the doctrine became more thoroughly established is possible, though scarcely, I think, probable.

Tatian speaks (*Orat.* 13; *Opp.* p. 62, al. 153 A) of "the [suffering] Deity." If the word "suffering" be spurious, Tatian was speaking of the Supreme Being. If it be genuine, he spoke of the subordinate deity. There is no difficulty in regarding him as having held the belief expressed in the passage. There is, however, great difficulty in supposing that he, or any fellow Christians of his era who held it, would have CALLED ATTENTION of heathens to the fact that one whom they regarded as a deity had been put to death by Roman soldiers. I mistrust that, after Tatian became a Gnostic, some member of the Orthodox party may, as a criticism on his change of views, have added the word "suffering," and that in course of time it crept into the text.

ing himself of reason, emitted his reason,[16] constituting it a distinct being. Through this "subordinate workman" he created all things save man. When man was to be created he said, " Let us make man." [17]

Tatian, the disciple of Justin Martyr, became eventually a Gnostic. Before becoming so he wrote his *Address to Greeks*. In it he maintains the unity of the Supreme Being [18] and represents the Logos as having received a separate existence before the creation, the work of which devolved on him.[19]

---

[16] The term Logos was used sometimes as identical with reason, sometimes with utterance, sometimes with fiat or executive energy. Compare *Judaism*, p. 358.

[17] "God, having his reason dwelling within him, gave it existence eliminating it with his own wisdom before [creation of] all things. He had this reason [or Logos] as a SUBORDINATE WORKMAN of the things produced by him, and he made all things through him." — **Theophilus**, *ad Autol.* **2**, 10; *Opp.* pp. 78 – 80 B C.

"God, by saying [**Gen. 1**, 26] '*Let us make man in our image and similitude*,' indicates first the dignity of man ; for God having made all [other] things by his Logos and having esteemed all [other] things a side matter, deems only what was immortal [namely] the making of man a work worthy of [his own] hands." — *Ad Autol.* **2**, 18; *Opp.* 108 C D. Compare Sibyl. Orac. **8**, 265, cited on p. 177. Theophilus had previously explained (**1**, 4) that the universe was made on man's account.

"For before anything came into existence [God] had this [Logos] as a counsellor, it being HIS OWN MIND AND THOUGHTFULNESS. But, when God wished to make what he had resolved, he brought into existence outside of himself this Logos, the first-born of the whole creation, he himself not being [thereby] emptied of reason." — *Ad Autol.* **2**, 22; *Opp.* 118 B.

[18] "Our God did not originate in time, being alone without beginning, and he himself being the beginning of all things." — *Orat. ad Græcos*, 4; *Opp.* p. 18 C.

"The Master of all things being himself the substance of the universe was, before the creation, ALONE. . . . With him existed through his reasoning power the Reason [or Logos] which was in him. By the will of his simple (*or* uncompounded) nature, the Logos sprung forth. But the Logos (*or* utterance of God), not going forth void (compare Is. **55**, 11), becomes the first-born of the Father. This Logos we know as the beginning of the world." — *Orat.* 5; *Opp.* 22 A – 24 B. Tatian tries, not very intelligibly, to explain the process by which the Logos was separated from the Father.

[19] "The Logos proceeding from the [reasoning] power of the Father did not render the Being who begot him void of reason, even as I speak and you hear, but I who address you do not, by the transmission of my utterance (Logos), become void of (Logos) speech. . . . The Logos, being begotten in the beginning, begot in turn our world." — *Orat.* 5; *Opp.* p. 26 B C. "The heavenly Logos, a spirit produced from the Father, and the (Logos) utterance of his rational power, in imitation of the Father who begot him, made man an image of immortality." — *Orat.* 7; *Opp.* p. 30 B C.

Athenagoras is very emphatic in affirming but one Supreme Being,[20] and in alleging the impossibility of two or more un-originated Gods,[21] yet he treats the Son as identical with the Logos, and as the instrument of creation.[22]

The **author of the Clementines**, who belongs to the time of Marcus Antoninus, condemns explicitly the deification of Jesus,[23]

[20] "God, the Maker of the world, was from the beginning One and Alone." — *Supplicat.* (or *Legat.*) 8; *Opp.* p. 42 C, edit. Otto. Compare 4, *Opp.* 20 B. "God is unoriginated, incapable of suffering and invisible, and therefore not compounded of parts." — *Supplicat.* 8; *Opp.* p. 38 D.

[21] "See as follows, that God, the Creator of this universe, was from the beginning [but] One, so that you may have the argument for our faith. If from the beginning there were two or more Gods, either they were in one and the same place or each in his own place. In one and the same place they could not be, not even if the Gods were similar, but because [also] unoriginated beings are not similar. Originated things [may be] similar to the pattern [after which they are made], but the unoriginated are dissimilar, being neither [produced from] any one nor after [the pattern of] any one." — *Supplicat.* 8; *Opp.* pp. 36-38 B C. "But the Maker of the world is above created things, supervising the world by his foresight for these [created things]. What place will there be for the other god or the remaining ones? not in the world, for it belongs to another; nor beyond the world, since above it is God the Maker of the world." — *Supplicat.* 8; *Opp.* pp. 38-40 D A.

[22] "It has been sufficiently shown by me that we are not atheists, believing as we do in one God, unborn, eternal, invisible, incapable of suffering, incomprehensible, not to be contained [by any locality], apprehended by the mind only and the reason, surrounded by light and splendor and spirit and power beyond narration, by whom the universe was produced through his Logos and [by whom] it has been adorned and is preserved.

"We understand also [that there is] a Son of God, and let no one deem it ridiculous in me [to say] that God has a son. For we do not think concerning God the Father, or concerning his son, after the fashion of your poets' fables, who represent the gods as in no wise better than men. But the Son of God is the utterance (Logos) of the Father as regards his thought and energy. For according to him and through him all things were brought into being, the Father and the Son being [in their purposes] one; the Son being in the Father and the Father in the Son, through the oneness and efficacy of [their] spirit. The Son of God [being] the intelligence and the utterance (Logos) of the Father." — *Supplicat.* 10; *Opp.* pp. 44 B-46 C.

[23] "Our Lord . . . did not proclaim himself God. He justly blessed him who called him Son of that God who perfected the beauty of the universe. . . . The Father is unborn; the Son is born. The born cannot compare with the unborn or self-born." — **Homily, 16,** 15, 16. "Denial of him (the One God) is for a professed Monotheist to allege until death another God, whether [as the Gnostics?] a greater, or [as those who deify Jesus?] a less." — **Homily, 3,** 7. The writer adds (see *Judaism,* p. 359) that eternal punishment awaited any one who should do this.

which he regards as introduced by converts from heathenism who yet clung to a multiplicity of gods.[24]

Hermias wrote a very short work [25] pointing out the inconsistencies of heathen teachers. It contains no allusion to the deification of Jesus, but its omission of this and other subjects hardly furnishes any ground for determining the author's views concerning them.

The **De Monarchia** has for a title the watchword of those Christians who utterly rejected the deification of Jesus. It seems impossible that its writer can have been a believer in that doctrine.

The **Oratio ad Græcos** is a simple and brief statement [26] by some convert from heathenism of the reasons for his change. These reasons are moral ones, a contrast being drawn between the views and conduct of heathens and of Christians. The tone of his argument renders it at least improbable that he sided with those who sought to win respect for Jesus by representing him as a pre-existent God.[27]

The **Cohortatio ad Græcos** is a much longer work [28] than either of the preceding. Had the writer regarded Jesus as a pre-existent deity the view could not have escaped mention in his systematic and elaborate statement of the differences in date and character between heathen and Christian views as to the Being or Beings whom they recognized as God. It may be assumed with certainty from his direct statement [29] and

---

[24] See quotations in *Judaism*, Ch. XI. note 60.

[25] The work with its Latin translation covers five folio pages in Maran's edition of Justin.

[26] The work covers pages 2 – 13 in Otto's (8vo) edition of Justin, each alternate page being occupied with a Latin translation and part of every page with notes.

[27] In ch. 5 (p. 11 C) Otto has retained a translation of Logos which seems to me the true one as meaning the divine teachings. A little further on the writer speaks of the divine teaching (Logos) as our supporter, but in this case Otto, following earlier editors, has retained in his translation the word Logos, understanding by it apparently a being. The connection is, I think, against such interpretation.

[28] It and its translation cover pages 12 – 111 in Otto's (8vo) edition of Justin.

[29] "No one existed earlier than God who could give Him a name, nor did He think it necessary to affix a name to himself, being one and alone, as He testifies through his own prophets, saying : 'I was God originally, and afterwards, and beside me there is no other.'" — **Cohortatio ad Græcos,** 21 ; Justin, *Opp.* **1,** 62 C. The quotation is from Isaiah **44,** 6.

from the whole of his argument, that he did not regard Jesus as a god either subordinate or in any way whatever.

The **Epistle to Diognetus** has been deferred to the last as being the latest of the works here quoted, and as belonging in all probability to a subsequent century. The writer is obviously a person of literary culture, who penned his work at a time when, or else in a locality where, he did not feel himself personally in danger. He writes with a self-confidence which states, rather than argues, and assumes that his reader Diognetus, who seems to have been an inquirer concerning monotheism, would scarcely need argument in order to share his conclusions. The document is marked by none of the almost tediously diffuse statement and argument which we find in Justin. Its writer seems rather to multiply short affirmations, as if thereby to emphasize his views, or to overpower his reader. This is less striking in his portraiture of the Supreme Being [30] than in his account of the Christians,[31] and of the embassy sent to man.[32]

---

[30] "For God the Master and Artificer of the universe, who made all things and arranged them in order, not only was a friend of man but very patient. This indeed he always is and will be, excellent and good and without anger and truthful ; and He only is good. Meditating a great and unuttered conception which he communicated to his only Son, so long as he continued to keep secret his wise counsel he seemed to disregard and neglect us, but when he revealed and made manifest through his beloved Son the things prepared from the beginning, he enabled us at [one and] the same time to partake of his benefits and to see [his principle of action]."— **Epistle to Diognetus**, 8 ; Justin, *Opp.* **2**, 490 C D.

[31] Epistle to Diognetus, cc. 4 – 6 ; Justin, *Opp.* **2**, 476 – 482.

[32] "God who is truly the All-ruler, the All-creator and Invisible, himself placed the Truth from heaven and his holy and uncomprehended Logos in men and established it in their hearts, not as any one might think probable, by sending to men some servant or angel, or any ruler of those who supervise earthly affairs, or one of those entrusted with the arrangement of things in heaven, but the artificer and artisan of the universe, THROUGH WHOM He created the heavens, BY WHOM he restricted the sea to its own bounds, whose secret [orders] all constituents [of the universe] faithfully obey, from whom they have received [injunctions] to guard the measure of each day's course, whom the moon obeys when he commands her to appear by night, whom the stars obey, following the course of the moon, by whom ALL THINGS are arranged and limited, and to whom they are subordinated : the heavens and the things in the heavens ; the earth and the things in the earth ; the sea and the things in the sea ; the fire, the air, the abyss, the things on high, those in the depths and the things between. This being He sent to them. Did he send him, as some man might think, to tyrannize, to cause fear and to ter-

Possibly the self-confidence of the writer may be due to personal peculiarities or to the locality where he lived, but it is more probable that he lived in the third century, and that when he wrote, Christians, instead of struggling for existence, found themselves able to assume a loftier tone. An additional reason for this view is placed in the note.[33] I suppose him to have written in the third century.

A summary of the case stands as follows. The writings of **Justin Martyr** render probable that in his mind the belief took root after publication of his first *Apology* and before writing the *Dialogue*, that is, after A. D. 150, a view corroborated by his evident mistrust of his own arguments in the latter work.[34]

The other writings which we have examined do not militate against, but rather favor, the same conclusion. Four of them ignore the doctrine: one writer condemns it. Three who teach it do not agree in their expositions of it, while their disuse of the words Jesus and Christ indicates that they wrote under some then existing bias. Had the doctrine originated earlier than the assigned date it would have been less ignored, and there would have been more unanimity among its supporters.[35]

---

rify? By no means, but in mildness and gentleness. As a king sending a royal son He sent him; He sent him as a god; He sent him as to men; as purposing to save He sent him; as desiring to persuade, not to compel, for there is no violence with God. He sent as if inviting, not prosecuting. He sent as one who loves, not who judges. . . . For who among men, before his coming, understood what God is!" — **Epistle to Diognetus**, 7, 8; Justin, *Opp.* 2, 484 – 488.

[33] In the third century the word Economy οἰκονομία was used by believers in the deity of Christ, or by some of them to designate what might be termed a household arrangement, by which the Deity had delegated, for a time at least, certain of his former cares and duties to the Son. The word, though frequently occurring in writers of the second century (Justin Martyr, *Dial.* 45, 67, 87, 103, 107, 120, 141; *Opp.* pp. 144 A, 224 E, 300 A, 346 A, 360 E, 398 B, 460 A; Theophilus, *ad Autol.* 2, 12, 15, 29; *Opp.* pp. 88 B, 102 A, 138 B; Tatian, *Orat.* 5; *Opp.* p. 24 B; Athenagoras, *Supplicat.* 21; *Opp.* p. 102 D) bears in no case, I think, this meaning. The Epistle to Diognetus (8; Just. *Opp.* p. 495 D), however, uses the adverb "economically" in a seemingly similar sense. Compare in the same work (7; Just. *Opp.* p. 484 B) the apparently vague use of ECONOMY.

[34] Justin in his deification of Jesus evidently felt that he was not treading on sure ground. See note 2.

[35] Among those acquainted with common interpretations of the introduction to John's Gospel, especially if they have access only to the common English version of it, the question may arise whether John held any

One or two additional considerations, though not bearing on the date when Jesus was deified, may not be without interest. Justin repeatedly (see p. 52, note 7), and oftener than other writers, designates the Father as the Master-God. He also applies to Jesus the term SERVANT. He lived in a city the headquarters of slaveholding, and expected to be read by its inhabitants. How far this influenced his interpretation of the Old Testament may be a question. In such a community menial offices were thought very derogatory to the deity. **Tertullian** says concerning God shutting the door of the Ark after Noah, which he includes, however, with certain other non-menial acts : " These things would not be credible concerning the Son of God unless written; perhaps they would not be credible concerning the Father, even if they were written." [36]

It will further be noticed that the extracts treat merely of TWO gods. Deification of the Spirit as a distinct and third person took place in the third century, being taught in that century by two writers only. One of these, as elsewhere remarked (see *Judaism*, p. 357), treats the majority of Christians who had been horrified at the introduction of a second god, as exclaiming, You are ALREADY introducing a third one!

---

view analogous to that of Justin and other writers. The tenor of John's writings is against such interpretation of his words. To the common English reader his meaning will be plainer by substituting for Logos the word Providence, the only English term analogous in triple meaning to the Greek one. It denotes God, his agency, and some of his attributes, but prominently supervision, rather than, as Logos, reason, fiat (Ps. 33, 6), creative energy, or planning. Compare on this subject *Judaism*, p. 358, note 59. Verse 3 admits two translations, which, for the reader's convenience, are put into parallel columns.

"In the beginning Providence existed and Providence was with God and Providence [compare on p. 195, Theophilus, *ad Autol.* **2,** 22] was God [himself]. It was in the beginning with God.

| Through it all things came to being, and without it not one created thing came into existence. | Through it all things came to pass, and without it not one occurrence took place. |

And Providence (God's interposition) took a human form and dwelt among us, . . . full of favor and of truth." — **John 1,** 1–14.

The use of "he" and "him" in the Greek depends on the termination of the word referred to, and would be equally necessary in referring to the word οἶκος, house, as in referring to an intelligent being.

If πάντα in verse 3 were preceded by the article τά, there would be more probability that John spoke of creation. As the text stands there is equal or greater probability that he was not thinking of it. Compare in Lactantius, **7,** 18, the use of γενομένοις as quoted from Hermes.

[36] Tertullian, *adv. Prax.* 16, p. 649 A, edit. Rigault.

The fabrication which the Christians circulated and quoted as a work of Hermes, indicates the views which many of them wished to spread. **Lactantius** says: "Hermes, in that book which is inscribed The Perfect (*or* Final) Discourse, uses these words: 'The Lord and Maker of all things, whom we are accustomed to call God, when He made a SECOND god; . . . when He made this one, first and only, and sole, [and when] he [the created being] appeared to him excellent and most filled with all good things, He consecrated him and loved him exceedingly as his peculiar child.'" [87]

NOTE N.

FIRST TWO CHAPTERS OF MATTHEW.

SOME Hebrew manuscripts of Matthew omitted the first two chapters. The narrative which they contain, moreover, is not easy to reconcile with that in the first two chapters of Luke,[1] and the name Jesus Christ without the article intervening (on which compare pp. 60, 61) is not to be found in the undoubted portions of Matthew. This raises the question whether they were prefixed to **Matthew's Gospel** by himself or by another. The question has been argued by more than one writer.[2] The chief object of the present Note is to bring out by its typography what these chapters profess to be. The typography commonly used fails to give it due prominence.

---

[87] Lactantius, *Div. Inst.* **4**, 6.

[1] The two chapters prefixed to Matthew represent that when Jesus was born wise men from the East came to Jerusalem (**2**, 1, 2); that they communicated with Herod before they had seen the child, and were warned by God that they should not communicate with him again. Herod sought the child's destruction, which was prevented by its parents taking it to Egypt, where they remained until Herod's death, after which they did not go (**2**, 22) to their former home, but turned aside into Galilee, and dwelt in a city called Nazareth.
According to **Luke** Nazareth was the home of Joseph and Mary. They were merely visiting (Luke **2**, 4, 5) in Bethlehem. After the child's birth they went openly into the temple and afterwards returned (**2**, 39) "to their own city Nazareth."

[2] See Norton's *Genuineness*, **1**, App. p. liii; abridged edit. p. 431.

BOOK OF

THE BIRTH OF JESUS CHRIST,

SON OF DAVID, SON OF ABRAHAM.

Abraham was the father of Isaac; and Isaac of Jacob; and Jacob of Judah and his brothers; and Judah was the father of Pharez and Zarah, by Tamar; and Pharez was the father of Hezron; and Hezron of Aram; and Aram of Aminadab; and Aminadab of Nashon; and Nashon of Salmon; and Salmon was the father of Boaz, by Rahab; and Boaz was the father of Obed, by Ruth; and Obed was the father of Jesse; and Jesse of David the king.

And David the king was the father of Solomon, by the wife of Uriah; and Solomon was the father of Rehoboam; and Rehoboam of Abiah; and Abiah of Asa; and Asa of Jehoshaphat; and Jehoshaphat of Jehoram; and Jehoram of Uzziah; and Uzziah of Jotham; and Jotham of Ahaz; and Ahaz of Hezekiah; and Hezekiah of Ma-

nasseh; and Manasseh of Amon; and Amon of Josiah; and Josiah was the father of Jeconiah and his brothers, at the time of the removal to Babylon.

And after the removal to Babylon, Jeconiah was the father of Salathiel; and Salathiel of Zerubbabel; and Zerubbabel of Abiud; and Abiud of Eliakim; and Eliakim of Azor; and Azor of Zadok; and Zadok of Achim; and Achim of Eliud; and Eliud of Eleazar; and Eleazar of Matthan; and Matthan of Jacob; and Jacob was the father of Joseph, the husband of Mary, of whom was born Jesus, who is called Christ.

So all the generations from Abraham to David were fourteen generations; from David till the removal to Babylon, fourteen generations; and from the removal to Babylon until Christ, fourteen generations.

Now **THE BIRTH OF JESUS CHRIST** took place as follows: While his mother Mary was betrothed to Joseph, before they lived together, she was found to be with child by the Holy Spirit. Joseph, her husband, being a just man and not wishing to expose her to shame, purposed to put her away privately. While he was considering this, lo an angel of the Lord appeared to him in a dream, saying, Do not fear to take Mary as thy wife [etc., to the close of Ch. 2].

NOTE O.
PUBLICATION OF MARK'S GOSPEL.

CHRISTIAN tradition says that Mark at Rome committed to writing what Peter had taught concerning the history of Jesus, and that afterwards, going to Alexandria, he published his Gospel in that city.[1] Two circumstances harmonize sufficiently with this statement to increase somewhat its probability.

1. The Gospel of Mark terminates,[2] as already said, rather abruptly with verse 8 of chapter **16**. This accords at least with the supposition of an interruption to his labors by the death of Peter or by the persecution of the Christians.

2. Three or four years later, when Vespasian was at Alexandria, aiming at imperial power, some of his adherents who had already perhaps tried to make him the subject of proph-

---

[1] **Irenæus** says: "After the death of these (Peter and Paul), Mark, the disciple and INTERPRETER of Peter, delivered to us in writing the things that had been preached by Peter."— *Cont. Hæres.* 3, 1, 1; *Opp.* 1, 423. Papias states: "The elder said this: 'Mark being the INTERPRETER of Peter, wrote WHAT HE REMEMBERED.'"— **Papias** quoted by **Eusebius**, *Ecc. Hist.* 3, 39. **Jerome** says: "Mark ... wrote a short Gospel according to what he had heard related by Peter ... taking the Gospel which he himself had composed, he went to Egypt, and at Alexandria founded a church of great note."— *De Vir. Illust.* 8; *Opp.* 2, 841–843, edit. Vallarsius; Lardner's trans.

[2] The subsequent verses, 9–20 (quoted in Ch. XI. note 10), "are not found in the Vatican manuscript. In the Codex Stephani η after the eighth verse, it is said, *The following also is extant*, which words precede a short conclusion undoubtedly spurious, and then come the words, *This also is extant;* after which follow the twelve verses in question. In more than forty other manuscripts they are accompanied by various remarks, to the effect 'that they were wanting in some, but found in the ancient copies'; 'that they were in many copies'; 'that they had been considered spurious, and were wanting in most copies'; 'that they were not in the more accurate copies'; and, on the other hand, 'that they were generally in accurate copies.' [The Sinaitic MS. discovered by Tischendorf also omits the passage.]

"In the other manuscripts of the Gospels beside those mentioned, the passage in question is found without remark; and likewise in all the ancient versions, with the exception of the Armenian, in the manuscripts of which, as appears, it is either omitted or marked as of doubtful credit, and likewise of the copy of an Arabic version preserved in the Vatican Library.

"The nineteenth verse is distinctly quoted by Irenæus as from the Gospel of Mark; and the passage in question appears to have been recog-

ecy,[3] undertook yet further to strengthen confidence in him by a couple of fictitious miracles, borrowed evidently from our Gospel narratives, or from Christian teaching concerning Christ. John's Gospel was not yet written. One of these miracles,[4] that of restoring sight after spitting on the eyes, is not mentioned in Matthew nor in Luke. It is found only in Mark, and gives plausibility to the surmise that the recent publication of Mark's Gospel may have caused discussion and suggested to Vespasian's adherents the character of the miracle which they attempted.

NOTE P.

THE BAPTISMAL FORMULA.

ANY baptisms mentioned in the New Testament were, as already stated,[1] into the name of Jesus. In the second cen-

---

nized as genuine by some other fathers.* But no part of it is quoted by Origen. According to Eusebius, almost all the copies of Mark's Gospel, including the most accurate, ended with what is now the eighth verse. Gregory of Nyssa states, that the passage was not found in the more accurate copies; and Jerome says, that it was but in few, being wanting in almost all the *Greek* manuscripts." — **Norton**, *Genuineness*, abridged edit. pp. 444 – 445; unabridged edit. Vol. **1**, App. LXX – LXXII.

[3] "Through the WHOLE EAST an ancient and uninterrupted opinion had gained thorough currency, as contained in the fates, that at that time PERSONS from Judea should obtain rule. That, as afterwards appeared from the event, was a prediction concerning a Roman commander." — **Suetonius**, *Vespas.* 4. The commander referred to is Vespasian. The plural form "*persons*" may have been due to an association of Titus with Vespasian as nominally joint emperors.

[4] "One of the common people of Alexandria, known to have a disease in his eyes, embraced the knees of the emperor, importuning with groans a remedy for his blindness. . . . Another who was diseased in the hand [compare Mark **3**, 1 – 5; Matt. **12**, 10 – 13; Luke **6**, 6 – 10] . . . entreated that he might be pressed by the foot and sole of Cæsar. Vespasian at first ridiculed the request. . . . Vespasian executed what was required of him. Immediately the hand was restored to its functions and the light of day shone again to the blind." — **Tacitus**, *Hist.* **4**, 81; Bohn's trans. According to Suetonius (*Vespas.* 7) Vespasian ANOINTED THE MAN'S EYES WITH SPITTLE. Compare Mark **8**, 23.

[1] See Ch. IV. note 22.

* Not, however, by Clement of Rome, nor Justin, who are cited as quoting it in the editions of the New Testament by Griesbach and Scholz, nor, I think, by Clement of Alexandria, who is also adduced." — *Ibid.*

tury — apparently before the deification of Jesus[2] and a full half-century before any deification of the Spirit[3] — we find a baptismal formula "in the name of the Father of the universe and Master-God, and of our Savior Jesus Christ, and of the Holy Spirit."[4]

The change of formula claims attention; and this is equally the case whether the baptismal precept (quoted on p. 49) be genuine or interpolated. In the former case we have the difficult problem of explaining non-attention to it in Apostolic times, while in the latter we need to explain the cause, or causes, which produced a change. Part of the change can be explained without difficulty. While Christians made converts only among Jews or monotheists, they felt no need of baptizing them into a belief in God, since they already believed in him. When Christianity was carried among heathens its converts were asked to confess belief in God as well as in Jesus.

Confession of belief in the Spirit admits more question as to its origin. The most probable explanation, though not Justin Martyr's,[5] is that some Christians of the second century PRIDED themselves on their alleged miraculous powers. Jesus had cautioned his Apostles against similar pride,[6] yet in the spu-

---

[2] The baptismal formula occurs in Justin's first *Apology*. On his views concerning Jesus at this date, see in preceding note pp. 191-193.

[3] No writers of the second century, and only two of the third century, namely, Tertullian and Origen, deify the Spirit as a person. Even at the close of the third century such deification must have made but little progress. The document attributed to Hermes Trismegistus, and first quoted by Lactantius, cannot be earlier than the second half of the third century. It mentions the formation of a second God, but in such a way as to exclude a third one. See Lactantius, *Div. Inst.* **4**, 6, cited at close of Note M. Also *Div. Inst.* **7**, 18, cited at close of Note K.

In the second century the author of the Clementine Homilies, as will be seen on p. 196, condemns severely those who deified any being save the Creator, but alludes to none who introduced more than one such additional.

[4] **Justin Martyr,** *Apol.* **1**, 61; *Opp.* **1**, 258 A, edit. Otto.

[5] **Justin,** after explaining (*Apol.* **1**, 61; *Opp.* **1**, 258 - 260 D, ed. Otto) that baptism was into the name of the "Father of the universe and Master-God," who had, and needed, no name, and into the name of Jesus Christ crucified under Pontius Pilate, adds (c. 61, 260 E): "into the name of the Holy Spirit, which through the prophets PREDICTED ALL THINGS CONCERNING JESUS." Belief in the Spirit seems in Justin's mind to have meant chiefly a belief in the predictions concerning Jesus which he regarded the spirit of God (the prophetic or holy spirit) as having uttered in the Old Testament. In regard to these predictions, and to prediction in general, see pp. 17, 37, 38, 72, and compare *Judaism*, pp. 345, 346.

[6] "Rejoice not, that the spirits are subject unto you; but rather rejoice, because your names are written in heaven." — **Luke 10**, 20.

rious addition to Mark's Gospel he is made apparently to encourage it.[7] This disposition of Christians[8] renders probable that baptism into the Spirit meant baptism into the possession of miraculous powers.

If we assume that the baptismal precept in Matthew (28, 19) is genuine, any explanation of its non-observance in Apostolic times is difficult and unsatisfactory.

NOTE Q.

THE MISSION OF JESUS.

§ 1. *Its main Object.*

IN the Preface Christianity is treated as a revelation. The writer supposes that this revelation was intended to give mankind a deeper assurance as to the existence and character of God and as to his relations with men, thus strengthening human sense of responsibility, encouraging human effort, and imparting to human existence the sunshine of hope and trust.

He is not unaware that large bodies of Christians hold other views as to the chief purpose of Jesus. Those who attach high importance to Church authority claim that his main object was to form an ecclesiastical organization with delegated powers.[1] In Protestant communities several active denominations hold that his main object was to make a sacrifice.[2]

---

[7] "These signs shall accompany believers : In my name shall they cast out demons ; they shall speak new languages ; they shall take up serpents ; and if they drink any deadly thing, it shall not hurt them ; they shall lay hands on the sick, and they shall recover." — **Mark 16,** 17, 18. Compare Acts of Pilate, § 15, text of Paris A.

[8] Justin tells Trypho : "From our works [of practical-monotheism] and from the δυνάμεως, MIRACULOUS POWER, consequent on them, all can understand that this [Jesus] is the new Law and the new Covenant." — **Just. Mart.** *Dial.* 11 ; *Opp.* **2,** 42 E, edit. Otto. Tertullian, with injudicious vehemence, dares the heathens to test the divinity of their gods. He is willing to stake the Christian exorcist's life on the result if he does not compel the fancied divinity to confess itself a mere demon. See Tertullian, *Apol.* 27, in *Underworld Mission,* p. 78 ; 3d ed. 74, 75.

[1] This view, transmitted from the Middle Ages, is unlikely to hold its own in communities which lay stress on individual religious responsibility.

[2] Prominent teachers of this theology allege that its chief doctrine, or

§ 2. Some Impediments to it.

At and before the Christian era many Jews expected a divine interposition in the form of a temporal ruler clothed with miraculous powers, who should establish order upon earth and facilitate, if not establish, a reign of holiness.[8] Not a few Christians retained this anticipation, and as their Master had

---

doctrines, cannot be found in the Gospels. **Archbishop Whately** says: "The Gospel which Jesus himself preached was not the same thing with the Gospel which he sent forth his Apostles to preach after his resurrection. . . . How, indeed, could our Lord, during his abode on earth, preach fully . . . his meritorious sacrifice as an atonement for sin? . . . Our Lord's discourses, therefore, while on earth, though they teach, of course, the truth, do not teach, nor could have been meant to teach, the WHOLE truth, as afterwards revealed to his disciples. They could not, indeed, even consistently with truth, have contained the main part of what the Apostles preached. . . .

"Our chief source, therefore, of instruction, as to the doctrines of the Gospel, must be in the apostolic epistles." — *Difficulties in the Writings of St. Paul*, pp. 65 – 67, 74.

Macknight says: "The chief doctrines of the gospel are more expressly asserted and more fully explained in the Epistle to the Hebrews, than in any other of the inspired writings." — *The Apostolic Epistles*, Vol. 5, p. 1.

Those who hold the foregoing view would probably, by calling themselves "Epistolary" instead of "Evangelical" Christians, convey to others a more correct idea of the ground on which they plant themselves.

This view as commonly held ignores the universe save the sandspeck on which we live. Were a human being to step outside of the solar system, not to any distant part of the universe, but to the nearest fixed star, he could not with the best of human telescopes discern the earth. Yet what is called Evangelical theology teaches, that on this sandspeck, and nowhere else in the universe, the Supreme Being found a need of being put to death, or for having a constituent part of himself put to death — whatever either expression may mean — before he could forgive his infant children who dwell there. Among the myriad millions of homes where his other children are trained, no such need arose.

[8] " . . . Then shall the mightiest kingdom
Of the Immortal King appear among men,
And a Sacred Prince shall come to hold the sceptre of the whole earth
To all ages of the time which approaches."
Sibyl. Orac. 3, 47 – 50.

"Then God will send a King from the East,
Who shall cause the whole earth to cease from wicked war,
By killing some, and administering binding oaths to others.
Nor shall he do these things by his own counsels,
But by obeying the excellent rules of the Great God."
Sibyl. Orac. 3, 652 – 656.

not fulfilled it they expected his reappearance to establish such a reign.[4]

Of course a temporal ruler, guided by God and clothed with power to crush injustice and oppression, might in the world's history more than once have demolished whatever obstructed open allegiance to God or the improvement consequent thereon. Probably such interposition would have diminished human sense of responsibility and human efforts, nor would mankind have learned the lessons which experience has taught them. It is plain at least that divine interposition has addressed only the individual conscience. Wherever correct views of God have depended for maintenance on supporters too few, too disunited or unfaithful, these views have been overpowered and civilization has retrograded or been driven out. This happened to Greek civilization — the child of monotheism — at Rome[5] and subsequently in Asia and North Egypt, as also to its offshoot the Saracenic culture in Spain.[6] A modern era witnessed but one small locality where reasonable freedom was allowed to the utterance of Christian truth and to the advocacy of human improvement.[7]

---

[4] See Norton, *Statement of Reasons*, Appendix, Note B. Compare *Judaism*, pp. 235, 236.

[5] See *Judaism*, pp. 11-14, 369, 387, 388.

[6] The Saracenic views of God must have been less defective than the misnamed Christian ones by which in Spain they were supplanted. Compare *Judaism*, p. 370.

[7] "To Europe and mankind, in the mean time, the success of the maritime provinces was of the greatest importance. . . . Resistance to those who were controlling religious opinions by fire and sword, and trampling upon constitutional privileges, had been successfully made.

"An asylum was opened for all those, of whatever country, who fled from persecution; from persecution of whatever kind. The benefit thus accruing to mankind cannot now be properly estimated, for we cannot now feel what it is to have no refuge and no means of resistance, while men are ready to punish us for our opinions, and are making themselves inquisitors of our conduct. It is known to have been one of the severest miseries of the later Romans, that they could not escape from their government; that the world belonged to their emperors.

"It was in the Low Countries that the defenders of civil and religious liberty found shelter. It was there that they could state their complaints, publish what they conceived to be the truth, and maintain and exercise the privileges of free inquiry. These were the countries to which Locke retired, and where William the Third was formed." — **Smyth**, *Lectures on Mod. Hist.*, Lect. XII. Vol. **1**, pp. 319-320. Even in the Low Countries the execution at a somewhat earlier date of Barneveldt and the imprisonment of Grotius indicate how slow men were in learning to respect the rights of others.

At present the number of Christian countries which more or less clearly acknowledge the rights of conscience, renders very improbable that these rights can again be totally abolished. Yet many impediments affect their free exercise.

In hereditary monarchies the character of the king and his surrounders may hinder growth.

Monarchical system excessively carried out may, even under a good sovereign, impede progress. The author has elsewhere quoted (*Judaism*, p. 367) the remark of an old philanthropist living under one of the most liberal monarchies of continental Europe ; that those in authority were sure to oppose efforts for improving society unless they themselves had been previously consulted and their approbation obtained.

Privileged classes, whether ecclesiastical or secular, may hinder not only growth of correct views touching God, but their application to human welfare. Even if the sentiment of such class be against existing evils there will be hesitation to commence innovations, whose limit cannot be foreseen.

In communities not qualified for self-government, though living under popular institutions, thoughtful citizens, to say nothing of the merely timid, will sometimes oppose a commendable innovation through fear of other changes which they might prove unable to hinder.

Again : War, though under exceptional circumstances a duty, is, even under conscientious commanders,[8] a severe interruption to religious development and human improvement. European standing armies absorb young men by hundreds of thousands, substituting camp influences for those of home.

False representations of Christianity by its advocates repel even yet not a few right-minded persons.

In most European monarchies the Church is more or less managed by the government. Many who identify Christianity with this organization imagine that the renunciation of

---

[8] **Archenholtz**, amid incidents, some of which might be attributed partly to generous sentiment, narrates the following : " The French, under General Mercieres, captured the Westphalian city of Bielefeld, celebrated for its linen manufacture, on which occasion the bleaching stations were plundered, though the General opposed these excesses. His conscience, however, told him that he could have acted more energetically. Therefore, in the year 1790, thirty-three years after the occurrence, he sent from Bayonne to the magistrate of Bielefeld a considerable sum of money, with the request to apportion it among the sufferers yet living, or if they were dead to appropriate the amount in some other way useful to the city." — *Geschichte des Siebenjährigen Krieges*, **1**, pp. 339, 340.

Christianity is requisite to republican institutions.[9] A generation or two may pass before this error can be unlearned.

In our own country its marvellously rapid development keeps multitudes in a state of anticipation and speculation unfavorable to thoughts of personal improvement.

Yet in spite of impediments those views of God for which Christianity furnished needed evidence have been taking deeper hold among mankind, even among many who have imbibed them without knowing the extent of their indebtedness to Christianity. Since the rights of conscience have been more acknowledged, the application of religious truth has been more easy and human progress more rapid. Many know but little of what was tolerated within a century.

In France, prior to the Revolution of 1793, the punishment of "Wheeling"[10] even for moderate offences had been rendered so atrocious that it would seem prompted by a conclave of demons.[11] The Revolution abolished it and similar barbarities in most French-speaking countries.

In Germany this mode of punishment[12] was retained in a

---

[9] This must not be confounded with the view of those who wish merely to dissolve connection between Church and State, a step from which some liberalists shrink. Compare in *Judaism*, note on pp. 369, 370.

[10] In English allusions to this punishment "Wheeling" is almost universally mistranslated "breaking on the wheel." Mrs. Hemans has been misled by such phraseology into representing the wife of Rudolph Von der Wart (Hemans's *Poetical Works*, 2, p. 101) as remaining by her husband during the hours when he was ON THE WHEEL.

The punishment of Wheeling was usually executed by fastening the subject to the ground and breaking his limbs either with a common wagon-wheel, or with one made for the purpose. The wheel seen by the writer at Freiburg, Switzerland, was much smaller than a wagon-wheel; was provided on one side with handles, and on the other side, for perhaps a fourth or a third of its circumference, with a sharpened iron or steel rim to facilitate breaking the limbs. His guide had seen a man executed with it in 1823.

[11] In France, though the term WHEELING was retained, the punishment was inflicted with an iron club, the victim being stretched in an iron frame. The directions to the executioner, which the author read many years ago, are here given from memory. These were: to begin with the left arm, commencing at the wrist; then with the left leg; then, after some delay, with the right leg, and then with the right arm. He was to mangle each wrist, elbow, ankle, and knee-joint with two blows, and the intervening portion of each limb with a specified number, not less, if memory serve me, than five or six. The executioner was further directed not to desist because of cries from the condemned person.

[12] In Germany, as I was informed by a Berlin lawyer, two forms of condemnation were recognized: wheeling FROM ABOVE DOWNWARDS, and

less brutal form so late, at least, as A. D. 1841, when a man was "wheeled to death in Prussia,"[13] at a spot southwest of Koenigsberg on the sea-coast.

In the United States burning to death as a LEGAL punishment must have been retained in a state so far northward as New Jersey until the middle of the last century,[14] while in some of the more Southern States this mode of punishment was in force so late at least as the second quarter of the present one.[15]

FROM BELOW UPWARDS. In the former case the first blow fell on the chest, and was expected to kill the victim, the limbs being afterwards broken for form's sake; in the latter case the limbs were first broken and the *coup de grace*, or finishing stroke, given afterwards, if at all.

[13] The following is extracted from p. 87 of a German newspaper furnished me by the **Burgomeister of Frauenburg**. The title of the paper does not appear on the slip sent me. "Braunsberg, July 7, 1841. This morning at half past six the death penalty of wheeling from below [upwards] was executed on the robber and murderer Rudolph Kühnapfel, ... in the vicinity of the village Nartz, near Frauenburg, in presence of a great multitude." The bracketed word is supplied from a different paper. I remember an extract from yet another paper which stated that Kühnapfel was ten minutes in dying. I suppose that his crime may have been treated as constructive parricide. The Bishop of Ermeland whom he murdered may have been regarded as his spiritual father. I was told that an attempt to murder the king could be punished in the same way, perhaps on the ground that he was the political father of his people, yet in aggravated cases the punishment may have been adjudged without stretching the meaning of language.

[14] The author has learned from one of his neighbors that when the uncle of that neighbor's father was killed in New Jersey by a slave, the slave was legally executed by burning. The father was born in 1750. Whether the execution took place before or after that date is unknown to his informant.

[15] **W. C. Bryant** informed me that the execution in South Carolina of a negro woman by burning in the year 1820, is mentioned by Stroud in his *Slave Laws*. He omitted to mention the page.

An intelligent colored man now resident in Meadville, and born he says in 1826 or 1827, tells the author that during his childhood his grandmother witnessed a similar execution of a man near Fayetteville, N. C. He remembers his grandmother's statement that the man (a white one he thinks) petitioned to have oil put upon the fagots.

The author himself distinctly recollects reading in early life the newspaper account of a similar execution in South Carolina, an account recollected also by one of his older relatives. The newspaper said that the driest of fagots had been procured in order to diminish the pain of execution. As a Charleston lady, with whom he conversed in 1839 at Geneva in Switzerland, was unaware of the execution, and as he has had a Charleston paper searched ineffectually for its record, he supposes it to have occurred in the interior of the State. Lest, moreover, the accuracy of his

The late Henry Colman of Massachusetts told me that he had in early life seen human beings carried down State Street, Boston, to be branded and to have their ears slit.[16]

The exigencies of war may sometimes be thought to palliate harsh treatment; but corporal punishment in the peace establishment of Frederick the Second equalled that of the most barbarous nations.[17]

If we consider that more than eighteen centuries ago Tiberius, educated partly by the monotheistic influences of Asia Minor, abolished corporal punishment,[18] it seems as if the world had received a discouraging back-set. But it is undoubtedly further advanced than in his time, for his views would

---

memory should be suspected, he will state some of the circumstances which corroborate it. He remembers conversing on the subject with his father, who expressed his opinion that it was in some States the specified form of punishment for a slave who killed his master. Also in one of his own letters to his father, dated Jan. 12, 1841, is the following : " In Prussia the punishment of the Wheel is still in use for persons who have killed near relations. . . . In Greece I see from the papers that the torture still exists. Whether we have so far got rid of such abominations in our own country as to have formally abolished the law in South Carolina ordaining burning to death as the punishment of a slave who kills his master, I do not know. I remember but one instance of such an execution, but that was one too many."

My father's opinion that the form of punishment was specified by law, cannot have been true of South Carolina. The late **W. C. Bryant** procured for me information taken from Stroud's *Slave Laws*, that in certain cases the *method* of punishment was left to the discretion of three magistrates.

[16] I learn from **Judge Hoar** that "branding and cropping the ears were abolished as punishments in Massachusetts, in 1805 ; whipping in 1826."

[17] "If the soldier committed a [military ?] crime he had to run the gantlet through a lane of two hundred, or rather to walk it. Six times was the least, thirty-six the highest number of these painful perambulations. The last-mentioned punishment was called ' FOR LIFE AND DEATH,' and was divided into three days, and on the last day the wrong-doer's coffin was brought with him on the parade." — **Archenholtz**, *Kleine Hist. Schriften*, **1**, pp. 27, 28. To prevent any acceleration of pace by the condemned man, a soldier with reversed musket under his arm preceded him so that he could not quicken his pace without running on the bayonet. This punishment his comrades must sometimes have been compelled to execute on one from whom they had received kindness and whom they would gladly have spared.

"The highest crime was breach of subordination. Even for the slightest faults of this kind [a soldier] was confronted by running the gantlet, or by the bullet. Whoever with weapon in hand carried his fault to practical acts was wheeled alive." — *Ibid.* p. 28.

[18] See Tac. *An.* **4**, 6, quoted in *Judaism*, p. 506.

now find a general sympathy which they then, in Europe at least, failed to receive. We must remember, however, that the existence of mankind on the earth has probably little more than begun. One cycle of the earth's motion requires more than a thousand centuries.[19] There must be stellar cycles for which a million centuries would be but a fraction of the required time. The hand which arranged these movements will probably permit a few of them to be studied before human existence shall cease on earth. The lesson learned in eighteen centuries will at some future day seem a brief one.

The Pagan nations of our own time have as yet come in contact chiefly with the worst traits of Christian communities. They have seen wars[20] by Christians for selfish ends, and have not found models of virtue in the crews of ships visiting their shores. Patience will be requisite that evil lessons may be unlearned, and that Christianity may appear a religion of virtue and of hope.

NOTE R.

THE MINISTRY.

In the first Christian congregations the office of teaching was not restricted to any one individual.[1] Several shared in

---

[19] "The perihelion . . . of the earth's orbit accomplishes its revolution in one hundred and eleven thousand years." — **Mitchell,** *Planetary and Stellar Worlds,* p. 177.

[20] Our own country during a century of independent existence has waged but two foreign wars. One of these would not have occurred save for a privileged class no longer existing, who wished to extend the area of that institution, Slavery, on which their privileges were based.

[1] "He sent to Ephesus, and called the ELDERS of the church." — **Acts 20,** 17. "Take heed . . . to all the flock over the which the Holy Spirit hath made you ἐπισκόπους, BISHOPS [i. e. overseers]." — **Acts 20,** 28. The word overseers in the common version is the same which is elsewhere translated bishops. "For this cause left I thee in Crete, that thou shouldest . . . ordain ELDERS in every city. . . . For a BISHOP must be blameless." — **Titus 1,** 5, 7. "Paul . . . to all the consecrated in Philippi with the bishops and deacons." — **Philip. 1,** 1. "If a man desire the office of a bishop, he desireth a good work." — **1 Tim. 3,** 1. "Likewise must the deacons be grave, not double-tongued."—**1 Tim. 3,** 8.

It will be noticed that in the last two instances the two classes of offi-

it. This plan was attended by some difficulties, to avoid which the custom was introduced of having but one teacher in each congregation. The latter plan has prevailed in most Protestant denominations, and has been so nearly universal that Christianity and the ministry have in the majority of minds become identified. Many persons would be mentally unable to dissociate the two, and the value of Christianity is estimated by them according to the worth of its supposed representatives and interpreters.

The Christian ministry has undoubtedly done excellent service, and been of importance to the religious progress of mankind.[2] It is at present, however, confronted by the following obstacle. In proportion as mankind become attentive to their moral and religious improvement, it becomes more and more impossible for any one human being to meet the wants of five hundred others.[3] Those whom he addresses are, if thoughtful

---

cers recognized in a single society are bishops and deacons, the former of whom are in preceding quotations identified with elders.

At a later date **Jerome** says : "Among the ancients [i. e. the earliest Christians] bishops and presbyters were the same since the former name [that is, overseer] indicates the office, [while] the latter designates the age [of the incumbents]." — *Epist.* 69 *ad Oceanum. Opp.* **1**, col. 415 A, edit. Vallars. Again : "Therefore a presbyter is the same as a bishop, and before by prompting of the Devil rivalries took place in religious matters and people said : I am of Paul, I of Apollos, and I of Cephas, the assemblies were governed by mutual agreement of the elders. But after each one thought those whom he had baptized to be his own [disciples], not Christ's, it was determined in the whole world that one selected from the elders should be placed above the others, to whom the whole care of the assembly should pertain, and [thus that] the seeds of division should be removed." — *Comment. ad Tit.* **1**, 7 : *Opp.* **7**, Part. I. col. 694, 695, edit. Vallars.

[2] The above remark must not be understood of the ministry while, or in so far as, its discourses were in an unknown tongue. The writer remembers listening to a lecture in which was quoted a regal admonition to the Anglican clergy, telling them to dispense with laziness and write their sermons in Latin. He has not had opportunity to hunt up this admonition, but thinks that it was issued by Charles II.

The literary folly which prompted such directions existed much later in European institutions of learning. Firmness equally as good sense may have been requisite in **Dr. George Campbell** when telling his pupils that he knew no reason why he should give himself more trouble in order to render his lectures less intelligible. "I should think it unpardonable to sacrifice the profit of the students to the parade of learning ; or to waste more time in composing, to no other end I may say, but to render the composition less useful." — *Lectures on Systemat. Theol.*, near close of Lecture 1.

[3] The above-mentioned difficulty may be illustrated by supposing that

for their own improvement, growing in a variety of directions, and need aid of very different kinds in order to facilitate their progress.⁴ Even the same individual may within a brief period go through experience of different kinds and need aid in the subject of his or her thoughts rather than to have them diverted to something else.

---

in mental education a teacher were required to instruct pupils in Mathematics and Metaphysics, Astronomy and Architecture, Surgery and Civil Engineering, History and Hygiene, Jurisprudence, Ancient Languages, Natural History, and other branches of modern study. Could any one expect a satisfactory result?
⁴ Whoever studies the moral and religious wants of life will find them diversified. A business man, witnessing the various avenues for dishonesty and the disguises which screen it, will deem firmness of condemnation requisite to uphold business rectitude in the community, or to guard his own mind against indifference.
One placed so as to notice the need of encouragement and kind speech may see most call for attention to these and for illustration of the manner in which they can best be given.
A person brought up under erroneous views of religion, and who has suffered much from such views, will highly esteem the teachings which dispel error.
One engaged in study of the Scriptures will desire the suggestions or information that assist comprehension of them.
Those engaged in benevolent work see constant opportunities of good to be done; of children to be rescued from vice or suffering, and of mature persons to be aided while struggling to keep the right path. They long for teachings which may guide their efforts or call others to their aid.
Some, disheartened amid daily duties and distractions, feel the need of raising their thoughts to the Source of strength, and of finding in communion with the Father of their spirits serenity and new strength to encounter harassing cares. They need to be called away from daily occupations rather than to have them more vividly presented.
Blended, often at least, with the foregoing is a dissatisfaction due to incorrect views of life. Persons look on its avocations as interruptions rather than as aids to self-development. To this class correct views of life would be an inestimable boon.
Some have had questionings as to whether Jesus were or were not authorized to make a revelation, and to them the question may be one of painful importance. The evidence which they need must be of that kind which they are most competent to appreciate.
Others, aside perhaps from questions about the authorization of Jesus, are striving to look beyond the term of human existence here and to catch some glimpses of a future one. Considerations which may give them confidence will prove of great value.
Some are occupied in a contest with social evils. They have had friends or relatives carried to ruin, and are more intent on combating the evils of this life than on thoughts of a future one. They need in many cases wise counsel to prevent feeling from overriding judgment.

Of course many ministers could by methodical study of their congregations meet wants which now go unsupplied. Were a minister to provide a list of his parish, and to append opposite each name what he deemed the chief wants of that individual; were he also, by observation, thought, and conversation, to correct his own judgments and alter his memorandum accordingly, he would have sketched out before him an approximate map of his work. By such effort he would meet the wants of his people far more nearly than if his pulpit themes were taken from the last question mooted in theological and secular journals.

Still the difficulty cannot be ignored that only a person gifted with more than average observation and reflection, and with more than average capacity of conveying his ideas to others, can in a thoughtful congregation hope to meet even a majority of its wants. The question, therefore, arises whether the present plan of meeting such wants can be supplemented or improved.

Let us suppose a well-selected library[5] of religious and moral literature, including clear-headed discussions on the various duties of a human being to himself and his fellows, and let us suppose a portion of time set apart when the congregation should meet for silent perusal of what is best adapted to each one's wants. A preliminary need would be an Index to the topics treated in the library, unless some one member happened to be so thoroughly posted that he could point out to others where the desired reading might be found.[6]

---

[5] A suitable library ought of course to contain not merely the subjects mentioned in the preceding note, but many others not there suggested. For study of the Scriptures there should be translations, commentaries, concordances, Bible dictionaries, and other critical aids. In selecting translations it would be well to have such as were made on different plans. The rendering best suited to a scholar is by no means always that most fitted for the average reader.

Fiction on moral topics, though not to be excluded from such a library, should be admitted with the utmost caution. Miss Sedgwick's *Live and Let Live* treats one class of human duties more successfully than could be hoped for in most cases from the pulpit. But this is more than can be said for many works of fiction even when written with moral intent.

[6] In the absence of printed Indexes some one might be employed to prepare a special Index for each library, or a dozen societies might conjointly employ some skilled person to make such a work. Printed Indexes would, however, soon come into existence if their want were generally felt. In them there should be marks to distinguish brief statements from copious articles.

The time devoted to silent reading should not preclude public devotional exercises, nor yet public instruction, which, in the absence of a minister, might be supervised by one or more members of the congregation.[7]

A chief risk with such a library would be the introduction of sensational works, dignified or not by the title of religious. A similar risk exists in the pulpit, but can there less readily than in a library escape attention from thoughtful members of the congregation. Much would depend on the judgment, attention, and earnest religious feeling of those by whom any such experiment were tried. A number of congregations, by communicating to each other the result of their experience, might eliminate mistakes and suggest improvements.

---

[7] Of course those best qualified to select hymns may not always be the ones best qualified to lead the singing. Those best qualified to decide on a discourse, or a series of extracts for public reading, may not be best qualified for reading aloud, and may need to intrust this duty to another.

INDEX I.

QUOTATIONS FROM SCRIPTURE.

Reference	Page
Gen. 1, 26	195
9, 4	46
49, 10, 11	22
Exod. 3, 2, 6, 14, 15	191
31, 16, 17	43
Psalms 8, 2	163
19, 5	23
22, 6	39
45, 3	41
Isaiah 1, 13	12
2, 3	81
44, 6	197
53, 2	39
53, 3, 4	40
53, 12	57
Jer. 31, 31, 32	66
Ezek. 20, 12	43
Zech. 11, 12, 13	112
Matt. 1, 1–20	202
3, 7	156
10, 3	158
10, 22, 23	78
11, 25	163
22, 32	31
24, 36	80
27, 1–11	89, 90
27, 15–20	87
27, 23–26	88
27, 51–54	88
27, 59–28, 5	88, 89
28, 10–16	89
28, 19, 20	49, 91
Mark 3, 18	158
6, 20	154
9, 41	60
12, 26, 27	31
13, 32	80
15, 28	57
16, 9–20	90, 91
Mark 16, 17, 18	206
Luke 1, 1, 2	182
2, 11	60
2, 39	201
6, 15, 16	158
10, 20	205
20, 37, 38	31
21, 12	78
22, 37	57
23, 2	60
24, 13, 15	90, 91
24, 32	38
24, 36	91
John 1, 1–14	200
1, 17	61
1, 25	48
3, 25, 26	49
4, 3	49
5, 39, 46, 47	38
9, 22	60
15, 20	78
16, 2	78
17, 3	60
20, 1, 14, 18	90
20, 19, 27	91
See also pp. 93–102	
Acts 1, 8, 9	91
8, 16	50
10, 48	50
11, 3	8
11, 26	55
15, 7	46
15, 10	10, 11
15, 28, 29	47
17, 18	67
19, 5	50
20, 17, 28	213
21, 20–24	10
Acts 22, 16	50
26, 28	55
Rom. 4, 9, 10	11
14, 3, 5, 14, 23	9
14, 20	28
1 Cor. 1, 22	67
4, 9	62
7, 21	64
8, 1–11	9
9, 24–26	62
10, 25–28	9
15, 32	62
Gal. 2, 2–5	9, 10
2, 11–13	11
4, 9, 10	12
5, 6; 6, 15	9
Eph. 6, 5	64
6, 12	62
Phil. 1, 1	213
3, 13, 14	62
Col. 2, 16, 17	12
3, 22	64
4, 1	64
1 Tim. 2, 9, 10	69
3, 1, 8	213
3, 15 ; 4, 2	73
6, 1	64
2 Tim. 2, 5	63
Titus 1, 5, 7	213
2, 9	64
Heb. 1, 13 ; 2, 4	91
8, 8, 9	66
12, 1	62
1 Peter 2, 18	64
3, 3, 4	69
4, 16	55
2 Peter 3, 7, 12, 13	36
John, Epistles	93–102

INDEX II.

CITATIONS FROM ANCIENT AUTHORS.

Reference	Page
ACTS OF PILATE, 5, 107 – 142	
§ 3	90
15	91
ANTONINUS, pseudo, 167,	168
APOSTOL. CONSTITUT.	
7, 23	45
ARNOBIUS, adv. Gentes,	
1, 1	18
" 27	14
" 57	1
7, 7	20
ASCENSION OF ISAIAH,	
3, 12 – 25	169, 170
7, 9 – 12	170
9, 13 – 18	170, 171
5, 40	170
11, 2 – 15	171
" 18 – 22	171, 172
" 41 – 43	170
ATHENAGORAS, Supplicat.	
7, 9	73
8	196
10	194, 196
AUGUSTINE, Epist. 54	161
BARNABAS, Epist. 15	32
BARUCH, 4, 36, 37	33
CELSUS	40
CICERO, de Nat. Deorum,	
1, 30	15, 81
" 111	15
3, 94	15
CLEMENTINE HOMILIES,	
3, 7	196
8, 20	24
11, 12	29
16, 15, 16	196
CLEMENT OF ALEXANDRIA,	
Protrept. 2	81
Pædag. 3, 25	47
Strom. 1, 18, 80	66
1, 64, 72, 87, 101	67
" 67	68
3, 92	188
6, 41, 66, 67, 156, 159	66
6, 80	68
CODEX THEOD. 2, 8	45
COHORTATIO AD GRÆCOS,	
14	67
15	179
21	197
COMMODIANUS, Instruct.	
6, 13	37
8, 8, 9	20, 37
CONSTANTINE, Edicts of,	45
CORPUS JURIS CIVILIS,	45
COUNCIL OF LAODICEA,	
29	45
DIO CASSIUS, 55, 7	82
DIOGNETUS, Epistle to,	
4	13
7, 8	198, 199
EPIPHANIUS, Hæres.	
29, 9	186
30, 3	186
ESDRAS 2d, 14, 15, 16	19
EUSEBIUS, Eccl. Hist.	
1, 13	40, 149, 150, 158 – 161
3, 37	184
" 39	31, 32, 203
4, 29	184
5, 1	63
" 9, 10	187
HERMES TRISMEGISTUS,	179 – 181
HOMILIES ON LUKE,	
Prologue to	189
IGNATIUS, Magnes. 9	44
IRENÆUS, cont. Hæres.	
3, 1, 1	203
3, 11, 7	184, 185
3, 11, 8	184
4, 15, 1	59
" 16, 1	43
" 16, 1, 2	13
" 16, 2	59
" 33, 11 – 12	40
5, 31, 2	30, 171
" 33, 2, 3	32
" 35, 1, 2	33
" 35, 1	34
JEROME, de Vir. Illust.	
2, 3	186
8	203
12	161
18	32
cont. Pelag. 3	186
Epist. 69 ad Oceanum	214
Comment. ad Tit.	214
Comment. in Matt.	
12, 13	186
JOSEPHUS, Antiq.	
18, 3, 2 – 4	153
18, 5, 1 – 3	154, 155
20, 9, 1	156, 157
JUSTIN MARTYR,	
Apology, 1, 6	190
Apology, 1, 13	190
" 14	192
" 20, 57, 60	36
" 35	105
" 44	67
" 48	2, 105
" 61	48, 49, 205
" 63	190, 191
" 66	49
2, 6	3, 27, 53
" 7	36
Dialogue, 2, 8	67, 68
10, 11, 21, 23, 27, 43	12
11	206
14	39, 40
24	173
48	190, 192
50, 56, 57, 58, 60	192
60, 61	192, 193
80	31, 32
92	12, 13
LACTANTIUS, Div. Inst.	
1, 6; 2, 11, 16	180
4, 6	201
" 9	180
" 13	180 – 181
6, 25	181
7, 4, 13, 18	181
LYONS AND VIENNE, Letter from	47
MINUCIUS FELIX, Octavius, 28	27
ORATIO AD GRÆCOS, 5	16
ORIGEN, Epistle	185
Comment in Matt.	
§ 100	41
10, 17	158
" 18	160
12, 43	33
Cont. Celsum.,	
1, 47	157
2, 13	157, 158
6, 75	40, 41
" 77	41
OROSIUS, 7, 9	79
ORPHEUS, pseudo	179
PAPIAS	31, 32, 203
PHILOSOPHUMENA, 5, 7	187
SENECA,	
Nat. Quæst. 7, 2	77
Pseudo Letters, 161 – 166	
SIBYLLINE ORACLES,	
1, 324 – 400	172 – 175
3, 47 – 50, 652 – 656	207

CITATIONS FROM ANCIENT AUTHORS.

	Page
SIBYLLINE ORACLES,	
6, 1-15, 16-28	175, 176
8, 256, 257	40
" 256-323	176-178
" 278	174
" 324-336	179
SUETONIUS,	
Augustus, 40	82
Vespasian, 4	204
Domitian, 9	82
TACITUS, Annals, **6,** 32	156
History, **4,** 81	204
TATIAN, Orat. **4,** 5, 7	195
13	194
18	24
25	15, 30, 36
40	67

	Page
TERTULLIAN,	
de Præscript. Hæret.	
15	185, 186
37	186
adv. Marcion, 4, 5	184
4, 22	73
adv. Prax. 16	200
adv. Judæos 2	43, 44
de Idololat. 1	29
Apology, 9	47
21	1, 3, 105
27	19
ad Nat. **1,** 7, 8	56
2, 2	68
Scorpiace, 10	56
de Orat. 18	45, 46

	Page
TERTULLIAN,	
de Baptismo, 13	49
THEOPHILUS, ad Autol.	
1, 5	14
" 14	67
2, 9, 10	72
" 10	195
" 17	71
" 18	20, 195
" 22	194, 195
" 37	67
3, 17	17
" 18	18
" 20	18, 19
VIRGIL, Æneid, **1,** 1	82
1, 282	82
Georg. **2,** 537	82

INDEX III.

WORDS AND SUBJECTS.

Words marked with an * will be found also in Index I. or Index II.

Abbot, E., v.
Abdel Leuarin Kasen, 151.
Abdus, 160.
Abdus, the son, 160.
Abel, 11.
Abgarus, 158, 159, 160; pseudo correspondence of, with Jesus, 4, 6, 149-150.
Abraham, 11, 12, 31, 59, 102; brought to life, 148.
Acabar, 151.
Achaia, 163.
Acrostics, 172.
Acts of the Apostles,* 21, 57, 62, 85, 90.
Acts of Pilate,* v, 2, 3, 4, 17, 50, 86, 87, 89, 105-142, 143, 145, 206.
Adam, 44, 59, 137.
Adamantius, 189.
Adas, 140.
Addas, 140, 141.
Ædilitian tribute, 62.
Æneas, 19.
Æon, 50, 171.
Æsculapius; see Esculapius.
Africa, 17, 61.
Ages, two, of Just Men, 59; middle, 206.
Agra, 151.
Agrippa, king, 156, 157.
Agrippina, 69, 81.
Albinus, 157.
Alexander, son of Simon, 129.
Alexander the Great, 165.
Alexandria, 70, 79, 157, 189, 202, 203, 204.
Alpheus, 158.
All-men, meaning of, 58.
All-Ruler, 52, 177, 198.
Amos, 170.
Ananias, the prefect, 6; the courier, 149, 150.
Ananus, 156; the younger, 156, 157.
Ancient Customs, Discipline, 194.
Angæus, 140, 141.
Angel of Christian Church, 169.
Angels, 24; evil, 23, 26.

Annas, high-priest, 107, 108, 116, 117, 118, 135, 147.
Antichrist, 34, 35; cp. Beliar.
Antioch, 11, 92.
Antiquity, iii, 18.
Antiquities, Jewish, 158.
Antoninus, Marcus, 63, 72, 75, 80, 190, 196; his reign reactionary, 193; pseudo letter of, 7, 167, 168.
Antoninus, Pius, 80, 190.
Apelles, 184, 185, 187.
Apoc. N. Test , 161, 182.
Apollinarius, 32.
Apollos, 214.
Apostolic Age, 8, 43, 50, 58.
Apronius, 165
Archelaus, 147.
Archenholtz, 209, 212.
Aretas, 154, 155.
Argus, 180.
Aristocracy, Jewish, 35, 55, 154.
Aristocracy, Roman, 14, 34, 35, 54, 82, 154, 156.
Ark 38, 200.
Armies, standing, 209.
Arnuphis, 167.
Ascension of Isaiah, v, 7, 77, 169-172.
Assembly (an æon), 50.
Asia, 55, 151, 208; the province, 62.
Asia Minor, 17, 61, 74, 77, 212.
Asiarchs, 62.
Atheism, 55.
Atheists, 55.
Athenagoras,* 15, 30, 52, 53, 68, 72, 75, 78, 193, 199
Atonement, vicarious, 29.
Attalus, 63
Atticus, M. V., 166.
Augustine,* 48.
Augustus, 54, 80, 82
Autolycus, 194.

Bacchus, 18, 22.
Bacis, 72.
Baptism, 48-50; of Jesus, 49, 175.

Baptism, vicarious, 48; into the spirit, 206.
Baptismal formula, 50, 83, 204-206.
Barabbas, 87, 88, 125.
Barbarians, 68.
Barnabas,* 9, 11, 21, 173; epistle of, 44, 173.
Barneveldt, 208.
Bartholomew, 186, 187.
Basilides, 185, 187.
Beelzebub, 109, 115.
Beliar, 34, 35; cp. Berial and Antichrist.
Bellerophon, 23
Berial, 169; cp. Beliar.
Berlin, 210
Beronice, 124.
Bethlehem, 115, 126, 171, 201.
Bib. Repository, 151, 152.
Bibliotheca Theolog., 151.
Bielefeld, 209.
Bishop, 213, 214.
Blaesilla, 189.
Blood, contains the soul, 46; eating of, 46-48.
Bondsman, Bondsmen, 64, 65.
Books, the written, 112.
Boston, 212.
Braunsberg, 211.
Bryant, 211, 212.
Burning, punishment by, 211, 212.

Cæsar, Julius, 80.
Cæsarea, 186.
Caiaphas, 107, 108, 116, 117, 118, 135, 138, 147.
Caligula (Caius), 15, 35, 81, 155, 156 165; abolishes public games, 63.
Calvin, 183
Cambridge, v.
Campbell, G , 183, 214.
Capito, jurist, 81.
Capito, consul, 164.
Carnutum, 167.
Carpocrates, 187.
Castor, a god, 163.
Castor, Agrippa, 187.

WORDS AND SUBJECTS.

Catholics, 21, 171; liberalist, 31, 33.
Celsus, 71, 75, 115.
Cephas, 214.
Ceremonial Law; *see* Law.
Cerinthus, 186, 187.
Charles II., 214.
Charleston, 211.
Charmus (Charinus), 26.
Chrestos, Chrestus, 55.
Christ, disuse of term, 75, 76, 193, 199, au æon, 50.
Christian, Christians, terms applied to, 54, 55, 56, 71; terms used by, 56-58; charges against, 18, 19; semi-Jewish, 12, 31, 33; Jewish, 28, 29, 31, 33, 42, 46; Gentile, 8, 9, 10, 43, 46, 47; Eastern, 45; Western, 45; Catholic, 21.
Church, Discipline, 73, 74; authority, 206
Church, Greek, Latin, Eastern, 46.
Churches, Gentile, Latin, 48.
Cicero, M. T.,* 62, 76, 77, 176, 180, 190.
Cicero, Quintus, 62.
City, the truly Holy, 33.
Claudius, 28, 63, 81; statue of, for the temple, 34, 35.
Clement of Alexandria,* 26, 26, 52, 53, 55, 63, 70, 77, 78, 179, 186, 189, 203.
Clement of Rome, 188, 203.
Clementines.* Clementine Homilies, 152, 189, 205.
Cohortatio ad Græcos,* 17, 52, 58, 68.
Colman, II., 212.
Colossians,* Ep. to, 28, 43.
Commodus, 80.
Conflagration, The, 36.
Constantine, edicts of, 45.
Corinthians,* Ep. to, 21, 28, 31, 48, 57, 73, 163.
Cotta, 180.
Council, 8, 28, 46, 47.
Creation of man, iv; of universe, 14.
Creator, term as used by Catholics, 194.
Crœsus, 25
Culture, Greek, iii, 81, 82; Saracenic, 208.
Cyrene, 129.
Cyrenius, 74.

David, 136, 171, 176, 184.
Deacons, 213, 214.
Death, 44.
Deity; *see* God.
Deity, Sabine, 34.
Deities, heathen, 14, 17, 18, 19, 21-29, 170; authors of evil, 71; no revelation from, 20; not predicted, 37.

Demas, 131, 132.
De Monarchia, 197.
Demons, 109, 143, 206, 210; *see* Deities, heathen.
Devil, 45, 66, 67, 214.
De Wette, 183
Diatessaron, 184.
Didymus, 189.
Dillmann, 170, 172.
Dio Cassius,* 14, 63, 69, 167
Dio Chrysostom, 69.
Diognetus,* Ep. to, 27, 43.
Dionysius, 165.
Divination, 23, 76.
Domitian, 55, 64, 80, 82.
Doxology, 137.
Dress 69, 70.
Dysmas, 128, 131.

Earth, growing old, 19; form of, 76
Earthquake, 133, 149; in Judea, 88, 137, 138.
East, 204; king from, 207.
Ebionites, 185, 186.
Eclipse, 76, 133.
Economy, a theological term, 199.
Edessa, 149, 150, 158.
Edessene Archives, 7.
Egypt, 61, 67, 77, 115, 122, 129, 132, 170, 173, 180, 188, 201, 203; North, 208.
Egyptians, 18, 122, 180, 186, 188, 189.
Eighth Day, 44, 46, 173.
Eighth Sphere, 173.
Eleatics, 68.
Elijah, 41.
Elysian Fields, 25.
Emaus, 5, 6.
Emmaus, 91.
Emperor, Roman, opponent of God, 34, 35.
Ennœas, 107, 108
Ennœus, 5, 106, 108.
Endor, 23
Enoch, 11, 12, 13; book of, 24.
Ephesus, 21, 62, 213.
Epicureans. 67, 68.
Epicurus, 66, 68
Epiphanius,* 187, 188, 189.
Ermeland, Bp. of, 211.
Esau, 192.
Esculapius, 181.
Esculapius (the god), 23, 109.
Eucharist, 49
Europe, 55, 193, 208, 213
Eusebius,* 7, 36, 85, 105, 186, 188, 189
Eustochium, 189.
Eve, 23, 70, 177.
Ezekiel, 32.

Fabricius 151, 161.
Fascial, 109, 110, 114.
Father of Justice, of the

heavens, of the universe, 52, 53.
Fathers, the, 2
Fayetteville, 211.
Festus, 157.
First-day, 44, 46.
Foreign Rites, 43.
France, 210.
Frauenburg, 211.
Frederick II., 212.
Freiburg, 210.
Frothingham, 183.
Fucinus, Lake, 69.

Galatians,* Ep. to, 43, 58, 163.
Galilee, 89, 95, 107, 139, 140, 141, 142, 171, 201.
Games, public, 61-63, 84; Christians sacrificed in, 63
Gaul, 61.
Gemalitis, 154.
General, a conscientious, 209
Genesis,* 8, 18, 192.
Geneva, 211.
Gentile, Monotheists, 3, 69. 115; Christians, 8, 9, 43, 46, 47.
Germany, 167, 210.
Gestas (Stegas), 131.
Gnostics, 20, 21, 70, 77, 184; Alexandrine, 50, Valentinian, 77, 173.
God, designations of, 51-53; a pilot, 14; the Creator, 15, 52; devoid of name, 36, 51; spherical form of, 16; whether corporeal, 15, 16, 81; Gnostic view of, 21; a spirit, 15; discussion of his antiquity, 18.
Gospel, meanings of term, 183.
Gospels, alleged uncanonical, 7, 182-189.
Greece, 61, 212.
Greek Church, 46.
Greek, Culture or Civilization, iii, 81, 82, 208; society, 69; dress, 82.
Greeks, adopted Jewish views of God, 81.
Gregory of Nyssa, 203.
Grotius, 208.

Hadrian, 65, 80.
Heavens, lower, 171; seven, 77, 171; seventh, 171; eighth, 173
Hebrews, antiquity of, 18; Lord's day of, 110; writer to, 166
Hebrews,* Ep. to, 166, 169, 207.
Hemans, Mrs., 210.
Heracleon, 185.

Hercules, 23, 145.
Heretics, 185.
Hermas, 49, 59.
Hermes Trismegistus,* 179, 180, 181, 200, 201, 205.
Hermias, 197.
Hermopolis, 180.
Herod, 107, 126.
Herod Antipas, 107, 127, 147, 154, 155, 156.
Herodias, 154, 156.
Hezekiah, 170.
Hoar, Judge, 212.
Holy of Holies, 33, 65.
Holy Spirit, 49, 169, 170; deification of, 50, 200, 204;
Homer, 19, 78.
Homilies * on Luke,186, 187, 188.
Hone, 161. 182.
Horeb, 12, 66.
Huet, 16, 27.
Hystaspes, 7, 36, 71, 72, 188.

Idol, 25.
Idolatry, 13, 18, 21, 25, 27 - 29, 83.
Images, 27.
India, 187.
Indians, 187.
Inspiration, 72, 73.
Irenæus,* 78, 173, 182, 183, 187.
Isaac, 148.
Isaiah,* 23, 32, 73, 197.
Isaiah, Ascension of,* 7, 77, 169 - 172.
Isis, 153.
Italy, 55, 61, 62, 79, 81, 83, 84, 85; religion of, 19; politics of, 84.

Jacob, 22, 31, 141, 148, 191, 192.
Jambres, 122.
James, 11, 156, 157, 158.
Jannes, 122.
Jeremiah,* 73, 90, 112.
Jerome,* 186, 189.
Jerusalem, rebuilding of, 31, 32, 33; the Heavenly, 33; Temple at, 32, 34, 35, 79; Council at, 8, 28, 46, 47.
Jesus, 153; birth of, 115, 116, 171, 190, 202; mission of, 27, 170, 206 - 213, 215; underworld mission of, 29, 85, 177; deification of, 50, 190 - 201, 204; personal appearance of, 39 - 42, 75, 152, 160; Deity of the O. Test., 38, 39; an angel, 190, 191, 194; an apostle, 190, 191; a subordinate God, 194; a servant, 192, 193, 200; a subordinate workman,

177, 195; duration of his ministry, 171; pre-existent, 170, 190, 192, 197; the Beloved, 170; temporary disuse of word, 75, 76, 193, 199.
Jews, Liberalist, 28; expulsion of, from Rome, 34.
John, Ep. of,* 58, 93.
John, Gospel of.* 31, 58, 65, 76, 111, 119, 123, 150, 184, 185, 188, 189, 199, 204.
John, style of, 92.
John, the Baptist, 38, 48, 49, 74, 94, 98, 101, 154, 155, 156, 173.
Jonathan, high-priest, 155.
Jones, 161.
Joppa, 95.
Jordan, 49; takes fire, 175.
Joseph, the carpenter, 108, 115, 116, 126, 132, 171, 202.
Joseph of Arimathea, 5, 88, 134, 135, 136, 138, 139, 140, 142.
Josephus,* 34, 65, 74, 79, 158; interpolations of, 6, 153 - 157.
Joshua, 193.
Judah, 22.
Judas Iscariot, 41, 89, 90, 112, 158.
Judas, 158, 159.
Jude, Ep. of, 57.
Judgment, The, 172.
Julian, 167.
Jupiter, 22; Capitolinus, 65; Pluvius, 167.
Justin Martyr,* 17, 19, 23, 34, 37, 43, 50, 51, 52, 75, 78, 130, 167, 175, 178, 189, 195, 197, 198, 199, 200, 203, 204.
Just Men, 12, 13, 44, 60; two ages of, 59.

Kaye, 19, 22, 23, 24, 25, 26.
King from the East, 207.
Koenigsberg, 211.
Kuhnapfel, Rudolph, 211.

Lactantius,* 18, 32, 174, 200, 205.
Lahore, 151.
Lamson, 2, 22, 23, 27, 70.
Laodicea, Council of, 45.
Lardner, 149, 167.
Laurence, 169.
Law, Ceremonial, Jewish, Mosaic, 6, 8, 9, 10, 11, 13, 46, 47, 56, 59, 60 66, 67,73, 119, 178; new, 111, 206; Roman, 64, 164; none given by heathen deities, 20; given through an angel, 24; book of the, 142; of God, 173, 175.

Law-less One, 32, 84.
Law-less, (heathen?) 56, 57, 174, 177.
Law-lessness, 56.
Lazarus, 111, 122, 125, 146.
Lebbeus, 158.
Lentulus, 6, 42, 84, 151.
Lexicon, Pierer's, 6.
Leyden, 80.
Library, 216, 217; Vatican, 203.
Liddell & Scott, 178.
Locke, 208.
Logos, 20, 47, 75, 76, 177, 190 - 197.
Longinus, 132.
Lord's Day, 44, 45, 84, 110, 137, 138.
Lord's Supper, 49, 50, 51, 74.
Love, altar to, 26.
Low Countries, 208.
Lucilius, 162, 163.
Luke, 74, 85, 90, 92; Gospel of,* 65, 74, 86, 95, 107, 112, 124, 154, 184, 185, 186, 187, 188, 189, 204.
Lusitanica, 151.
Lyons, 47, 63.
Lystra, 21.

Macedonian Months, 74.
Macherus, 155.
Macknight, 207.
Mæcenas, 82.
Man, an æon, 50; creation of, iv.
Manasseh, 169, 170.
Mandelium, 109, 110.
Marcion, 77, 107, 184, 185, 187.
Marcionites, 185, 188.
Mark, 92, 202; Gospel of,* 44, 47, 49, 65 86, 92, 124, 184, 185 186 202 203, 204, 205; Epitome subjoined to, 90, 91.
Mary, 88, 89, 108, 115, 116, 130, 132, 135, 171, 202.
Mary Magdalene, 88, 89, 90.
Massachusetts, 212.
Master-God, 52, 200, 205.
Matthew, 92, 201; Gospel of,* 33, 47, 57, 60, 65, 86, 92, 124, 132, 140, 154, 182, 184, 185, 186, 187, 188, 189, 201, 204, 206.
Matthias, 187.
Meat offered to idols, 8, 9, 21.
Mercieres, 209.
Mercury, a planet, 76.
Mercury; see Hermes.
Messala, 164.
Michael, 169.
Middleton, 144.
Millennium, 31, 32.
Minos, 25.
Minucius Felix,* 26, 47.

WORDS AND SUBJECTS. 225

Miracles, iv, 2, 3, 4, 122, 123, 124.
Mitchell, 213.
Money, the Sacred, 153
Monotheism, 16, 19, 57, 58, 67, 73, 81, 208.
Monotheist, Monotheists, 14, 15, 16, 19, 57, 58, 69, 114, 124, 134, 196, 205; the twelve, 115, 116, 117, 125; see Gentile.
Moral Ruler, acknowledged by communities only which believe in revelation, iii.
Moses, iii, 8, 10, 12, 13, 18, 19, 22, 38, 41, 43, 47, 59, 67, 73, 120, 122, 148, 191, 192.
Mosheim, 15, 183.
Mystics, 188.

Nartz, 211.
Nazareth, 171, 201.
Nazarenes, 152, 186.
Nero, 35, 65, 102, 163, 164, 165.
New Jersey, 211.
New Testament, Apocryphal, 161, 182.
Nicodemus, 106, 107, 108, 121, 122, 123, 125, 134, 135, 142; Gospel of, 4, 5
Noah, 12, 13, 18, 39, 59, 148, 200.
Norton, 21, 41, 50, 71, 78, 92, 132, 184, 186, 201, 203, 208.

Octavius, 27, 47.
Ogdoad, 50.
Old Testament, predictions in, 7, 14, 17, 37, 38, 39, 85, 205.
Ophites, 188.
Oracles, 24.
Oratio ad Græcos,* 197.
Origen,* 16, 26, 39, 47, 68, 71, 78, 186, 187, 189, 203, 205.
Orion, 148.
Orosius,* 65, 80.
Orpheus, pseudo,* 179.
Orthodoxographa, 143, 144, 145, 151.
Orthodox, 194.

Paley, 62.
Palm-Sunday, 84, 110.
Pantænus, 187.
Papias,* 31, 32.
Paradise, 132.
Passover, 133
Patriarchs, 38, 59, 148, 192.
Paula, 189.
Paul, 9, 21, 28, 43, 44, 47, 62, 63, 69, 73, 85, 91, 161 – 166, 188, 214.

Paullinus, C. S., 166
Pegasus, 23.
People, 31, 115, 173
Peripatetics, 68.
Perseus, 23.
Peter. 8, 11. 46, 50, 56, 69, 90, 92, 112, 187, 188, 202, 203; Ep. of,* 56, 57, 73.
Pharaoh, 122, 126.
Pharisees, 88, 112.
Philemon, Ep. to, 64.
Philip, king, 165.
Philip, apostle, 184; daughters of, 184.
Philippi, 213.
Philo, 67.
Philosophers, 67, 68; physical, 68.
Philosophumena,* 15, 188.
Philosophy, 66 – 68; Greek, 66 – 68; Hebrew, 67; origin of, 66, 67; antiquity of, 66, 67.
Phineas, 141.
Pierer's Lexicon, 6.
Pilate, surrender of, 146, 149; wife of, 87, 114, 115, 121; see Acts of Pilate.
Pilate's Report, 5, 17, 105, 142 – 149.
Plato, 19, 68, 78, 81; his views of demons, 26; treatise of, 76.
Platonics, 68
Platonists, 68.
Pleroma, 77.
Pliny Sen., 15, 69.
Plutarch, 64.
Pollio, Vitrusius, 168.
Pollux, 163.
Polycarp, 55.
Pompeianus, 167.
Pomponius, 69.
Practical - monotheism, or Practical piety, 57, 58, 73, 146, 148, 180.
Prætorium, 114, 118, 119, 120, 129, 145.
Preaching of Peter, 188.
Predictions, 1, 72; see Old Testament.
Preparation, 137.
Procla; see Pilate, wife of
Prophet, true, or of truth, 152.
Prophets, 59, 67, 120.
Proselytes, 116.
Providence, 200.
Prussia, 211 212
Psalms,* 132, 152
Pyriphlegethon, 25.
Pythagoreans, 68
Pythian Priestess, 25.

Quadratus, 184.

Race, Third, 56; Jewish, 127, 146.
Rachaab, 109.

Rasos or Rosos, 130.
Reason 47, 195, 196.
Reate, 163.
Regions, Lower, 171.
Religion, Greek, Roman, 106.
Renovation, 36.
Resurrection, 15, 30, 31, 45, 174; of Jesus, 85, 88, 106, 120, 137, 138, 139, 142; of Lazarus, 125, 146; of saints, 88, 148, 149; of the Just, 31, 34; physical, 30, 31; Jewish view of, 30, 31; Stoic view of, 30; Christian view of, 30, 31; body spherical, 16.
Revelation, through Moses, through Jesus, iii; none from heathen deities, 20.
Rhadamanthus, 25.
Rheinwald, 45, 46
Robinson, Prof. E., 151.
Roman, Empire, 61; society, 69; masters, 118; rule, 119; power, 159; government, 208.
Romans, Ep. to,* 43, 58.
Romaus, 56, 82, 173, 208.
Rome, 17, 28, 34, 6*, 156, 202; destruction of, 33.
Routh, 46, 47.
Rufus, 129.

Sabbath, 9, 11. 12 13. 32, 42 43 44 45, 84, 108, 109, 118, 123, 136, 137, 138, 146, 147, 148; term for Sunday, 44; cessation from labor on, 42, 111.
Sacrifice or Sacrifices 9, 13, 21, 25, 206
Sadducees, 157.
Samael, 169, 170.
Samaria, 34
Samaritans, 34.
Samuel, a prophet, 23.
Sanhedrim, 133, 157.
Satan, 23, 70, 170.
Saturn, a god, 37; a planet, 173.
Savior, 22, 76, 95, 149; the æon, 171.
Sedgwick, 216.
Semler, 68.
Senate, 15, 19, 20, 61, 167.
Seneca,* pseudo letters of, 4, 161 – 166
Septuagint, 33, 132.
Serapion, 187.
Seventh day, 32, 173.
Sexes, relations of, 8.
Shiloh, 22.
Sibylla, 7, 19, 71, 72, 188.
Sibylline Oracles,* writings, verses, 19, 20, 65, 71, 80, 81, 85, 172 – 179.
Sibyllists, 71.
Sibyls, 145.

Silianus, A. L. N., 166.
Simeon, sons of, 142.
Simon, 34.
Simon, the Cyrenian, 129.
Simon Magus, 34, 187.
Slavery, 64, 65, 213.
Smith, Dict. of Biog., 82, 176, 191.
Smyth, Lect. on Mod. Hist., 208.
Socrates, 19.
Sodom, 176.
Son of God, 117, 121, 125, 131, 143, 150, 152, 158, 159, 172, 173, 174, 179, 190, 196, 200.
Soul, in the blood, 46.
South Carolina, 211, 212.
Spain, 61, 208.
Spirit, Divine, 73; prophetic, 191, 205; see Holy Spirit.
Standards, homage of, 85, 113, 114.
Statue, of Claudius, 34, 35; of Simon Magus, 34; of a Sabine Deity, 84.
Stegas, 128.
Stoics, 19, 36, 58, 66, 68, 106.
Stroud, 211, 212.
Suetonius,* 85.
Suidas, 167.
Sunday, 44, 45, 46, 173; edicts concerning, 45; not the Sabbath, 44, 45; Palm, 84, 110.
Supreme Being, 15, 16, 173, 180, 194, 207.
Switzerland, 210, 211.
Syria, 17, 61, 74, 154, 156.

Tacitus,* 34, 69, 85, 212.

Tatian,* 23, 52, 53, 68, 75, 78, 182, 183, 184, 199.
Telesinus, C S., 166.
Temple, 119, 120, 174, 175; burned, 79; destruction of, 32, 79, 85; statue in, 34.
Tertullian,* 2, 17, 25, 26, 30, 39, 63, 69, 77, 142, 145, 146, 167, 187, 205, 206.
Thaddeus, 158.
Thaddeus, pseudo. 85, 150, 158, 159, 160, 161.
Theodoret, 184.
Theodosius, 5, 6.
Theophilus,* 68, 75, 78, 182, 199, 200.
Thessalonians, Ep. to, 57, 85.
Thilo, 4, 5, 6, 90, 91, 106, 107, 110, 124, 126, 133, 142, 143, 145, 146.
Thomas, 158, 187.
Tiber, 34.
Tiberius, 3, 5, 54, 63, 74, 81, 105, 114, 117, 120, 125, 126, 142, 143, 145, 146, 149, 154, 155, 156, 161, 194, 212.
Timothy, Ep. to,* 95.
Tischendorf, 182, 203.
Titus, 9, 10; Ep. to,* 57.
Titus, emperor, 65, 79, 204.
Tobias, 158, 159.
Toparch, 5, 106, 107.
Trajan, 80.
Trinity, doctrine of, 50.
Trismegistus; see Hermes.
Troas, 95.
Trogyllium, 95.
Truth, 93, 94, 101, 119.

Trypho, 12, 31, 190, 192, 206.

Unbelief, prosecutions for, 14, 15, 54
Unbeliever, Unbelievers, 54, 55, 56.
Underworld, The, 5, 29, 35, 44, 142, 148, 160, 174, 177, 178.
Universe, spherical, 16.
United States, 211.

Valentinians, 77, 171, 185, 187, 188.
Valentinianus, Flavius, 6.
Valentinus, 185.
Vaticnus, 163.
Venus, 76.
Vespasian, 203, 204.
Victorinus of Pettaw, 32.
Vienne, 47, 63.
Virgil,* 82.
Virgin, 177; sacred, 174.
Vitellius, 154, 155, 156.
Von der Wart, Rudolph, 210.

Walch, 151.
War, 65, 209, 212; under Hadrian, 65, 80, 126, 173, 190.
Wesley, 183.
Whately, 207.
Wheeling, a penalty, 210, 211.
William III., 208.
Wisdom of Solomon, 27.
Wise men, 201.

Xavier, Francis, 151.

www.ingramcontent.com/pod-product-compliance
Lightning Source LLC
Chambersburg PA
CBHW031751230426
43669CB00007B/571